Crown
West
16.95

OLD M...

AN...

OLD MORMON
KIRTLAND
AND
MISSOURI

HISTORIC PHOTOGRAPHS
AND GUIDE

RICHARD NEITZEL HOLZAPFEL
and
T. JEFFERY COTTLE

FOR
LEONA MCDANIEL,
ROBERT AND ARLEEN HOLZAPFEL,
AND
TOM AND MARYLOU COTTLE

Book Design by Thomas Child and Scott Knudeson
Front and back cover photograph credits given where they appear in the book.

Library of Congress Catalog Number: 91-073601
ISBN: 1-879786-02

Printed in the United States of America

Fieldbrook Productions, Inc.
1901 E. Fourth Street, Suite150
Santa Ana, California 92705

PREFACE

During the 1990-91 academic year, we participated in two important history conferences, the John Whitmer Historical Association Annual Meeting (September 1990) in Independence, Missouri, and the Brigham Young University Missouri Symposium (March 1991) in Provo, Utah. We presented papers on the use of photographs in Mormon history and George Edward Anderson's 1907 photographic mission to Missouri. This book continues our previous efforts to study, identify, and publish the earliest photographic record of important Mormon historical sites.

Although historians cannot reconstruct the past, they do attempt to bring together information that helps us better understand the past. Diaries, letters, newspapers, books, and other materials are the hidden treasures on which modern historical writing is based. We believe that historic photographs are an important resource that has not been fully utilized in past historical work. The following narrative documents the early photographic history of Mormon sites in Ohio and Missouri.

The Kirtland Temple was the daguerreotype studio of James F. Ryder in the 1840s, though no known Ryder photograph was taken of the temple itself. The earliest-known photograph of the Kirtland Temple was taken in the early 1860s by Thomas Sweeny from Cleveland, Ohio. Another early photograph was taken in the 1870s by W. A. Faze from Painesville, Ohio.

Beginning in the 1870s, Mormons from Salt Lake City were among those visiting Church historical sites in Ohio and Missouri as pilgrims. Sometimes these visitors obtained photographs of Church historical sites. For example, Joseph F. Smith acquired J. T. Hicks' photograph of the Liberty Jail, Liberty, Clay County, Missouri, while visiting David Whitmer in 1878. Many of the visitors also took photographs of the historic places. Among these were four well-known Mormon historians, Andrew Jenson, B. H. Roberts, Edward Stevenson, and Junius F. Wells. Although they were not professional photographers, Jenson, Roberts, Stevenson, and Wells, along with Sweeny and Faze, preserved a few important glimpses of the Mormon past in Ohio and Missouri.

Some of the earliest photographs of Church history sites are stereographs; these stereographic views (two stereoscopic pictures designed to give a three-dimensional effect when viewed through a stereoscope) were sold house to house throughout North America and England by various companies.

James Ricalton, a professional photographer, traveled throughout the world to produce photographs for several companies, including the firm of Underwood and Underwood. In 1904, Ricalton made his way to the Far East from New York. As he journeyed toward the Pacific Ocean, he photographed Mormon historical sites, beginning in New York and finishing in Salt Lake City. Shortly thereafter, the firm of Underwood and Underwood produced a set of thirty-six stereo views from Ricalton's work. Among the views published were several taken in Ohio and Missouri.

These stereoscope images were the first attempts by a professional photographer to document the LDS Church's history, beginning in New York and ending with the settlement in Salt Lake City. According to one scholar, the Mormon Church is "the only religious group that may be said to have a pictorial history in stereo." [1]

George Edward Anderson's celebrated photographic pilgrimage to Missouri and Ohio in 1907 was not the first nor the last visit to Church historical sites by persons interested in Mormon history. Nor was Anderson the first individual to photograph these places of historic interest. However, his views are counted among the most memorable images of these sites.

Anderson's photographic work of Church historical sites was more than a passion; it was a deeply felt religious mission. "I selected points that I thought would make good views and show the temple ground [Independence, Missouri] from the outside so you could see how it was to the eye. I feel it a privilege to be in this land which the prophet of the Lord designated as the center stake of Zion where the great temple of our God should be raised." [2]

Numerous professional and amateur photographers have been adding images to an increasingly large photographic collection of Mormon historical sites. Many of these views can be seen in several books and articles, including our previous works, *Old Mormon Nauvoo and Southeastern Iowa* (1990) and *Old*

Mormon Palmyra and New England (1991).

Our intent is to provide a verbal and pictorial tour of Mormon historic places in Ohio and Missouri in this book. Although we cannot possibly return to the past, these early photographs allow a visual window to the past in a way other documents cannot. The early Saints' own words that we have selected help restore the life of this period, as do the photographs we have included. In our quotations from journals, letters, and diaries, obtained from either holographic writings or printed editions, we have oftentimes spelled out abbreviated words and made corrections in spelling and punctuation to make the material more readable.

Many of the nineteenth- and early twentieth-century photographs in this book are the earliest-known photographs of their respective sites. When early photographs of sites were not available, we used contemporary illustrations and a few recent photographs. We have also included two appendices—a section on the Missouri "extermination order" and a list of photographic sources and collections. The selected bibliography of published material lists the most important publications concerning this period of Church history.

Many individuals encouraged and helped us during our research and writing. Although their contributions have made this work better than it would have been, we must take full responsibility for the end result. We thank Charles Allen, Gina Alton, Karl Anderson, Paul Anderson, Milton V. Backman, Suzanne Barnard, Ron Barney, Barbara Bernauer, Lamar C. Berrett, Susan Easton Black, Dave Calkins, Lyndon Cook, Ed Davis, Lyman Edwards, Jesse E. Ehlers, Ron Fuenfhausen, Dean Jessee, Brant Jones, Jess Kohlert, Mary Ann Lyman, Veneese Nelson, Max Parkin, Bruce Pearson, Michael S. Riggs, Ron Romig, Dana Roper, Bill Slaughter, Steve Sorenson, Calvin Stephens, Patricia Struble, Bruce Van Orden, and John Waldsmith. We give a special thanks to Ted D. Stoddard, our editor, and Tom Child our designer.

Many institutions have graciously provided copies of photographs and permission for their reproduction. We thank Amherst Historical Society; Ashtabula Historical Society; Boone County Historical Society; the Brigham Young University Harold B. Lee Library Archives; The Church of Jesus Christ of Latter-day Saints Church Historical Department; The Church of Jesus Christ of Latter-day Saints Visual Resources Library; Cincinnati Public Library; Clay County Museum and Historical Society; Cole County Historical Society; Dewitt Historical Society; Gallatin Publishing Company; Geauga County Historical Society; Jackson County Historical Society; Kansas State Historical Society;

Lake County Historical Society; Missouri Historical Society; Oberlin College; Oberlin Historical Society; Orange Historical Society; Ray County Historical Society; the Reorganized Church of Jesus Christ of Latter Day Saints Library Archives; Shaker Historical Society; United States Department of Agriculture National Archives and Records Service; United States Library of Congress; the Utah State Historical Society; Village of Mantua; Western Reserve Academy; Western Reserve Historical Society; and Willoughby Historical Society.

We have used the writings and statements of those who lived in these historic places whenever possible. The early members of the Church, like ourselves, believed that their religious experiences were real and worthy of recording. Because they believed in these experiences, we have treated them as real. Although many non-Mormon readers may want to read interpretative studies of these events, this work will allow them to at least understand what the participants in these events believed themselves and how they described their experiences in Ohio and Missouri.

George Edward Anderson, one of the earliest photographic pilgrims to Church historical sites, wrote, "I feel impressed with the necessity of making the [photographic] views. I can see what a blessing they would be to our people in arousing an interest in this land [Missouri]."[3] In this spirit, we have prepared a photographic guide to Old Mormon Kirtland and Missouri.

CONTENTS

1

PERSONAL VOICES:
An Intimate History of the Church

In 1851, Charles Mackay, an English author, published a small engraved work that he claimed was the first public history of "that new religion" founded in America by Joseph Smith, Jr. (1805–1844), "one of the most remarkable persons who has appeared on the stage of the world in modern times."[1]

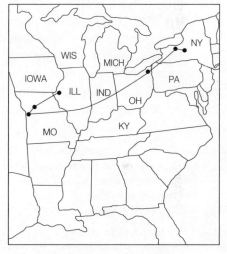

Although Mackay certainly was not the first to write a public history of the Mormons, he was right when he stated that Joseph Smith was a remarkable person. Since the founding of the Church of Christ in Fayette, New York, in 1830, a veritable avalanche of material has been published about Joseph and the church he founded. Of that which has been written and published, the contemporary letters, diaries, and personal reminiscences of those who witnessed the rise of this new-world faith are most interesting. The following excerpts from the "personal voices" of those who participated in the story themselves share an intimate view of Church history.

While Joseph Smith, Sr. (1771–1840) and Lucy Mack Smith rented a piece of farm land from Joseph's father-in-law, Solomon Mack, in Sharon, Vermont, Lucy delivered a son, named after her husband, on 23 December 1805. Dr. Joseph

Adam Denison's diary reported the birth of a son at the Smith home. A note written at a later date was placed on this entry stating, "If I had known how he was going to turn out I'd have smothered the little cuss."[2] Although Denison was somewhat chagrined about how the young baby boy "turned out," others reacted quite differently. Brigham Young reflected on Joseph's life by expressing the following sentiments:

> Who can say aught against Joseph Smith? I do not think that a man lives on the earth that knew him any better than I did, and I am bold to say that, Jesus Christ excepted, no better man ever lived or does live upon this earth. I feel like shouting Hallelujah all the time, when I think that I ever knew Joseph Smith, the Prophet.[3]

At a young age, Joseph discovered that "how he was going to turn out" would elicit such divergent opinions about his life and mission. From his birth in 1805 until early 1820, however, his life did not attract such notice.

The Smith family moved numerous times. Joseph Jr. lived for a while in New Hampshire and made a short visit to Massachusetts while recovering from a leg operation before moving to Palmyra, New York, with his family in 1816. Just two years later, his father bought a farm in Manchester township, just south of Palmyra. A Smith family neighbor, Mrs. Palmer, related the following information:

> My father owned a farm near that of the Smith family, in New York. My parents were friends of the Smith family, which was one of the best in that locality— honest, religious and industrious, but poor. The father of the family was above the average in intelligence . . . Mrs. Smith was called "Mother Smith" by many. Children loved to go to her home.

> My father loved young Joseph Smith and often hired him to work with his boys. I was about six years old when he first came to our home. I remember going into the field on an afternoon to play in the corn rows while my brothers worked. When evening came, I was too tired to walk home and cried because my brothers refused to carry me. Joseph lifted me to his shoulder, and with his arm thrown across my feet to steady me, and my arm about his neck, he carried me to our home.[4]

Young Joseph's interest in religion increased during this period. Although the family members were not united in their religious beliefs or practices, they were deeply concerned about personal salvation. Joseph's religious experiences occurred during a period of renewed religious sentiment. These personal experiences with God culminated in Joseph's being led to the "golden plates" in a

Joseph Smith, Sr. Farm, Manchester, New York
(Site of Joseph Smith's First Vision in 1820)
LDS Historical Department—George E. Anderson, 1907

hill not far from his home, later known as the Hill Cumorah. The plates contained a religious history of a family who left the Holy Land in 600 B.C.

Orlando Saunders, another Smith neighbor, recalled that "[Joseph] was always a gentleman when about my place . . . He always claimed that he saw the angel and received the book."[5] Other neighbors were less likely to accept Joseph's sincerity. Long-time Palmyra resident Thomas Taylor supported Smith and characterized the antagonists as "a set of damned liars. I have . . . been here, except when on business, all my life—ever since I came to this country—and I know these fellows. They make these lies [about] the Smiths."[6]

Hill Cumorah, Manchester, New York
(Joseph Smith obtained the Golden Plates here in 1827)
Utah Historical Society—unknown, before 1910

Joseph's antagonists attempted to stop his translation work, so Joseph moved first to Pennsylvania and then to Fayette, New York, to complete an English translation of the plates.

The completed manuscript was taken to a book publisher in Palmyra for

Joseph and Emma Smith Home, (center part is original) Harmony, Pennsylvania
(Much of the Book of Mormon translation occurred here)
LDS Historical Department—George E. Anderson, 1907

printing. E. B. Grandin published Joseph's translation in 1830. *The Book of Mormon*, the title given to the work, became an additional witness to the early Saints that God still was working among men.[7] Within a few weeks, Joseph organized the Church of Christ, later known as The Church of Jesus Christ of Latter-day Saints, on 6 April 1830.[8]

Important as the founding meeting at Fayette, New York, was to the future of the Church, it was also significant for the Smith family. All living members of the Smith household belonged to the same church for the first time. The occasion was so emotional that Joseph's eyes filled with tears as he grasped his father's hand following his father's baptism in a small stream near the Whitmer farm home in Fayette. "Oh, my God! have I lived to see my own father

E. B. Grandin Building, Palmyra, New York
(Book of Mormon was printed here in 1830)
LDS Historical Department—unknown, before 1920

baptized into the true church of Jesus Christ." Joseph Knight, a family friend and participant at this meeting, later recalled that Joseph "burst out with grief and joy and [it] seemed as though the world could not hold him. He went out into the lot [near the home] and appeared to want to get out of sight of everybody and would sob and cry and seemed to be so full that he could not live." Knight finally went after him to bring him back to the home. "He was the most wrought upon that I ever saw any man," Knight wrote. "His joy seemed to be full."9

Peter Whitmer, Sr. Farm, Fayette, New York
(Church organized here in 1830)
LDS Historical Department—George E. Anderson, 1908

Many, like Sarah Leavitt, came to believe that Joseph Smith's religious experiences were not only significant for the Smith family but also for themselves. She wrote, "It came to my mind in a moment that this was the message . . . for me and not for me only, but for the whole world, and I considered it of more importance than anything I had ever heard.10

Many new believers flocked to Kirtland, Ohio, where the Church began to gather in 1831. Joseph Smith moved to Ohio in early 1831, following a revelation that asked the Saints living in the small New York state branches to "go to the Ohio."11 Persecution in New York and the unexpected growth of the Church in the Western Reserve area of northeastern Ohio necessitated the move of Church headquarters. Joseph established several places of gathering for new converts during the first decade of the Church's existence, first in Kirtland.

The Saints began the long trek from New York to Ohio, while others continued on to Missouri, another Church gathering point, known as Zion. Traveling to a new Church gathering place presented many difficulties to the

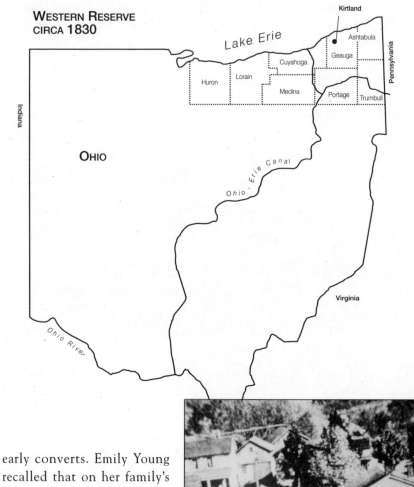

WESTERN RESERVE
CIRCA 1830

Lake Erie

Kirtland

Ashtabula

Geauga

Cuyahoga

Huron   Lorain

Medina

Portage   Trumbull

Pennsylvania

Indiana

OHIO

Ohio - Erie Canal

Virginia

Ohio River

early converts. Emily Young recalled that on her family's way to Missouri, they encountered ice coming down the river "so thick that the boat could not proceed." The family was forced to abandon the boat and look for a suitable place to spend the night out of the freezing weather. The only shelter available was a cabin occupied by a poor black

*Kirtland Flats Section of Kirtland, Ohio
(Newel K. Whitney Store, upper right)
LDS Visual Resources Library—unknown,
before 1910*

Temple Lot, Independence, Missouri
(Dedicated by Church Leaders in 1831)
LDS Historical Department—George E. Anderson, 1907

family. "On the banks of the river [near Arrow Rock] was a log cabin occupied by Negroes," she wrote. The cabin consisted of two rooms without windows. An open door allowed light into the home. The black family, with much kindness, let Emily's mother and another woman have one room. More than fifteen moved into the cabin for a three-week stay before they began their journey again.

The quarters in the slave cabin were cramped, but "there was a fireplace in the room [and] we could have a good fire and so kept from freezing."[12] Such hospitality was unusual, but always welcomed.

The Church built two main centers in Ohio and Missouri between 1831–39. Joseph Smith sent missionaries across the United States and Canada to seek out converts. This missionary activity meant that at any given time a large number of men were away from their families on missionary journeys. The women of the Church knew from experience what a call to the priesthood entailed—a mission assignment. Caroline Crosby related her own experience:

> Shortly after our arrival [in Kirtland], my husband was ordained to the office of an elder, and chosen into the second quorum of seventies. I well recollect the sensations with which my mind was actuated when I learned the fact that my husband had been called and ordained to the Melchizedek priesthood and would undoubtedly be required to travel and preach the gospel to the nations of the earth.[13]

In many instances, Joseph Smith was among the early missionaries who left family and home to preach the message of the restoration. Joseph stopped at the home of Alva Beaman in New York while on such a trip. Mary, Beaman's daughter, recalled,

> In the spring of 1834, Brother Joseph Smith came from Kirtland, Ohio, to my father's New York estate, which he had purchased at Avon, Livingston County. This was the first time I ever beheld a prophet of the Lord, and I can truly say at the first sight that I had a testimony within my bosom that he was a man chosen of God to bring forth a great work in the last days . . . While he was there, Sidney Rigdon, Joseph and Brigham Young, Luke and Lyman Johnson, and twelve or fourteen of the traveling elders had a council at my father's place. I, in company with my sisters, had the pleasure of cooking and serving the table and waiting on them, which I considered to be a privilege and a blessing.[14]

While Joseph and the missionaries made trips to visit new members who had joined the Church in other locations, many disciples came to Church headquarters to meet Joseph Smith, even though the disciples were not moving there at the time. Recent converts were eager to meet the man they believed to be a prophet. Some, like Brigham Young, later recalled their first meeting. Young recalled,

> In the Fall of 1832, Brothers Heber C. Kimball, Joseph Young and myself started for Kirtland [from New York] to see the Prophet Joseph. We went to his father's house and learned that he was chopping wood. We immediately went to the woods, where we found the Prophet and two or three of his brothers. Here my joy was full at the privilege of shaking the hand of the Prophet of God, and I received the sure testimony, by the spirit of prophecy, that he was all that any man could believe him to be, as a true prophet. He was happy to [meet] us, and made us welcome.[15]

Not all those who visited the young prophet were as impressed. In a letter, Charlotte Haven, a non-Mormon, wrote the following reflection to her sister:

> Joseph Smith is a large, stout, man, youthful in his appearance, with light complexion and hair, and blue eyes set far back in the head . . . I, who had expected to be overwhelmed by his eloquence, was never more disappointed than when he commenced his discourse.[16]

Even some early converts expected something different from what they found upon meeting Joseph. Jonathan Crosby wrote, "I thought he was a queer man for [a] Prophet, at first. He didn't appear exactly as I expected to see a prophet of God . . . I found him to be a friendly, cheerful, pleasant [and] agreeable man. I could not help liking him [though]."[17]

Joseph Smith organized Zion's Camp when difficulties between Church members and their Jackson County, Missouri, neighbors erupted into violence in 1833. Heber C. Kimball recalled,

> Our brethren in Jackson County, Missouri, also suffered great persecution. In 1833, about twelve hundred were driven, plundered and robbed. Their houses were burned, and some of the brethren were killed. The next spring, Joseph gathered together as many of the brethren as he could, with what means they could spare, to go to Zion [Missouri], to render assistance. We gathered clothing and other necessaries to carry to our brethren.
>
> Our wagons were about full of baggage, etc. Consequently, we had to travel on foot. Every night before we went to bed, we united in our tent and offered up our prayers before the Lord for protection. This was done by all the companies at the sound of the trumpet; and at the sound of the trumpet in the morning every man was upon his knees, each one in every tent being called upon in his turn to be mouth in prayer.[18]

Zion's Camp was unable to assist the Missouri Saints in their efforts to return to their homes in Jackson County. Nevertheless, the gathering in Missouri continued, but now in Clay County. The Saints in Missouri continued to meet together to pray and sing as they worshiped. An early convert recalled "We never missed a meeting [of the Church] for we loved the Saints and had confidence in them."[19]

The Church grew numerically and organizationally during this period (1833–38), both in Missouri and in Ohio. Despite economic problems and religious persecution, the Saints were able to construct a temple in Kirtland, Ohio. Built at great sacrifice and incorporating various design styles and forms, the temple was more than a church building. It was the House of God. George Burkett recorded his feelings about the structure when he wrote in his diary, "It is truly marvelous to see the greatness of the House and the beauty of the work."[20]

Kirtland Temple, Kirtland, Ohio
(Joseph Smith conducted the dedication ceremonies in 1836)
LDS Historical Department—probably W. A. Faze, 1870

The dedication was filled with excitement and religious meaning for the Saints gathered in the spring of 1836. Joseph Smith dedicated the Kirtland Temple on 27 March 1836. During the next few weeks and months, several manifestations of the spirit occurred there. Zebedee Coltrin, an early Church leader, recalled,

> In the Kirtland Temple I have seen the power of God as it was on the day of Pentecost, and cloven tongues of fire have rested on the brethren, and they have spoken in other tongues as the Spirit gave them utterance. I saw the Lord high and lifted up. The angels of God rested upon the Temple and we heard their voices singing heavenly music.[21]

Although members of the Church experienced much joy and satisfaction with the completion and dedication of the temple, they were quickly reminded of their status as a minority in a country still coming to grips with the notion of political, social, and religious pluralism. On many occasions, the abuse and persecution were on a very personal level. Joseph invited a Baptist minister to spend the night at Joseph's home in Kirtland. The clergyman, a former acquaintance in New York, spent the night and, after eating breakfast on the following day, blew up in a fit of rage against Joseph and called him a "hypocrite, a liar, an imposter and a false prophet." Luke S. Johnson, a local officer of the law who witnessed the incident, recalled,

> Joseph boxed his ears with both hands and turning his face towards the door, kicked him into the street. The clergyman immediately went before a magistrate and swore out a writ against Joseph for assault and battery. I saw the operation, and as an officer of the law I followed the minister into the Squire's office and demanded a writ for his apprehension, for provoking an assault. The clerk filled up the writ I called for first. The minister, fearing trouble, paid for his writ and withdrew without it, and made his way posthaste for Cuyahoga County. I followed him on horseback, making him travel pretty lively until he got a few rods over the line, where I overtook him and said, "Sir, you are lucky to have got over the line, and out of my jurisdiction, or I should have arrested you."[22]

Although abuse and persecution from nonbelieving neighbors were often harsh and unrelenting, the abuse and persecution from within the Church were almost greater challenges to bear. Some members, led by Warren Parrish, Joseph's former secretary, left the Church and founded an alternative organization that sought to overthrow Joseph Smith's leadership role in the final days of the Mormon Kirtland period (1838). Caroline Crosby "felt very sorrowful, and gloomy" by these events, but she said she "never had the first idea of leaving the Church or forsaking the prophet." She elaborated on the personal nature of such strife and conflict from within:

As to poverty we could endure that patiently, but trials among false brethren, who can endure with patience? Many of our most intimate associates were among the apostates . . . These were some of our nicest neighbors and friends. We had taken sweet counsel together and walked to the house of God as friends. They came out boldly against the prophet.[23]

In spite of the serious nature of these difficulties and others, Joseph and the Saints found ways to release the pressure from life in a frontier environment. In 1838, Joseph Smith and several young people "were playing various outdoor games, among which was a game of ball," recalled Edwin Holden, a teenager at the time. Joseph said to them, "Let us build a log cabin." The cabin was for a widow who had no home. Soon, the young men went off with Joseph to erect the log cabin. "Such was Joseph's way, always assisting in whatever he could."[24]

Joseph Smith enjoyed life, whether he was playing ball as he "took turns knocking and chasing the ball" with the young men of the community or working along side them.[25] Another teenager influenced by Joseph during this period was Benjamin F. Johnson. "As a companion," Johnson wrote, "[Joseph] was kind, generous and mirth loving." Johnson recalled the moments so memorable to a young man. He wrote,

> For amusements, he would sometimes wrestle a friend, or others; would test strength with others by sitting upon the floor with feet together and stick grasped between them . . . Jokes, rebuses, matching couplets in rhymes, etc., were not uncommon. But to call for the singing of one or more of his favorite songs was more frequent. Of those, "Wives, Children and Friends," "Battle of River Russen," "Soldier's Tear," "Soldier's Dream," and "Last Rose of Summer" were most common.[26]

Although the Saints found time to relax and to enjoy the simple pleasures of life, they were constantly reminded of the temporary nature of mortality. Death stalked the Saints wherever they located. Particularly difficult was the death of young children. Hyrum Smith's three-year-old daughter, Mary, died in his arms. He wrote:

> Mary was called from time to eternity on the 29th day of May [1832]. She expired in my arms—such a day I never before experienced, and O may God grant that we may meet her again at the great day of redemption to part no more.[27]

Increased trouble in Kirtland caused many of the Saints to leave their homes, fields, temple, and loved ones' graves to seek a place of rest in Missouri.

The Temple Site, Far West, Missouri
(Church Headquarters in 1838)
RLDS Archives—unknown, 1920

The Kirtland Church center was abandoned; the last group to leave was the "Kirtland Camp" in July 1838. The preparations were well underway when Joseph and Sidney Rigdon fled the city seeking safety from their enemies in Kirtland. Their destination was Far West, Missouri, another Mormon community in northern Missouri. From Kirtland, Hepzibah Richards wrote a letter to family members in Massachusetts describing the evacuation of the remaining Saints in Ohio:

> I must give you some account of the plans and prospects of this Church relative to emigration. Many families have already left. Those that remain are going up [to Missouri] in camp. They design to start the first of May, but may not before the 10th or later. Probably an hundred and twenty-five families or more remain [in Kirtland]. They will go in large wagons covered [and] will take their clothing, beds, and cooking utensils and tent by the way . . . They will travel five days in a week; stop on Saturdays to bake and wash. Sabbath hold meeting. Will be eight or ten weeks on the road. They design to take along the poor and the lame, deeming it wrong to leave those who have a desire to go, but have no means . . . The camp will move but slowly. The men will walk much of the way.[28]

Hepzibah's observations were correct; the journey was slow and tedious. While on the trip to Far West, Missouri, John Smith, a participant in the Kirtland Camp, wrote, "We are like the ancients wandering from place to place in the wilderness . . . [We] moved our tent today."[29]

Unknown to the Saints, their move to the Missouri settlements in Caldwell and Daviess counties would not end their trouble and would only be temporary gathering places.

Those first pioneers to arrive in the new Mormon settlements in Caldwell and Daviess counties described their life as happy and blissful, unaware of the approaching civil war between themselves and their neighbors. Sarah Rich described those early, peaceful days in her autobiography:

> Far West was a place everybody lived in log houses so my husband had built a nice little hewed log house and made it ready to live in by the time we were married. It was four miles from Far West near my husband's father's [home]. So I left my father's home in Far West and we moved to our cozy and happy home and we thought we were the happiest couple in all the land. My husband had a beautiful prospect for a nice farm with plenty of timber and water and our plans were laid for a comfortable and happy home in the near future and our religion being [the] first with us in all things.[30]

The tranquil life found in Missouri was short lived when conflict arose in the area between the Saints and nonmembers of the Church. In the face of continued conflict with their Missouri neighbors in 1838, the Saints abandoned their homes in the outlying communities and went to Far West, the main Mormon settlement, in an effort to protect themselves. The struggle to meet the most basic needs only intensified as new converts arrived daily in the area of conflict. Food and shelter were at a premium. During these difficult days, a member of the Church living at Far West wrote,

> A meeting was called this day [19 October 1838]. The brethren here consecrated beef, corn, wood, and finally they do freely impart to those that have need. Finally here is a time and place that tries men's souls.[31]

During the final confrontation between the Saints and the Missourians, Church leaders were arrested and incarcerated. On 2 November 1838, a cold and rainy Friday, Church leaders were marched to the town square in Far West; and a few, including Joseph Smith, were allowed to visit their families before being taken to Richmond for trial. After a short visit, Joseph was forced into the street with young Joseph still holding on to his father's legs. The soldier separated them with his sword and said, "You little brat, go back. You will never see your father no more."[32]

While many of their leaders were held for trial, the Saints were expelled from the state and were forced to leave their homes and farms. Several thousand

Joseph Smith Home Site, Far West, Missouri
(Traditionally identified as the Joseph Smith home site in Far West)
LDS Historical Department—George E. Anderson, 1907

Saints left Missouri during the winter of 1838–39 and went to Illinois and Iowa, seeking refuge from the mobs and state militia in northern Missouri. Their escape to Illinois was accomplished as fast as eight days and as long as three weeks. The usual trip took between ten and eleven days. Some of the last Saints out of Far West found camp poles and wood for fires all along the way, provided by the Church's Committee for Removal. One man returning from Illinois to Far West reported over two hundred wagons between the Mississippi River and Far West, all heading for safety in Illinois. Among those who fled Missouri were Joseph Smith's wife and children.

Emma made her departure from Far West on 7 February 1839 with a group of Saints. She later recalled,

> No one but God, knows the reflections of my mind and the feelings of my heart when I left our house and home, and almost all of everything that we possessed excepting our little children, and took my journey out of the State of Missouri, leaving [my husband] shut up in that lonesome prison. But the reflection is more than human nature ought to bear, and if God does not record our sufferings and avenge our wrongs on them that are guilty, I shall be sadly mistaken.[33]

Emma finally arrived at the western shore of the Mississippi River, which had frozen. Emma, somewhat fearful of the thin ice, separated her two horses and walked apart with two-and-one-half-year-old Frederick and eight-month-old Alexander in her arms. She had Julia hold securely to her skirt on one side and positioned young Joseph on the other side.

Emma also carried Joseph's manuscripts of his Bible translation in heavy bags, along with her husband's other personal papers fastened securely to her waist. She then walked across the frozen river to safety in Illinois.

The people of Illinois, particularly the citizens of Quincy, reached out to help the refugees from Missouri. Elizabeth Barlow wrote her friends in the East and mentioned the help the Saints had received:

> The people of Quincy have contributed between four and five hundred dollars for the poor Mormons. God had opened their hearts to receive us. May heaven's blessing rest upon them. We are hungry and they feed us, naked and clothed us. The citizens have assisted beyond all calculation.[34]

Quincy, Illinois
(Mormons sought refuge here from Missouri persecution in 1838-39)
Missouri Historical Society—C. Rogers, 1848

The Saints continued to gather to the Illinois and Iowa shores awaiting word of the fate of their leaders who languished in jail in Missouri. Eventually, the Missouri prisoners escaped and found safety across the Mississippi River in Illinois. Soon, a site was selected for a new Church center several miles north of Quincy in a small village named Commerce (which was later changed to Nauvoo). Members arrived by the thousands; and the community began to change as brick homes began to replace the log and frame buildings.

The effects of the Missouri persecutions and the swampy conditions along the Mississippi River took a heavy toll upon the Saints. Many died during the first two years; others watched their loved ones fade away, both old and young. Nancy Tracy wrote, "It seems almost impossible to raise a child in Nauvoo."[35]

Eventually, the settlement developed; and the drainage ditches that were dug allowed an unprecedented growth to take place in Nauvoo.

The Church in Nauvoo was much different from the Church as it had been in New York when only a few members had been baptized. In New York, the Saints used the *Bible* and the *Book of Mormon* as their printed scriptures. During the early period of the Church's existence, Joseph Smith and Oliver Cowdery acted as the first and second elders, the only general Church organization. As the Church increased in membership, a complex leadership organization developed, including a Church First Presidency (three presiding leaders), Twelve Apostles, Seventies, and Church patriarchs. In Nauvoo, the development continued, both doctrinally and administratively.

Nauvoo Temple above the Town of Nauvoo
(Church gathering place from 1839-46)
LDS Historical Department—Lucian Foster, 1846

Church ordinances included those revealed in the New York period—baptism, sacrament, and priesthood ordinations. In Nauvoo, additional religious ordinances became part of Church practice, particularly as they related to temple worship. In the temple, Joseph planned to introduce proxy baptisms, washing and anointing, and sealing rites (eternal marriage).

The Church in Nauvoo had additional publications, including newspapers, hymnals, and an additional book of scripture, *The Doctrine and Covenants*, which included many of Joseph Smith's revelations. (An earlier version of *Doctrine and Covenants* was published in Kirtland in 1835.)[36] Joseph expanded the organization of the Church when he established the Nauvoo Female Relief Society in 1842. An early member of this women's organization, Elizabeth Ann Whitney, remembered,

> During our residence in the brick store the Relief Society was organized, March 17, 1842, and I was chosen counselor to the President of the society, Mrs. Emma Smith. I was also set apart under the hand of Joseph Smith the Prophet to administer to the sick and comfort the sorrowful. Several other sisters were also set apart to administer in these holy ordinances . . . President Joseph Smith had great faith in the sisters' labors, and ever sought to encourage them in the performance of the duties which pertained to these societies, which he said were not only for benevolent purposes and spiritual improvement, but were actually to save souls.[37]

Joseph and Emma Smith Mansion, Nauvoo, Illinois
(Joseph and Emma lived here beginning in 1843)
RLDS Archives—unknown, before 1920

In Nauvoo, priesthood holders were assigned to visit each member of the Church on a regular basis. One teenager had the unusual experience of being called to be the home teacher to the Prophet himself. This seventeen-year-old youth, William Cahoon, was somewhat apprehensive about his new calling. "I felt my weakness in visiting the Prophet and his family," he later recalled.

> I almost felt like shrinking from duty. Finally I went to his door and knocked, and in a minute the Prophet came to the door. I stood there trembling, and said to him, "Brother Joseph, I have come to visit you in the capacity of a teacher, if it is convenient for you." He said, "Brother William, come right in, I am glad to

see you; sit down in that chair there and I will go and call my family in." [The family arrived and sat down.] I said, "Brother Joseph, are you trying to live your religion?" He answered, "Yes." I then said, "Do you pray in your family?" He said, "Yes." "Do you teach your family the principles of the gospel?" He replied, "Yes, I am trying to do it." "Do you ask a blessing on your food?" He answered, "Yes." "Are you trying to live in peace and harmony with all your family?" He said that he was. I then turned to Sister Emma, his wife [and asked the same questions]. To all these questions she answered, "Yes, I am trying to do so." . . . As a teacher, I then left my parting blessing upon him and his family and took my departure.[38]

The Nauvoo period was also a time of healing and reconciliation for many former members of the Church who left the organization during the trying days in Missouri and Ohio. One brother who not only left the Church but also became a bitter enemy and assisted in the persecution of the Saints wanted to return to the fold. Daniel Tyler recalled that the man came to Nauvoo seeking forgiveness. Joseph saw the man from the front window:

As soon as he turned to open the gate, [Joseph] sprang up from his chair and ran and met him in the yard, exclaiming, "O Brother, how glad I am to see you!" He caught him around the neck, and both wept like children.[39]

While in Nauvoo, the Saints constructed their second temple, the Nauvoo Temple. In many ways, it was very similar to the earlier temple built in Kirtland; but the House of the Lord in Nauvoo included several new features, including a basement with a baptismal font supported by twelve oxen, representing the Twelve Tribes of Israel. A Canadian convert wrote,

The Temple is indeed a noble structure, and I suppose the architects of our day know not of what order to call it: Gothic, Doric, Corinthian or what; I call it Heavenly.[40]

The turbulent months preceding Joseph and Hyrum Smith's murders were marked by many diverse experiences. Converts continued to stream into the Nauvoo area; and the building projects, including the temple, business structures, and homes, continued unabated. From the dock at Nauvoo, Church leaders and missionaries left to near and distant destinations. Curtis Bolton, a member of the Church living in New York, visited Church headquarters for five weeks in 1844. Boarding a steamboat for his return trip home, Bolton saw Joseph Smith for the last time. Bolton wrote,

He was standing with his youngest boy in his arms at the brow of the hill on the west side of the Nauvoo House in the middle of the street. No one was near

Nauvoo Temple, Nauvoo, Illinois
(The Nauvoo Temple was the focal point of the Church from 1841-46)
LDS Historical Department—Lucian Foster, 1846

him. He was the most beautifully formed man, and was laughing pleasantly to the brethren on board the steam boat, who were leaving to go a preaching. I never in this life shall look upon his like again.[41]

Following his return to Long Island, Bolton heard the news of the death of the Smith brothers at Carthage, Illinois, on 27 June 1844.

After Joseph Smith's death at the hands of a mob, the Saints rallied to continue to fulfill Joseph's vision of their future as a people. Between 1844–46, additional missionaries were sent to various states within the United States, north to Canada, and to the British Isles. Literally thousands of Saints made their way to Nauvoo, some by land and many others by steamboat up the Mississippi River.

The effort to complete the temple was redoubled, and home construction increased. A period of peace existed in the county between the Saints and their enemies, but eventually mobs gathered to force the Saints away from their homes when the anti-Mormons began to realize that Joseph's death was not the undoing of Mormonism. Shortly after the Mormon exodus in 1846, J. H. Buckingham, a gentleman from Boston, visited the abandoned town of Nauvoo, expressing the reaction of many visitors to the "City of Joseph," as it was called by the Saints following Joseph's death:

> [T]he rise and progress of Nauvoo, will be, if it should ever be written, a romance of thrilling interest. No one can visit Nauvoo, and come away without a conviction that . . . the body of the Mormons were an industrious, hardworking, and frugal people. In the history of the whole world there cannot be found such another instance of so rapid a rise of a city out of the wilderness—a city so well built, a territory so well cultivated . . . Joe Smith, the Prophetleader, was, although an uneducated man, a man of great power, and a man who could conceive great projects.[42]

2

THE CHURCH IN OHIO

Ohio was settled long before the first Europeans arrived in the area. Archaeological evidence shows that native American Indians inhabited the area a thousand years before white settlers. The Mound Builders, Adena, Hopewell, and Fort Ancient Indian cultures grew crops, traded, crafted jewelry, and left impressive burial mounds during their existence.

When the French arrived, Ohio was home to four Indian tribes—the Delaware, Miami, Shawnee, and Wyandot. The French and Indian War resulted in the British occupation of French possessions east of the Mississippi in 1763. However, the Indian resistance did not finally subside until 1794, when General "Mad" Anthony Wayne defeated the Northwest Indian Confederation.

After the American Revolutionary War, Great Britain ceded Ohio lands to the United States. The Northwest Territory was created soon thereafter in 1787. The first governor, General St. Clair, moved the governmental office to Marietta in 1788 and then to Cincinnati in 1799. The northeastern portion (an area of approximately four million acres) was known as the Connecticut Western Reserve.

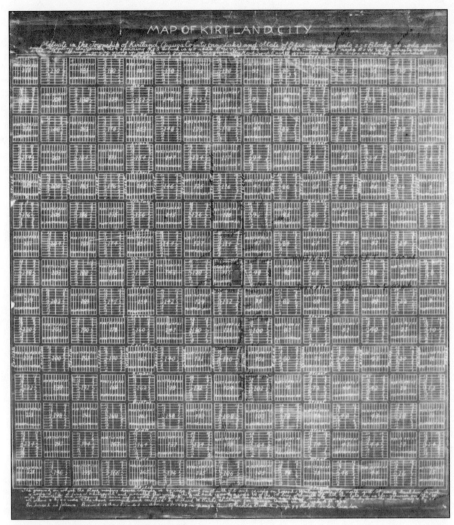

1836 Kirtland Plat Map, Kirtland, Ohio
(Mormon Kirtland proposed layout in 1830s)
RLDS Archives—Joseph Smith, 1836

In 1796, directors of the Connecticut Land Company commissioned Moses Cleveland, one of its original investors, to survey and divide the area into five-mile townships. A few years later, Turhand Kirtland, a land agent for the Connecticut Land Company, surveyed several townships in Geauga County (now in Lake County). Although settlement of the area proceeded rapidly, with almost seventy-two thousand white settlers arriving in 1800, political dissent postponed Ohio's admission to the Union until 1803, when Ohio was admitted as the seventeenth state.

Kirtland, Ohio

Kirtland, Ohio, is located approximately twenty-five miles northeast of Cleveland, Ohio. In 1811, the first white settlers arrived in Kirtland and organized a township in 1818. Kirtland began to expand with the establishment of a mill in 1820 and Newel K. Whitney's general store in 1823. Mail service to the area commenced sometime in 1825. By 1826, Kirtland, along with the entire state, was experiencing considerable growth and development. By the end of the year, almost three hundred thousand American settlers had arrived and had built communities in Ohio. The following year saw the construction of the Peter French Tavern in Kirtland. An early resident described the area thus:

> The country for many miles around had been for centuries the hunting-ground of the Indians, and surely their most vivid imagination could have portrayed nothing more desirable or delightful concerning their celestial hunting-grounds. The forest-trees were of endless variety and of the tallest kinds. A thick growth of underbrush grew beneath, flowers of rare beauty blushed unseen, birds of varied plumage filled the air with their music, the air itself was fragrant and invigorating.[1]

The building of several canal systems added to the growth of the area during the 1820s and 1830s. A year before the Church was organized in New York, Warren Corning of Mentor erected a log distillery at Kirtland Flats (lowlands just north of Kirtland). Residents hoped that such a business would bring great benefits to the Kirtland area, including a continued influx of settlers. Although this business was financially profitable, it was opposed by a group of 239 citizens who organized the Kirtland Temperance Society on 6 October 1830. The by-laws of the society included the prohibition on members' selling "grain of any kind to a distiller of whisky."[2]

During this period, the first Mormon missionaries arrived in the Western Reserve area from New York. Oliver Cowdery, Peter Whitmer, Ziba Peterson, and Parley P. Pratt arrived in Mentor, Ohio, in the latter part of October 1830. They were on their way to the Indian Territory on a proselyting mission and stopped at the home of an acquaintance of Parley P. Pratt, a restorationist preacher by the name of Sidney Rigdon. Rigdon was somewhat apprehensive of their new scripture, the *Book of Mormon*; nevertheless, he allowed them to preach at his Reformed Baptist Church in Mentor.

Main Street, Mentor, Ohio
(Sidney Rigdon lived in Mentor in 1830 when the first Mormon missionaries arrived)
Lake County Historical Society—unknown, c1910

After their visit to Mentor, the missionaries continued their work at the farm of Isaac Morley in Kirtland. Both in Kirtland and in Mentor, the missionaries' successes were immediate and remarkable. "The people thronged us night and day," Parley P. Pratt remembered, "insomuch that we had not time for rest or retirement." Some came "for curiosity, some to obey the gospel, and some to dispute or resist it."[3]

The missionaries did not have sufficient copies of the *Book of Mormon*; and, as a result, those who desired to read it had to borrow one of the few copies. Mary Elizabeth Rollins Lightner, a young girl at the time, described her own efforts to borrow a *Book of Mormon*:

> Quite a few residents of Kirtland accepted baptism . . . About this time, John Whitmer came and brought a Book of Mormon. There was a meeting that evening, and we learned that Brother Morley had the book in his possession—the only one in that part of the country. I went to his house before the meeting and asked to see the book. As I looked at it, I felt such a desire to read it that I could not refrain from asking him to let me take it home while he attended meeting. He finally said, "Child, if you will bring this book home before breakfast, tomorrow morning, you may take it." My uncle and aunt were Methodist, so when I got into the house, I exclaimed, "Oh, Uncle, I have got the 'Golden Bible.'" We took turns reading it until late at night. As soon as it was light enough to see, I was up and learned the first verse in the book. When I reached Brother Morley's house, he remarked, "I guess you did not read much in it." I showed him how far we had read. He was

surprised, and said, "I don't believe you can tell me one word of it." I then repeated the first verse, also the outline of the history of Nephi. He gazed at me in surprise and said, "Child, take this book home and finish it. I can wait."[4]

Sidney Rigdon met with his friends and neighbors on Sunday, 14 November 1830, at the Methodist meetinghouse in Kirtland. He announced his intentions of joining with the Saints. This sermon lasted about two hours, "during most of which time both himself and nearly all the congregation were melted into tears."[5] A local newspaper, *Painesville Telegraph*, reported that "some person came along here with the book [of Mormon], one pretends to have seen angels and assisted in translating the plates." News of the success in Kirtland had already reached the editor, as he concluded his report with the information that "in the neighboring township of Kirtland, we understand that twenty or thirty have been immersed into the new order of things, many of whom had been previously baptized."[6] By the end of the year, many members of Sidney Rigdon's congregation had embraced the new faith.

Within a month of their first visit to the Kirtland area, the four missionaries continued their journey west. Before their departure, some 130 individuals were baptized; and a branch of the Church was organized at Kirtland. Even after the missionaries left Kirtland, missionary work continued in northeastern Ohio through the efforts of the Ohio converts. Thus, Church membership continued to increase. Ohio was the fastest-growing area for the new Church; and by early 1831, four branches of the Church had been established. In New York, the Prophet Joseph Smith had received important revelations concerning the gathering that was to take place in Ohio. Soon, the New York branches prepared to move to Ohio,

Kirtland Area, Kirtland, Ohio
(Approaching Kirtland some two miles away)
John Waldsmith Collection—W. A. Faze, c1872

further augmenting the number of members in the area.

The advantages to such a move included allowing the new converts to learn about Church organization and facilitating Church teachings, thus assuring doctrinal and administrative uniformity. Easy access to other areas of the United States constituted another advantage. In addition, Ohio was a step closer to Zion (Missouri).

Joseph and Emma Smith were among the first of the Saints to make the journey to Kirtland, where they arrived in February 1831. Later, several emigrant groups of Saints arrived from New York. Lucy Mack Smith, the Prophet's mother, arrived at the Morley farm one evening in May 1831. Emma greeted her mother-in-law with surprise and relief, for Emma thought that Lucy was dead. Local newspapers had reported that a boat carrying emigrating members of the Church from Colesville, New York, had sunk in Lake Erie and that all passengers had drowned.

Panoramic View of Kirtland, Ohio
(Gathering place of the Saints from 1831-38)
LDS Historical Department—George E. Anderson, 1907

Since Kirtland was still a frontier community, living conditions were difficult. During the early period of Kirtland's settlement, the Saints built many frame and log homes, typically measuring sixteen or eighteen feet by twenty-two or twenty-four feet. The door was usually placed in the front side at about the middle. A few log homes had back doors on the opposite side. For light, many families used greased-paper windows by the side of the door. The lighting from these windows was poor, especially on dark and cloudy days. Eventually, glass from Pittsburgh arrived, although much of it was broken in transit and it was often thin and of poor quality. It was also expensive and often could not be obtained at any price. At night, candles provided light for those living in small cabins. The use of "tallow-dip candles" was economical; each candle consisted of a cotton rag tied around a button and set in a saucer filled with lard. An alternative source of light was to burn hickory bark in the fireplace. By occasionally feeding the fire with bark, the family obtained enough light to read in the evening.

At one end of the typical log home was a seven- to eight-foot area of logs that was cut out about six feet high. The opening created by this procedure was then filled with a stone wall. On this wall at each end was laid a timber sufficiently large to support the chimney to the fire chamber floor beam, which extended about four feet from the end of the house and two feet higher than the wall.

The chimney was built along these timbers and was composed of flat sticks, some two or three inches wide, laid up in clay mortar and plastered inside and outside. The chimney narrowed as it went up out of the peak of the roof, from six by four to three by two. This construction allowed light to enter the cabin from above.

The hearth, usually six by eight, was made of clay that was pounded down five or six inches lower than the floor. Flat quarry stones were then laid on the clay, bringing the hearth up even with the floor. A trammel or other device was used to hang the pot or kettle and to raise or lower it as the occasion required. In the fireplace was a large back log, five or six feet long; and smaller wood could be piled on to warm the whole house.

Cooking utensils included a five-pail brass kettle, an eight-quart brass kettle, a one-pail iron pot, an iron teakettle, and a frying pan with an iron handle three or four feet long. Bread was baked out of doors in a Dutch oven. Eating utensils were few during the early period.

The buttery was located on a few shelves in one corner of the room. A ladder accessed the upper loft; or, when lumber was available, the settlers built stairs. If the cabin had a cellar, a trap door was placed in the floor; and a small hole was dug in the ground for storing vegetables and other items. The bedrooms were partitioned off, originally by blankets hung up around the beds. Initially, most homes had a few items of furniture, some of which were homemade.

Although a necessity for cooking and heating, the open fireplace was a constant source of danger in pioneer homes. While Lorenzo and Persis Young were away from home one day in August 1836, their daughter, Lucy, "age three years and ten months . . . suffer[ed] short but excruciating [pain]. Her clothes took fire in the absence of the family, and notwithstanding her shrieks, no one arrived in time to extinguish the flames and save the child! So the morning flower, which but yesterday bloomed in all its native liveliness, was cut down and withered in an hour."[7]

Many converts came into the Church through relatives. One of these converts was Milo Andrus, a New York resident, who wrote:

> One month and nine days previous to my baptism, I was united in marriage to Abigail Jane Daley, whose father had been baptized into The Church of Christ about one year before. We were married February 21st, 1833, baptized April 12th, 1833. I was ordained an elder May 5th, 1833, under the hands of Joseph Wood.[8]

Typical of most male converts, Andrus soon left his home and began a "mission" for his new-found faith. He recalled, "[I] started on my first mission in June 1833, in company with Joseph Wood, traveled a distance of seventy miles preaching every day and baptized three." Eventually, Andrus and Wood "came to Kirtland where the Prophet Joseph Smith resided with his family." Many early Saints wanted to meet the Prophet and traveled long distances to see him. While in Kirtland, Andrus witnessed a Church quarterly conference. Besides being religious meetings, these conferences also gave Church leaders the opportunity to make administrative changes. Although many missionaries had great success, Andrus and his companion enjoyed less success on their mission to southern Ohio:

Peter French Tavern, Kirtland, Ohio
(Traditionally identified as the first brick building in Kirtland)
LDS Visual Resources Library—unknown, unknown

> [I] changed my traveling companion, and I was coupled with Ova Truman. Joseph Wood and his fellow laborer went to Philadelphia, and I with my new companion was sent to the southern part of the state of Ohio, to return in three months to the next quarterly conference. We were not very successful and baptized only two persons.[9]

The mass immigration of the Saints prevented many new community members from finding adequate housing and gainful employment. However, some were fortunate enough to have the money to buy property and build homes.

Among these more fortunate ones were Caroline Crosby and her husband Jonathan, who arrived in Kirtland from Massachusetts in the fall of 1835. "My husband purchased a lot west of the temple and began to make preparation for building," she later wrote.

While they built their home, they rented the home of Parley P. Pratt, who was on a mission. This occasion was the first time in their one and one-half years of marriage that they were able to live alone as a couple.

She described her joy at "housekeeping." She said, "I felt like a child with a new set of toys. I cleaned the house from stem to stern, and arranged everything in the best of order." She felt blessed since "several families came in at that time . . . [and] houses were very hard to be rented, every place being filled."

Eventually, they too had to share living space again, this time with a Sister Granger. Even among the Saints, these close living quarters were somewhat difficult. The difficulty is evident, as Sister Crosby described Sister Granger's having "had many peculiarities, which in some respects were not as agreeable to us, as we could wish."

Soon, the Crosbys had their own home near the temple "enclosed, and a loose floor, no windows, but my anxiety was so great," she recalled, "to get away by ourselves, that I determined to move in at all events." After they moved in, the work to finish the home continued at redoubled speed. "My husband continued his labors incessantly until he got the doors and windows in, and then we thought ourselves highly blessed."

These "pioneers" were thankful for many simple things. Caroline Crosby listed a good cellar, a nice cooking stove, and a "well, close to my door" as "three great conveniences." Eventually, "we got our house a little more comfortable, the floor planed, and made very tight, a partition through, and floor over head."[10]

Like many, including the Crosby family and Wilford Woodruff, the arrival of Saints in Kirtland was an occasion to meet the Prophet for the first time. Woodruff arrived in Kirtland in April 1834 with Harry Brown, Warren Ingalls, John Murdock, and Orson Pratt. Woodruff recorded,

> We continued to travel towards Kirtland and arrived there at night on the 25 of April 1834. There for the first time I had a view of our beloved Brother Joseph Smith the prophet and seer which God hath raised up in these last days through whom the Saints receive Revelations from time to time. Brother Joseph invited us to take up our abode with him and accordingly we did and boarded at his house most of the time for a week.[11]

Safety Society Building, Kirtland Temple, and Methodist Church
(Three significant structures in Kirtland during the 1830s)
RLDS Archives—unknown, c1890

Another important visitor was Brigham Young, who in February 1835 was called to the Quorum of the Twelve as organized by Joseph in Kirtland. Young recalled his first visit by saying, "We went to his father's house, and learned that he was in the woods, chopping." Near the home, Brigham Young and Heber C. Kimball saw the Prophet with two or three of his brothers chopping wood. "Here my joy was full," Brigham stated, "at the privilege of shaking the hand of the Prophet of God, and received the sure testimony, by the Spirit of prophecy, that he was all that any man could believe him to be, as a true Prophet."[12] The Prophet welcomed them and brought them to his home for the next seven days.

The news concerning difficulties in Jackson County, Missouri, another important Church center, reached Kirtland on 25 November 1833. This information was a factor in prompting Joseph Smith to organize "Zion's Camp" in 1834. This group of men walked nearly nine hundred miles through Ohio, Indiana, Illinois, and Missouri to Zion. The original purpose of the trip to Missouri was to reinstate the Missouri Saints on their Jackson County lands from which mobs had driven them beginning in July 1833. However, this original goal was never accomplished.

The initial preparation for Zion's Camp began when several small groups left Kirtland for New Portage, about fifty miles south, as early as May 1834. At New Portage, Joseph Smith organized about 130 men into Zion's Camp. Their march to Missouri officially began on 8 May 1834. At Salt River, Missouri, Joseph's group met Hyrum's group from Michigan. At this point, the group numbered 224 individuals. Later, at Fishing River, Joseph received a revelation commanding Zion's Camp not to pursue further the "redemption of Zion" at that time.[13] After several individuals fell ill with cholera, the group finally disbanded soon thereafter.

Although Zion's Camp did not fulfill its intended goal, the experience acquainted Joseph Smith with many of the male members of the early Church. It also provided the Church with tested men, many of whom later became its leaders. Many of the first Quorum of the Twelve Apostles and all of the Seventy, another priesthood body, were selected from the men of Zion's Camp.

After the destruction of the Church's printing establishment in Independence in July 1833, *The Evening and the Morning Star* continued publication in Kirtland from December 1833 through September 1834.[14] Thereafter, several different newspapers were published in Kirtland, including the *Latter Day Saints' Messenger and Advocate*,[15] *The Elders' Journal of The Church of Latter Day Saints*,[16] and the *Northern Times*. Although they featured different formats and sizes, they were dedicated to Church service. Sometimes this service included responding to other publications or newspaper articles. One example of this service was a response to a story printed in the *New York Mercury*. This newspaper claimed that Joseph Smith, in an attempt to give baptismal services more solemnity, promised that an angel would appear on the river bank at each baptism. The newspaper account continued:

> The rite was administered in the evening in Grand River, near Painesville, not by the Prophet in person, but by his disciples. In agreement with the prediction of the Prophet, on each occasion a figure in white appeared in white [and] was seen on the opposite bank and the faith of the faithful was thereby greatly increased . . . [At] length . . . a company of young men (unbelievers of course) . . . secreted themselves, they awaited its arrival. Their expectations were soon realized, by its appearance in its customary position, and rushing from their lair, they succeeded in forcing it into the stream . . . bearing triumphant to the opposite side of the stream, when who should this supposed inhabitant of the upper world be, but the Mormon Prophet himself![17]

The *Messenger and Advocate* responded and called this article a "slanderous slip."[18]

When the Church held important conferences or administrative meetings in Kirtland, the Kirtland newspapers served as a means of communicating this information to missionaries. "We request to inform," a notice stated in the March 1835 edition, "Elders Thomas B. Marsh and Orson Pratt, that they are desired to

Kirtland Flats, Kirtland, Ohio
(French Tavern and Newel K. Whitney Store)
LDS Historical Department—unknown, unknown

attend a meeting of the elders in this place on the 26th of April next. We hope that circumstances may render it convenient for them to attend, as their presence is very desirable."[19]

Life among the Saints revolved around their religious commitment to the restored gospel; but like other individuals who migrated to the frontier, the Saints in Kirtland had to confront the problems common to those struggling to survive in the harsh frontier environment. Death was common in frontier communities like Kirtland. Contemporary newspapers, journals, and letters frequently mentioned the death not only of older people but also of children and young people. The *Messenger and Advocate* for February 1835 ran this notice:

> DIED in this place on the evening of 19th inst. elder SETH JOHNSON, aged 30 years. Elder J. was a young man of promising talents, and of strict religious principles; ever manifesting, by his acts, the warm affection of a

Looking North from the Temple, Kirtland, Ohio
(Chillicothe Road and the Joseph Smith Home)
LDS Historical Department—unknown, c1900

heart devoted to the cause of God, and to the most dear to him of all things, the religion of the Lord Jesus; but his Master has accepted his work and taken him home, where he can receive that reward promised to the pure in heart. Though dust returns to dust, and his spirit has fled to Christ, we drop this as a tribute to his worth—HE WAS A SAINT.[20]

Joseph and Emma lost three children (two natural children and one adopted) during the Kirtland period. When Joseph and Emma arrived in February 1831, Emma was six months pregnant with twins. The babies, a boy and girl, were delivered on 30 April but lived only three hours. This death was a severe hardship for Joseph and Emma, who had already lost one child, Alvin, in Harmony, Pennsylvania, in 1828.

Looking North from the Temple (Joseph Smith Home), Kirtland, Ohio
(Joseph Smith lived here in 1835)
RLDS Archives—unknown, c1920

Death touched the Smiths again when Joseph Smith, Sr.'s mother, Mary Duty Smith, died during her visit to Kirtland in 1836. "She had come five hundred miles to see her children," Joseph Smith wrote. It was a joyous reunion, as she was introduced to her great-grandchildren. Several days after her arrival, Mary Duty died on 27 May at the age of ninety-three. "My Grandmother," Joseph noted, "fell asleep without sickness, pain or regret. She breathed her last about sunset, and was buried in the burial ground near the Temple, after a funeral address had been delivered by Sidney Rigdon."[21]

Although the death of a child was a painful reality to many of the Saints, the children themselves often showed astonishing faith in the face of death. Naomi Harmon, eleven years of age, comforted her parents just before her death saying that they should "not weep for [me], or in other words, not to feel bad, for she said, that it was better for her to go than to stay! for she knew that she should be happy, she wanted to go and be with Christ and her brothers that had died and gone before her." She died 15 June 1836 at her home in Kirtland with her parents and brothers and sister at her side."22

Along with the daily toil and drudgery of life and death in Kirtland also came moments of joy. In Oliver Cowdery's sketch book, a diary of his activities in Kirtland, he recorded the following experience:

> Wednesday the 20th [January 1836] copied blessings until evening, at which time I went, in company with my wife, to Elder John F. Boynton's wedding: a large company assembled, and after the services we were treated with wine and cake very sumptuously. While these things were passing, and joy filled each heart . . . O may the Lord my God roll on the day of peace and rest!23

Looking South from the Temple, Kirtland, Ohio
(The temple quarry is approximately two miles)
RLDS Archives—unknown, c1920

Other moments of great happiness occurred at marriages. Wilford Woodruff and Phoebe Carter's marriage was solemnized by Frederick G. Williams, and a blessing was given by Patriarch Joseph Smith, Sr. "In the name of the Lord," Wilford wrote, "and pronounced great Blessings upon us and our posterity." The wedding occurred at 2:00 P.M. at Joseph Smith's home. Two hours later, the company, consisting of about thirty-two individuals, assembled at Sidney Rigdon's to witness another wedding. Woodruff reflected on the event in these words:

> The sun in the east arose to gladden earth and shed over nature his pleasing beams to welcome the return of a delightful spring that dreary winter might be forgotten. No day more pleasing than April thirteenth 1837 while all nature smiled without friendship purest joys were felt beneath a prophet's roof where the bride and bridegroom found a welcome reception. While by law with the nuptial cord their hands were bound their congenial hearts in one, lay cemented bearing the seal of Eternal Life. Their friendship formed from principle pure, virtue unsullied, bid refinement over those hearts to rule, possessing the love of God the only foundation of true friendship.

He finished his entry for the day with the Latin phrase, *Vera amicitia est sempiterna*, meaning "True friendship is eternal."[24]

Woodruff's mention of the "delightful spring" arriving in Kirtland echoes public notices regarding the changing season. "The weather begins to look like spring," an editorial in the local newspaper stated. "[O]ur feathered songsters have greeted us with the sound of their voices once more, and nature is about to put on her summer dress. Our winter has not been as severe as in some places to the south, and with all, we think that the never changing goodness our God ought to inspire our hearts with increased devotion toward him."[25] At other times, the Saints observed heavenly wonders. Joseph recorded the following in his own journal:

> [13 November 1833] In the morning at 4 o'clock I was awoke by Brother Davis knocking at my door saying, "Brother Joseph come get up and see the signs in the heavens" and I arose and beheld to my great joy the stars falling from heaven, yea they fell like hail stones, a literal fulfillment of the word of God as recorded in the holy scriptures and a sure sign that the coming of Christ is close at hand. Oh how marvelous are thy works, oh Lord, and I thank thee for thy mercy unto me thy servant. Oh Lord save me in thy kingdom for Christ sake, Amen.[26]

The Saints also witnessed miracles of a more personal nature. Ebenezer Robinson recalls the conversion of an insane resident of Kirtland:

> There was a family by the name of Newcombe, residing about one mile south of the temple in Kirtland. His wife's brother, (a man we should judge about thirty years of age) was a raving maniac of the most violent kind. He had to be kept chained in an outhouse by himself, and clothed with strong, coarse clothing, for when he could, he would tear his clothing from him. He would also rave and rage exceedingly

whenever any person came near him excepting his sister, Mrs. Newcombe, she had control over him. We saw him [at] different times, but it was a distressing sight.

In the latter part of November or in December, 1836, several brethren took his case in hand, and went to Brother Newcombe's and commenced to fast and pray for power over the evil spirit, and deliverance for the man from his power. Joseph Smith, Sen. (father of Joseph Smith, Jr., the translator of the Book of Mormon), had charge, assisted by Brethren John P. Green, Oliver Granger, and others. They continued in fasting and prayer for three days and nights, with occasionally, one at a time, taking a little respite, when Brother [Joseph] Smith, Sen., told them to bring the man into the room where they were, which they did. They laid their hands upon him in the name of the Lord Jesus Christ, and rebuked the evil spirit by which he had been bound, when the man wilted down, and became as a little child. Brother Joseph Smith, Sen., ordered them to take the chains from off him. He was healed, to the great joy of all, and they felt to render thanksgiving and praise to our Heavenly Father, to whom be glory and honor forever and ever, amen.

The man continued sane and well, and during the winter attended church with the family at different times. It was customary in the Church in those days to give an invitation and opportunity for anyone who wished to unite with the Church by baptism, to make it manifest by rising to their feet. This invitation was given at the close of the morning sermon each Sunday. One Sunday in March, 1837, this man who had been healed, sat next to me at my right hand in the same pew with me, in the temple at meeting, and when the invitation for baptism was given out, he arose, and was afterwards baptized.[27]

Looking West from the Temple, Kirtland, Ohio
(A large residential area existed west of the temple)
RLDS Archives—unknown, unknown

Kirtland was the Church center, but other communities in Ohio had branches and members of the Church. Activity in these communities included missionary and church work as well as business and political duties.

During this early period of Church history, the Saints who had emigrated from New England retained many of their traditional practices and beliefs regarding dancing, theater, and other recreational activities. Most Christian churches at the time discouraged such activities. The Kirtland Saints by and large held views similar to those held by members of other Christian churches. On 22 October 1837, twenty-two members of the Church were "disfellowshipped" until they made "satisfaction for uniting with the world in a dance the Thursday previous." Over the next several days, "nine more of the brethren and sisters were reported to the Church as having been engaged in the recreations." These activities occurred during a period of retrenchment, when steps were taken against the "use of ardent spirits," "lounging about the streets," and "unruly children."[28]

An editorial in the Church newspaper entitled "Children" spoke rather frankly about various activities engaged in by the youth in Kirtland. "The practice of suffering boys and girls," the article stated, "to be strolling about the streets without any business, is unrighteous, and leads to vice; to vicious habits; to laziness; to profanity and disobedience, and, without speedy repentance, will leave many souls to reap the reward of their folly."[29]

Annual celebrations and holidays, often discouraged in New England Churches, were similarly insignificant in the lives of the Kirtland Saints. For most of the Saints, even Christmas was nothing more than a routine day. Instead of these activities, the men, women, and children participated in other kinds of diversions.

Joseph Smith III, who was the first surviving child of Joseph and Emma, was born in Kirtland. Though just five years old when he left Kirtland for Missouri with his family, he recalled several youthful activities in which he participated. For a brief time, the Smiths lived in a home "on the west side of the street which runs from the Temple down to the Chagrin River and was not very far from the ford across this little stream," he recalled. He went down to this creek "with a number of other boys who engaged in fishing for the small edible fish the stream afforded. Seeing their success I, too, wanted to fish. My mother, to gratify me, procured a little pole and attached a thread thereto, with a bent pin for a hook, and away I marched to the creek." He continued:

> I threw my hook without bait into the water and the little fishes gathered to it as it fell. By some strange chance one became fastened to it and was drawn to the shore. In great excitement I dropped the pole and gathering the fish in my hands rushed

to the house with it, shouting, "I've got one! I got one!" Whether or not the fish was cooked for delectation or whatever became of it, I have not the remotest remembrance. It was of the variety known as horned chub, about six inches long, round and attractive. I have seen such fishes in the same stream in later years.[30]

As it did in the life of young Joseph, nature played an important role in the Saints' lives, not only as a source of food but also as an impetus for solemn reflection and as an escape from the drudgery and demands of the frontier life. On 4 October 1835, Joseph Smith wrote the following in his journal:

Main Street, Ashtabula, Ohio
(Joseph Smith visited this community near Kirtland)
Ashtabula Historical Society—unknown, 1861

[S]tarted early in the morning with Brother J. Carrell to hold a meeting in Perry, Ohio when about a mile from home we saw two deer playing in the field, which diverted our minds by giving an impetus to our thoughts upon the subject of the creation of God. We conversed upon many topics and the day passed off in a very agreeable manner and the Lord blessed our souls.[31]

Joseph's other activities included visiting many of the lakes of the region. Among these visits was a trip to Lake Erie where Joseph went to fish and to visit friends in April 1834. During the summer of 1837, Joseph and several others visited Ashtabula, a town about thirty miles northeast of Kirtland. Joseph recorded, "[We were] enjoying ourselves very much in walking on the beach and bathing in the beautiful, clear water of the lake."[32]

Skating and sleighing during the winter and swimming, fishing, and horseback riding in the summer figured among the Saints' leisure activities. The youth were often engaged in playing ball, marbles, and dolls. In the winter, the children of Kirtland built forts and snow figures and had snowball fights. Family activities also included conversing, playing, singing, and studying together in the evenings. Writing and publishing poetry and religious hymns were other activities in which many Saints engaged and with which the Saints occupied themselves. Short verses like the following appeared on an almost regular basis in local newspapers:

> Love the Lord and keep his commandments without being reminded of it every day. Love your neighbor as yourself, and make his welfare your welfare, and the Lord will reward you for it. Love labor, and whatever you do, remember the poor and needy. Thank the Lord for the blessings you daily enjoy from his holy hand. Thank the Lord for all things for his goodness is endless.[33]

Church leaders introduced educational opportunities for the Saints during the Kirtland period. At the Newel K. Whitney store, Joseph established a "School of the Prophets." The school had several purposes, including the preparation of missionaries for their assignments. On 27 December 1832, Joseph Smith received a revelation known as the "Olive Leaf."[34] This revelation instructed the Saints to organize their first school, later known as the School of the Elders. This school was the beginning of a major educational program that eventually came to include both adults and children. The Saints not only studied theology but also studied mathematics, Latin and Hebrew, English grammar, writing, government, geography, ancient and modern history, and philosophy. As many as 130 young men and women attended the Kirtland School. The following notice appeared in the Kirtland newspaper, *Messenger and Advocate*:

> Notice—The spring term of the "Kirtland School" will commence on the 20th of April next. Young gentlemen and ladies from a distance can obtain board, in respectable families for $1.00 to $1.25 per week. The Trustees of this institution design to introduce the higher branches of English literature, at as early a period as possible.[35]

These schools were similar to the first high schools organized in America a few years earlier. Several small groups met in the homes of individuals to study singing, debate, and geography.

All these schools and classes were influenced by the restoration and therefore included discussions of the gospel in addition to the presentation of the secular subjects listed above. Occasionally, doctrinal issues were debated and resolved in the classroom. Brigham Young, although not a member of the school, recalled the situation at the time:

> When they [the School of the Prophets] assembled together in this room [Newel K. Whitney store] after breakfast, the first thing they did was to light their pipes, and while smoking, talk about the great things of the kingdom, and spit all over the room, and as soon as the pipe was out of their mouths a large chew of tobacco would then be taken. Often when the Prophet entered the room to give the school instructions he would find himself in a cloud of tobacco smoke.[36]

This situation did not go unnoticed. The Kirtland Temperance Society, a group of Saints and others in the community, opposed the use of alcohol, tobacco, and the consumption of too much meat. Almost daily, Emma Smith was faced with the task of cleaning the room after the meetings. While some of the women thought it "would be a good thing if a revelation could be had declaring the use of tobacco a sin, and commanding its suppression," the men retorted, "that a revelation should also provide for a total abstinence of tea and coffee drinking, intending this as a counter dig at the sisters."[37] The Prophet made the issue a subject of prayer; and to the chagrin of almost all involved, on 27 February 1833, he received a revelation known as the "Word of Wisdom." The revelation advised against the use of strong drinks, coffee, tea, and tobacco.

Other significant doctrinal developments occurred during the Kirtland period, including the publication of *The Doctrine and Covenants* (a collection of revelations, statements, and articles relating to the Saints' beliefs and practices).[38] On 25 October 1831, the Saints held an important conference at the home of Sirenus Burnett in Orange, Cuyahoga County, Ohio. William McClellan states in a letter:

> On the 25th October I attended a conference. General peace and harmony pervaded the conference and much instruction to me. From thence I went home with Joseph and lived with him about three weeks; and from my acquaintance then and until now I can truly say I believe him to be a man of God. A Prophet, a Seer and Revelator to the Church of Christ.[39]

At this conference, Joseph Smith received a revelation for McClellan.[40]

The construction of the temple was another important event in the lives of the Kirtland Saints. The completion of the temple in 1836 coincided with a great "pentecostal season" in Kirtland among the Saints. On 21 January 1836, just months before the temple was dedicated, Joseph Smith and several other brethren of the Church met in the nearly completed temple. About forty men entered the temple and climbed the spiral stair past the large assembly halls on the first and second floors to the third-floor "attic." The attic was divided into

Kirtland Temple Attic, Kirtland, Ohio
(Known as the President's Room and site of 21 January 1836 vision)
LDS Historical Department—unknown, unknown

five separate rooms with the presidency room located in the west end. This room had been consecrated a few weeks earlier as a place of learning and at the time served as a Hebrew classroom and a translating room. Some of the approximately forty priesthood holders met in this room, while others met in adjoining rooms.

Those in attendance included Sidney Rigdon, Oliver Cowdery, Frederick G. Williams, Joseph Smith, Sr., Hyrum Smith, David Whitmer, W. W. Phelps, John Whitmer, Warren Parrish, Edward Partridge, Isaac Morley, John Corrill, Newel K. Whitney, Vinson Knight, Reynolds Cahoon, and several others. Earlier in the day, these same men had met in the printing office to receive the washing and anointing ordinances.

At this meeting, some of the brethren encircled the seated Father Smith; and all raised their right hands. His son, Joseph Smith, Jr., holding a bottle of olive oil, blessed and consecrated it in the name of Jesus Christ. Joseph then anointed his father and invoked the blessings of heaven upon him. Following this blessing, each man in turn blessed Father Smith. Anointings of other men in the group followed. After the anointings of his father, Joseph Smith, Jr. testified,

> The heavens were opened upon us and I beheld the celestial Kingdom of God, and the glory thereof, whether in the body or out I cannot tell. I saw the transcendent beauty of the gate through which the heirs of that Kingdom will enter, which was like unto circling flames of fire, also the blazing throne of God, whereon was seated the Father and the Son. I saw the beautiful streets of that Kingdom, which had the appearance of being paved with gold. I saw father Adam, and Abraham and Michael and my father and mother, my brother Alvin that has long since slept, and marveled how it was that he had obtained an inheritance in that Kingdom, seeing that he had departed this life before the Lord had set his hand to gather Israel the second time and had not been baptized for the remission of sins. Thus came the voice of the Lord unto me saying all who have died with[out] a knowledge of this gospel, who would have received it with all their hearts shall be heirs of that Kingdom for I the Lord will judge all men according to their works according to the desires of their hearts. And I also beheld that all children who die before they arrive to the years of accountability, are saved in the celestial Kingdom of Heaven.[41]

The revelation continued as Joseph saw the "12 Apostles of the Lamb, who are now upon the earth who hold the Keys of this last ministry in foreign lands, standing together in a circle much fatigued, with their clothes tattered and feet swollen, with their eyes cast downward, and Jesus standing in their midst and they did not behold him." "Many of my brethren," the Prophet concluded, "who received this ordinance with me, saw glorious visions also. Angels ministered unto them, as well as myself, and the power of the highest rested upon us. The house was filled with the glory of God and we shouted Hosannah to God and the Lamb."[42]

The meeting concluded past midnight with singing and prayer. Joseph's journal indicates that he retired between one and two o'clock in the morning. Although the Hebrew school convened as usual on the following day, the brethren spent the entire morning discussing the visions of the preceding evening.

Wilford Woodruff had arrived in Kirtland in April 1834 and departed on a mission to New England after the Zion's Camp experience. He returned in the fall of 1836, just after the temple had been completed. He described his first view of it in his journal:

November 25 [1836] Took the parting hand with Elder Sherwood. I then set out in company with Elder Smoot on foot in a hard snowstorm for Kirtland. We came in sight of the Temple of the Lord before we reached the village and I truly felt to rejoice at the sight as it was the first time that mine eyes ever beheld the house of the Lord built by commandment and Revelation. We soon entered the village and I spent one of the happiest days of my life at this time in visiting Kirtland and the House of the Lord and the Presidents and Elders of the Church. I was truly edified to again strike hands with President Joseph Smith Jr.[43]

Local opposition to the Church spread during this period. However, the newspaper articles, pamphlets, and books against the Church published during this period oftentimes actually served to increase the public's interest in the message of Mormonism.

Sarah Leavitt recalled how she and her family subscribed to a "Free-will Baptist" paper while living in Canada. For a brief period of time, the newspaper published several antagonistic articles about the "new sect." Sarah read about this "sect" with great interest since "it had a prophet that pretended he talked with God." "They had built a thing they called a meetinghouse, a huge mass of rock and wood," the article stated. "In this Joe would go talk, he said, with the Lord and come out and tell them what the Lord said," she recalled. Sarah initially felt that the events recorded in the articles "were too big lies for anyone to believe." However, after she eventually obtained a copy of the *Book of Mormon* and a copy of *The Doctrine and Covenants*, she began to have faith that the stories

Panoramic View of Temple Area from the Flats, Kirtland, Ohio
(Joseph Smith's variety store on right side)
RLDS Archives—unknown, c1910

were true. She said that "it was the book of Doctrine and Covenants that confirmed" her faith that God had spoken again through a prophet.[44]

During the Kirtland period, the Church obtained several ancient Egyptian mummies and papyrus scrolls. As in most communities, rumors in Kirtland sometimes had to be corrected. "The public mind has been excited," John Whitmer wrote in the *Messenger and Advocate*, "by reports which have been circulated concerning certain Egyptian Mummies, and a quantity of ancient records, which were purchased by certain gentlemen in this place, last summer." The rumors in Kirtland said that the mummies were actually "Abraham, Abimelech, the king of the Philistines, Joseph who was sold into Egypt, &c &c. for the purpose of attracting the attention of the multitude." This rumor was, of course, "utterly false."[45]

The Egyptian manuscript, which Joseph Smith described as "beautifully written on papyrus, with black, and a small part red, ink or paint, in perfect preservation,"[46] was a source of the Book of Abraham that Joseph later published in Nauvoo, Illinois.[47] The purchase of these mummies enhanced the Church's interest in antiquities. Apparently, the Saints had an interest in anything ancient—they studied Hebrew and ultimately attempted to produce an Egyptian alphabet and grammar. Nevertheless, the Church leaders were also practical men who were concerned about their own era.

One of the problems facing the Saints as they struggled to build a gathering place and a temple to God was the lack of money and credit. After Andrew Jackson abolished the National Bank in 1837, individual states were more responsible for the creation of state and private banks. The Saints in Kirtland believed that the establishment of their own private bank would facilitate the completion of their ambitious building projects.

However, the Ohio legislature rejected the Saints' proposal. The Saints then established a safety society or anti-bank. The Kirtland Safety Society failed during the nation-wide panic of 1837. A combination of the failure of the Safety Society and the accompanying depression agitated dissenters in Kirtland and caused bitterness in the community of the Saints. Many members of the Church blamed Joseph Smith for the failure of the Safety Society and called him a fallen prophet. During this period, Brigham Young commented, "This was a crisis when earth and hell seemed leagued to overthrow the Prophet and Church of God. The knees of many of the strongest men in the Church faltered."[48]

Like other growing frontier communities, Kirtland attracted certain "less-desirable" individuals, many of whom were seeking to take advantage of the

Saints' willingness to share with their brothers and sisters of the Church. In one instance, the Church alerted the brethren to the presence of such an individual in their midst:

> We are under the painful necessity of saying to the branches of the church of Latter Day Saints abroad, as well as to all good people to whom this notice may come, that DAVID B. GILBERT a Botanic practitioner of medicine, was regularly received into the church in this place, and after obtaining the almost unlimited confidence of said church through the influence of some of the official members, he has in a shameful, and wicked manner, forfeited all confidence, by involving himself in debt deeply, borrowing money, and it is more than suspected, that he has stolen some and has now absconded to parts unknown. Said Gilbert is about five feet eight inches high, slim built, ruddy complexion, dark eyes; and walks rather slow for a man of his years, being, as we judge, about 28.[49]

Joseph Fielding, a recent convert from Canada, wrote of his sorrow upon his arrival in Kirtland during the troubling time of 1837–38:

> On my arrival at Kirtland I was much cast down and troubled. I found the Saints were far from being all righteous. There was great contention among them. This together with another circumstance which I forbear to mention, caused me much sorrow of heart. During two or three weeks stopping there I witnessed several unpleasant circumstances.[50]

Temple and Rigdon Home, Kirtland, Ohio
(Looking north, Chillicothe Road runs between the temple and Rigdon home)
RLDS Archives—unknown, c1910

Nevertheless, Joseph Fielding also found some joy during his stay in Kirtland, particularly when his sister Mercy married Robert Thompson, "a Priest in the Church." Fielding's call to travel to England, the Church's first mission outside of North America, was another significant event.

During this critical period of trial, Joseph Smith looked to God for an answer to his prayers to save the Church from the unsettling dissension. The answer came a few days later when he found Heber C. Kimball in the temple. Joseph whispered to him, "Brother Heber, the Spirit of the Lord has whispered to me, 'Let my servant Heber go to England and proclaim my Gospel and open the door of salvation to that nation.'"[51] Kimball's immediate and highly successful missionary success in England greatly strengthened the Church.

Kirtland's position as the center of the Church did not last very long, although Kirtland enjoyed a period of remarkable growth that peaked during 1835–37. The *Messenger and Advocate* announced the following under a column entitled "Our Village":

> Nothing can be more gratifying to the saints in this place and their friends and brethren abroad than to contemplate the scene now before them. Every Lords day our house of worship is filled to the overflowing with attentive-hearers, mostly communicants.

> In the evening following the singers meet under the direction of Brother L. Carter and J. Crosby Jr. who give instruction in the principles of vocal music. On Monday evening the quorum of high priests meets. They transact the business of their particular quorum, speak, sing, pray, and so worship the God of heaven. On Tuesday evening the Seventies . . . [speak] of the goodness and power of God. On Wednesday evening the rooms are occupied by the quorum of Elders . . . On Thursday P.M. a prayer meeting is held in the lower part of the house . . . [It] is conducted by Joseph Smith senior, the patriarch of the church.

> During the week a school is taught in the attic story of the house, denominated the "Kirtland High School" . . . On the streets are continually thronged with teams loaded with wood, materials for building the ensuing season, provisions for the market, people to trade, or parties of pleasure to view our stately and magnificent temple. Although our population is by no means as dense as in many villages, yet the number of new buildings erected the last season, those now in contemplation and under contract to build next season, together with our every day occurrences, are evincive of more united exertion, more industry and more enterprise than we ever witnessed in so sparse a population, so far from any navigable water and in this season of the year.[52]

A short period after this positive review of Kirtland, disaster struck in the form of economic depression and the failure of the Kirtland Safety Society. As a result, tensions increased between the faithful Saints and dissenters who were in league with anti-Mormon forces. Ultimately, many members lost faith and left the Church. Finally, in 1838, internal strife and persecution from non-Mormons caused the Saints to abandon their homes, shops, farms, schools, and beautiful temple. Joseph Smith and his family were among the first to leave Kirtland for Missouri in January 1838. Small groups of Saints soon followed, and the last group—the five-hundred-member Kirtland Camp—left in early July.

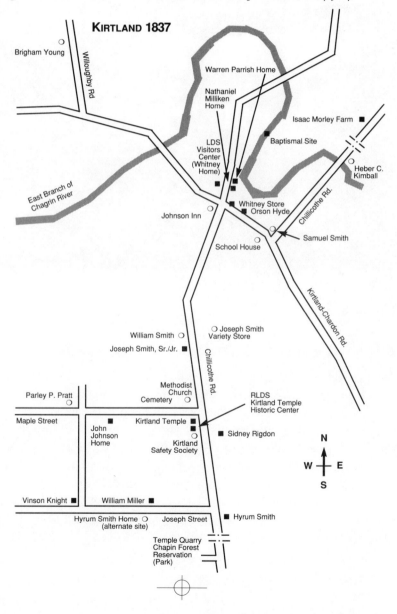

Newel K. Whitney Store

The Newel K. Whitney store is located north of the Kirtland Temple and is situated on the northeast corner of Chillicothe and Kirtland-Chardon roads.

Newel K. Whitney Store and Orson Hyde Home, Kirtland, Ohio
(The Store was the birthplace of Joseph Smith III in 1831)
LDS Historical Department—unknown, c1910

Historical Background

Around 1 February 1831, Joseph and Emma Smith arrived in Kirtland from New York, having traveled overland by sleigh. Joseph sprang from the sleigh and entered the Gilbert Whitney store. Extending his hand to the junior partner as though he were a familiar acquaintance, Joseph said, "Newel K. Whitney! Thou art the man!" A somewhat astonished Newel Whitney said, "Stranger you have the advantage of me. I could not call you by name, as you have me." Joseph replied, "I am Joseph the Prophet, you've prayed me here. Now what do you want of me."[53] Sometime earlier, Newel and his wife Elizabeth Ann had prayed for direction from the Lord. They saw this event as a direct fulfillment of their prayers.

Lucy Mack Smith recalled another experience at a meeting held at the store:

Joseph took all the male portion of our family into the . . . school room and administered to them the ordinance of washing of feet; after which the Spirit fell upon them, and they spake in tongues, and prophesied. The brethren gathered together to witness the manifestations of the power of God. At that time I was on the farm a short distance form the place where the meeting was held, and my children being anxious that I should enjoy the meeting, sent a messenger in great haste for me. I went without delay, and shared with the rest, the most glorious outpouring of the Spirit of God, that had ever before taken place in the Church.[54]

Another joyous event that took place in Kirtland for Joseph and Emma was the birth of their first surviving child, Joseph Smith III. In his memoirs, Joseph Smith III recalled this time:

I was born in the early morning of November 6, 1832, in the little town of Kirtland, Geauga (now Lake) County, Ohio. My mother, with her small family, was living in an upper room in the northwest corner of a store occupied by Newel K. Whitney. The comforts were meager and makeshift, but the life which my parents had been compelled to live, constantly harassed by vexatious persecution and moving about from place to place on what was then the frontier of the westward march of civilization, had inured them to hardships and strengthened their powers of resistance against apparently overwhelming difficulties.[55]

Newel K. Whitney Home, Kirtland, Ohio
(Elsa Johnson was healed here in 1831)
LDS Historical Department—
George E. Anderson, 1907

NEWEL K. WHITNEY HOME

The Newel K. Whitney home is located on the northwest corner of Chillicothe and Kirtland-Chardon roads. It is situated across the road from the Newel K. Whitney store.

Historical Background

Newel K. Whitney was born on 5 February 1795 at Marlborough, Windham County, Vermont. He married Elizabeth A. Smith on 20 October 1822. Whitney was baptized in November 1830 at Kirtland, Ohio.

Newel K. Whitney had prayed for direction in this home. Elizabeth

Ann related,

> One night—it was midnight—as my husband and I, in our house at Kirtland, were praying to the Father to be shown the way, the spirit rested upon us and a cloud overshadowed the house . . . We saw the cloud and felt the spirit of the Lord. Then we heard a voice out of the cloud saying: "Prepare to receive the word of the Lord, for it is coming!" At first we marveled greatly, but from that moment we knew that the word of the Lord was coming to Kirtland.[56]

This was also the home where John Johnson met Joseph and Emma Smith. Johnson had come to Kirtland to investigate reports concerning the new restoration church. Several individuals, including Johnson's wife, Elsa, who had chronic rheumatism and was unable to lift her hand to her head, and Ezra Booth accompanied him to see the Prophet. While visiting with Joseph in the Whitney home, one visitor said, "Here is Mrs. Johnson with a lame arm. Has God given any power to man now on the earth to cure her?" Joseph Smith rose, walked across the room, grasped the hand of Elsa Johnson, and in a solemn and impressive manner said, "Woman, in the name of the Lord Jesus Christ I

Orson Hyde Home, Kirtland, Ohio
(Orson Hyde became one of the first apostles; before his conversion, he worked in the Whitney store)
LDS Historical Department—George E. Anderson, 1907

command thee to be whole." According to several witnesses, Mrs. Johnson immediately lifted her arm and no longer suffered from any impairment.[57]

ORSON HYDE HOME

The Orson Hyde home is located immediately east of the Newel K. Whitney store and is situated on the north side of the Kirtland-Chardon Road.

Historical Background

Orson Hyde was born on 8 January 1805 at Oxford, New Haven County, Connecticut. He married Marinda N. Johnson on 4 September 1834. He was baptized on 30 October 1831 at Kirtland, Ohio. Hyde was ordained one of the original members of the Twelve Apostles on 15 February 1835.

NATHANIEL MILLIKEN HOME

The Nathaniel Milliken home is located immediately north of the Newel K. Whitney store and is situated on the east side of Chillicothe Road.

Nathaniel Milliken Home, Kirtland, Ohio
(Wilford Woodruff met his future wife at a party here in 1837)
Authors' Collection, Richard Neitzel Holzapfel, 1990

Historical Background

Nathaniel Milliken was born on 25 December 1793 at Buxton, York County, Maine. He married Mary Fairfield Hayes on 22 April 1819. He arrived in Kirtland sometime in 1834. He received his anointing in the Kirtland Temple on 30 January 1836 and was a doorkeeper of the temple. Milliken was appointed a member of the Second Quorum of Seventy in 1836 and signed the articles of the Kirtland Safety Society in 1837. He left the Church in 1838.

Wilford Woodruff wrote, "April 8th [1837] Spent day in writing my Journal spent the evening at Elder [Milliken's] in good company."[58] Later, Woodruff reflected upon another evening social at Milliken's home because he met his future wife, Phoebe W. Carter, there. He recorded:

> My first acquaintance with Miss Phoebe W. Carter was on the eve of the 28th of Jan. 1837 at which time I was introduced to her at Elder Millikens by the politeness of Elder M. Holmes. After two and half months acquaintance we were joined in Matrimony.[59]

WARREN PARRISH HOME

The Warren Parrish home is located immediately north of the Nathaniel Milliken home and is situated on the east side of Chillicothe Road.

Warren Parrish Home, Kirtland, Ohio
(Early church leader and later opposition leader to Church)
Authors' Collection, T. Jeffery Cottle, 1990

Historical Background

The birth date of Warren Parrish is unknown. He married Martha H. Raymond on 3 December 1835. He was a member of Zion's Camp in 1834 and was ordained a member of the Seventy in 1835. Parrish acted as a scribe for Joseph Smith from 1835–37 and signed the articles of the Kirtland Safety Society in 1837. Parrish was accused of embezzling twenty-five thousand dollars from the Society. He led a group of about thirty men who formed the "Church of Christ" and who tried to install David Whitmer as their president.

Parrish accomplished several missions during this period. He reported his mission in the southern states in 1835 in the local newspaper:

> Dear Brother in Christ:—I am happy to inform you, that through the blessing of God, I have returned from my mission in the South.[60]

Wilford Woodruff, one of Parrish's missionary companions, returned to Kirtland the following year. Woodruff found a shortage of living quarters in the rapidly growing community. As a result, Woodruff lived with Parrish before Woodruff's marriage and also after his marriage. Wilford Woodruff's journal documents the overcrowded conditions he encountered upon his arrival:

> Nov 25th [1836] . . . we spent the day with Elder Parrish.
>
> Nov 26th . . . Elder [Parrish's] house and spent the day in writing.
>
> Nov 29th . . . meeting closed spent the night with Elder W. Parrish.
>
> Dec 1st . . . spent the evening at Elder [Parrish's] accompanied by Brother Joseph Smith which was an interesting interview.
>
> [Dec] 4th . . . I spent the night with Elder Parrish.[61]

The following year, Woodruff was married and again found himself without lodging. He wrote,

> May 1st [1837] Mrs. Woodruff with myself removed our boarding place to Elder W. [Parrish's] where we tarry for the present.[62]

OLD SCHOOL HOUSE SITE

The old school house site is located approximately two hundred yards east of the Newel K. Whitney store and is situated on the south side of the Kirtland-Chardon Road.

Historical Background

During 1835, the Saints gathered for weekly meetings held on Tuesday evenings and Sunday mornings and afternoons in the schoolhouse on the flats. Joseph's history records the following entries about these meetings:

> Tuesday, November 3.—In the evening I preached in the school house, to a crowded congregation.

> Tuesday, November 17.—This evening, at candle light, I preached at the schoolhouse.

> Sunday, December 27.—At the usual hour, attending meeting at school house. President Cowdery delivered a very able and interesting discourse. In the afternoon, Brother Hyrum Smith and Bishop Partridge delivered each a short and interesting lecture, after which Sacrament was administered.

> Tuesday, December 29.—At early candle-light I preached at the school house to a crowded congregation, who listened with attention about three hours. I had liberty in speaking. Some Presbyterians were present, as I afterwards learned; and I expect that some of my sayings sat like a garment that was well fitted . . . I pray God that it may be like a nail in a sure place, driven by the master of assemblies.[63]

ISAAC MORLEY FARM

The Isaac Morley farm is approximately one mile northeast of the Newel K. Whitney store. From the Newel K. Whitney store, travel east on the Kirtland-

Isaac Morley Farm, Kirtland, Ohio
(Joseph and Emma Smith lived here in a log home in 1831)
Authors' Collection, Karl Anderson, 1990

Chardon Road. Take the Chillicothe Road at the fork. The farm is located on the north side of Chillicothe.

Historical Background

Isaac Morley was born at Montague, Hampshire County, Massachusetts, in 1786. He married Lucy Gunn in 1812. Morley was baptized in November 1830 in Kirtland, Ohio. He settled in Kirtland in 1812. He allowed the New York Saints to settle on his farm in 1831. Morley was ordained a high priest in 1831.

Shortly after the Saints' arrival in Ohio, Joseph received a revelation that stated, "It is meet that my servant Joseph Smith, Jun. should have a house built, in which to live and translate."[64] Isaac Morley, in obedience to the revelation, began building a home on his farm for Joseph and Emma. The Smiths lived here until they moved to Hiram, Ohio.

During this period, members and other visitors frequently visited the Morley farm. Wilford Woodruff attended a meeting in a log cabin above the Morley farm. He later recalled this meeting:

> On Sunday night the Prophet called on all who held the Priesthood to gather into the little log school house they had there. It was a small house, perhaps 14 feet square. But it held the whole of the Priesthood of the Church of Jesus Christ of Latter-day Saints who were then in the town of Kirtland . . . When we got together the Prophet said, "Brethren, I have been very much edified and instructed in your testimonies here tonight. But I want to say to you before the Lord, that you know no more concerning the destinies of this Church and kingdom than a babe upon its mother's lap. You don't comprehend it." I was rather surprised. He said, "It is only a little handful of Priesthood you see here tonight, but this Church will fill North and South America—it will fill the world."[65]

John Johnson Inn

The John Johnson Inn was located on the southwest corner of Chillicothe and Kirtland-Chardon roads.

Historical Background

The inn was originally built by Peter French. It was the first brick building in Kirtland. Eventually, in the spring of 1833, it was purchased by the Church and given to John Johnson.

In the summer of 1833, Church leaders in Kirtland learned that the Church printing press in Missouri had been destroyed by mob action on 20 July. By 1 October of the same year, Oliver Cowdery was on his way to New York with

John Johnson Inn, Kirtland, Ohio
(Church printing operation located here
briefly in 1833)
LDS Visual Resource Library—unknown,
before 1910

John Johnson Inn, Kirtland, Ohio
(Church leaders met here to conduct Church
business)
LDS Historical Department—unknown,before 1910

eight hundred dollars to purchase a new printing press. He returned in December with a press and other necessary printing equipment. A temporary printing office was established at the John Johnson Inn.

Oliver Cowdery wrote Church printer W. W. Phelps on 21 January 1834 that "Our office is yet in the brick building, though we expect in the spring to move on the hill near the Methodist-Meeting house."⁶⁶

Besides being used for a printing office, the inn displayed the Egyptian mummies and served as a community gathering place. For their first mission, the Twelve Apostles left from the inn.

BAPTISMAL SITE

The primary baptismal site was located east of the Warren Parrish home toward the Chagrin River and approximately two hundred yards north along the Chagrin River.

Chagrin River, Kirtland, Ohio
(Traditionally identified as early baptismal site)
LDS Historical Department—unknown, unknown

Historical Background

The baptisms performed in Kirtland usually took place in the Chagrin River in a large pool where the river was dammed to provide power for a mill. The early Saints were eager to be baptized regardless of the weather. Willard Richards, for example, was baptized by his cousin Brigham Young on 31 December 1836. Richards recalled, "Heber C. Kimball and others spent the afternoon in cutting the ice to prepare for the baptism."[67] Another convert, Ebenezer Robinson, related the following experience:

> I then went to the printing office [with Joseph Smith], he to his council room which adjoined the room where we worked, and I to my work in the printing office. I worked until well on to the evening, feeling very anxious all the time, for it seemed that I could not live over night without being baptized; after enduring it as long as I could, I went to the door of their room, and gently opened it, (a thing I had never presumed to do before.) As soon as Mr. Smith saw me he said, "yes, yes, brethren, Brother Robinson wishes to be baptized, we will adjourn and attend to that." We repaired to the water, (the Chagrin river which flows through Kirtland,) and, after a season of prayer, Brother Joseph Smith, Jr., baptized me by immersion, and as I arose from the water it seemed that everything I had on left me, and I came up a new creature, when I shouted aloud, "Glory to God." My heart was full to over flowing, and I felt that I had been born again in very deed, both of water and of the spirit.[68]

After the Mormon expulsion from Missouri in 1838 and 1839, some new converts and others seeking refuge returned to Kirtland. The earliest "refugees" arrived in March 1840 and stayed until the fall of 1841. The Prophet began teaching baptism for the dead[69] at the new Church headquarters in Nauvoo, Illinois, in 1840. The Kirtland Saints performed this ordinance in the river in Kirtland. The Kirtland Elder's Quorum minute book includes the following entry for 22 May 1841:

> The several quorums and whole conference, by a unanimous vote, accepted and resolved to uphold the first presidency at Nauvoo, [Illinois] . . . During the sittings of the conference, the greatest harmony prevailed. About 25 baptisms took place, the most of which were for the dead.[70]

WILLIAM SMITH HOME SITE

The probable site of William Smith's home is approximately one hundred fifty yards north of the temple on the west side of Chillicothe Road. The home was adjacent to the Joseph Smith, Sr./Joseph Smith, Jr. home.

William Smith Home, Kirtland, Ohio (Traditionally identified as the home used for Church meetings)
LDS Historical Department—unknown, unknown

Historical Background

William Smith was born on 13 March 1811 at Royalton, Windsor County, New York. He married Caroline A. Grant on 14 February 1833. Smith was baptized on 9 June 1830. He was a member of Zion's Camp and was ordained one of the Twelve Apostles on 15 February 1835.

Apparently, several meetings were held at the William Smith home. The Prophet Joseph Smith records:

[12 December 1835] At evening attended a debate at Brother William Smith's. The question proposed to debate on was as follows: Was it necessary for God to reveal himself to man in order for their happiness. I was on the affirmative and the last one to speak on that side of the question, but while listening with interest to the ingenuity displayed on both sides of the question, I was called away to visit Sister Angeline Works, who was supposed to be dangerously sick. Elder Corrill and myself went and prayed for and [laid] hands on her in the name of Jesus Christ. She appeared to be better. Returned home.[71]

Four days later, on Wednesday, 16 December 1835, the Prophet records the conclusion of the debate:

This evening according to adjournment I went to Brother William Smith's to take part in the debate that was commenced on Saturday evening last. After the debate was concluded and a decision given in favor of the affirmative of the question some altercation took place upon the impropriety of continuing the School fearing that it would not result in good.[72]

JOSEPH SMITH, SR./JOSEPH SMITH, JR. HOME

Scholars and researchers disagree whether the Smith home was the residence of the Joseph Smith, Sr. family or the Joseph Smith, Jr. family. The Smith home is located approximately one hundred yards north of the temple and is situated on the west side of Chillicothe Road.

Joseph Smith, Sr./Jr. Home, Kirtland, Ohio
(Church Headquarters in 1835)
LDS Historical Department—George E. Anderson, 1907

Historical Background

Joseph Smith, Sr. was born in 1771 at Topsfield, Essex County, Massachusetts. He married Lucy Mack on 24 January 1796.

Joseph Smith, Jr. was born on 23 December 1805 at Sharon, Windsor County, Vermont. He married Emma Hale on 18 January 1827 at South Bainbridge, New York. He was baptized on 15 May 1829. Following his "First Vision" in the spring of 1820 and after succeeding visions and revelations, Joseph translated the *Book of Mormon* and organized the Church of Christ on 6 April 1830. He was sustained as the "First Elder" and eventually as President of the Church.

Visitors constantly came to meet Joseph Smith, Jr. at his home. He conducted much of the Church business from this residence. The following accounts from Joseph's journal relate a few of these activities:

[Thursday 29th October 1835], Bishop Whitney and his wife, with his Father and Mother, called to visit us. His parents having lately arrived here from the East, called to make enquiry concerning the coming forth of the Book of Mormon. Bishop Partridge and some others came in [and] I then set down and related to them the history of the coming forth of the book, the administration of the Angel to me, the rudiments of the gospel of Christ. They appeared well satisfied and I expect to baptize them in a few days, or this is my feelings upon the subject although they have not made any request of this Kind at present.

Went to the Council, the Presidency arose and adjourned. On my return Elder Boynton observed that long debates were bad. I replied that it was generally the case that too much altercation was indulged in on both sides and their debates protracted to an unprofitable length.

We were called to supper. After being seated around the table, Bishop Whitney observed to Bishop Partridge that the thought had just occurred to his mind that perhaps in about one year from this time they might be seated together around a table on the land of Zion. My wife observed that she hoped it might be the case that not only they but the rest of the company present might be seated around her table in the land of promise. The same sentiment was reciprocated from the company round the table and my heart responded, "Amen!" God grant it, I ask in the name of Jesus Christ.[73]

Thursday, 26th [November 1835] At home. We spent the day in transcribing Egyptian characters from the papyrus. I am severely afflicted with a cold. Today Robert Rathbone and George Morey arrived from Zion.

Saturday, 28th [November 1835] At home. Spent the morning in comparing our journal. Elder Josiah Clark called this morning to see me. He lives in Campbell County, Kentucky about three miles above Cincinnati.

I am considerably recovered from my cold. I think I shall be able in a few days to translate again with the blessing of God. The weather is still cold and stormy. The snow is falling and winter seems to be closing in. All nature shrinks before the chilling blasts of a frigid winter.[74]

[Wednesday 16 December 1835], Returned home, Elder [McClellan], Elder Brigham Young and Elder Jared Carter called and paid me a visit with which I was much gratified. I exhibited and explained the Egyptian Records to them and explained many things to them concerning the dealings of God with the ancients and the formation of the planetary system. They seemed much pleased with the interview.[75]

JOSEPH SMITH VARIETY STORE SITE

The location of the Joseph Smith variety store is about 150 yards north of the temple. The store is situated on the east side of Chillicothe Road. Tradition and some evidence suggest that the building standing on this site used the Joseph Smith store foundation.

Historical Background

Joseph's daily labors included his religious calling as well as many secular pursuits. In an effort to stabilize his financial standing in Kirtland, Joseph

Joseph Smith Variety Store, Kirtland, Ohio
(Joseph Smith operated this store while living in Kirtland)
Utah State Historical Society—unknown, unknown

operated a variety store. Brigham Young recalled the situation:

> Joseph goes to new York and buys 20,000 dollars' worth of goods, comes into Kirtland and commences to trade. In comes one of the brethren, "Brother Joseph, let me have a frock pattern for my wife." What if Joseph says, "No, I cannot without money." The consequence would be, "He is no Prophet," says James . . . After awhile, in comes Bill and sister Susan. Says Bill, "Brother Joseph, I want a shawl, I have not got the money, but I wish you to trust me a week or a fortnight." Well, Brother Joseph thinks the others have gone and apostatized, and he don't know but these goods will make the whole Church do the same, so he lets Bill have [the] shawl. Bill walks off with and meets a brother. "Well," says he, "what do you think of brother Joseph?" "O Joseph is a first-rate man, and I fully believe he is a Prophet. See here, he has trusted me this shawl." Richard says, "I think I will go down and see if he won't trust me some." In walks Richard. "Brother Joseph, I want to trade about 20 dollars." "Well," says Joseph, "these goods will make the people apostatize; so over they go, they are of less value than the people."[76]

Brigham later remarked, "I know persons . . . would turn round and say, 'What is the matter brother Joseph, why don't you pay your debts; you must be a bad financier; you don't know how to handle the things of this world.' At the same time the coats, pants, dresses, boots, and shoes that they and their families were wearing came out of Joseph's store."[77] Joseph probably operated this store less than one year.

The Smith family had substantial financial needs, as their everyday financial burdens were augmented by both the time and money Joseph spent defending himself against legal harassments and the time spent fulfilling his calling as the Prophet of the Church. Another small example of the people's abuse of Joseph's position was the practice of individuals sending letters to him with postage due. Eventually, Joseph published the following announcement in the newspaper:

> To the Editor of the Messenger and Advocate: Dear Brother—I wish to inform my friends and all others, abroad, that whenever they wish to address me thro' the Post Office, they will be kind enough to pay the postage on the same. My friends will excuse me in this matter, as I am willing to pay postage on letters to hear from them; but am unwilling to pay for insults and menaces,—consequently, must refuse all, unpaid.
>
> Yours in the gospel, JOSEPH SMITH, jr. Kirtland, December 5, 1835.[78]

Obviously, the problem continued, for in an 1837 issue of the *Messenger and Advocate,* Joseph wrote, "Owing to the multiplicity of Letters with which I am crowded, I am *again* under the necessity of saying . . . that I will *not* hereafter, take *any* letters from the Post-office, unless they are post paid.[79]

METHODIST MEETING HOUSE SITE

The Methodist meeting house site is located at the Kirtland Cemetery north of the temple.

Methodist Church, Kirtland, Ohio
(Sidney Rigdon announced his conversion to Mormonism during a talk here)
RLDS Archives—unknown, c1900

Historical Background

On 14 November 1830, Sidney Rigdon invited his friends and neighbors to the Methodist meeting house in Kirtland. The *Painesville Telegraph* reported the meeting in its 15 February 1831 issue. According to the newspaper account, Rigdon was "much affected and deeply impressed . . . exceedingly humble [and] confessed the sins of his former life." Mormon missionary Parley P. Pratt said the talk lasted two hours, during which time "both himself and the congregation were melted into tears."[80] Rigdon was baptized on the following day by Oliver Cowdery.

KIRTLAND CEMETERY

The Kirtland Cemetery is located immediately north of the Kirtland Temple and is situated on the west side of Chillicothe Road.

Kirtland Cemetery, Kirtland, Ohio
(Many early Saints and their
descendants are buried here)
LDS Historical Department—George E.
Anderson, 1907

Historical Background

Many Saints are buried in the Kirtland Cemetery, including Mary Duty Smith, the Prophet's grandmother; probably Joseph and Emma's twin children, Louisa and Thaddeus; Jerusha Smith, Hyrum Smith's wife; Oliver Granger; John Johnson; and several other individuals.[81] The turmoil and anxiety of losing a loved one or friend could be compounded by grave robbers. Such was the case in Kirtland for a period of time.

Kirtland Cemetery from Temple Tower, Kirtland,
Ohio
(Joseph's grandmother, Mary Duty, was buried here
in 1836)
LDS Historical Department—unknown, before 1915

A medical college was founded in the nearby community of Willoughby during this period. Many of the Saints believed that medical students from Willoughby considered the "Mormon" dead as violable and sought cadavers in the public and private cemeteries in Kirtland. Helen Mar Whitney wrote,

RLDS Memorial Marker, Kirtland Cemetery,
Kirtland, Ohio
(Dedicated to the memory of Saints buried in
unmarked graves)
Authors' Collection, Richard Neitzel
Holzapfel, 1990

There are no doubt many still living who remember the perilous times in Kirtland. I can recollect a time when it was unsafe for a woman or child to be found alone on the street after sundown, and when the graves had to be closely guarded or they were robbed by students who came from Willoughby, and thought it no sacrilege to dissect a "Mormon" dead or alive . . . Several [Johnson family members died]. [T]hey had to be guarded and I was informed that for weeks they were in the habit of tying a strong rope to a bier, which was turned over the grave and the other end to the arm of someone who slept.[82]

The college was eventually closed in 1847 by the residents of Willoughby, who also charged the medical students with grave robbing.

John Johnson Home

The John Johnson home is located west of the temple approximately four lots and is situated on the south side of Maple Street, which runs between the cemetery and the Kirtland Temple.

Historical Background

John Johnson was born on 11 April 1778 in Chesterfield, Cheshire County, New Hampshire. He married Elsa Jacobs on 22 June 1800. He moved to Hiram,

Ohio, in approximately 1818. Johnson was appointed a member of the Kirtland High Council on 17 February 1834.

The following account in Joseph Smith's journal relates a marriage that occurred at John Johnson's home:

> [20 January 1836] At evening I attended at John Johnson's with my family, on a matrimonial occasion, having been invited to do so, to join President John F. Boynton and Miss Susan Lowell in marriage. A large and respectable company assembled and were seated by Elder's Orson Hyde and Warren Parrish in the following order: The Presidency and their companions in the first seats, the Twelve Apostles in the second, the 70 in the third and the remainder of the congregation seated with their companions.

John Johnson Home, Kirtland, Ohio
(Joseph Smith performed a marriage here in 1836)
Authors' Collection, Richard Neitzel Holzapfel, 1990

After the above arrangements were made, Elder Boynton and his Lady with their attendants, came in and were seated in front of the Presidency. A hymn was sung, after which I addressed a throne of grace. I then arose and read aloud a license granting any minister of the gospel the privilege of solemnizing the rights of matrimony. After calling for objection if any there were against the anticipated alliance between Elder Boynton and Miss Lowell and waiting sufficient time, I observed that all forever after this must hold their peace.

I then invited them to join hands and I pronounced the ceremony according to the rules and regulations of the Church of the Latter-day Saints. In the name of God and in the name of Jesus Christ, I pronounced upon them the blessings of Abraham, Isaac, and Jacob and such other blessings as the Lord put into my heart. Being much under the influence of a cold I then gave way and President Sidney Rigdon arose and delivered a very forcible address suited to the occasion and closed the services of the evening by prayer.

. . . Joy filled every bosom and the countenances of old and young alike seemed to bloom with the cheerfulness and smiles of youth and an entire unison of feeling seemed to pervade the congregation. Indeed, I doubt whether the pages of history can boast of a more splendid and innocent wedding and feast than this. For it was conducted after the order of heaven, who has a time for all things. This being a time of rejoicing, we heartily embraced it and conducted ourselves accordingly. Took leave of the company and returned home.[83]

PARLEY P. PRATT HOME SITE

The Parley P. Pratt home site is located near the northeast corner of Maple and Cowdery streets.

Parley P. Pratt Home, Kirtland, Ohio
(Traditionally identified as home of Apostle Parley P. Pratt)
LDS Historical Department—George E. Anderson, 1907

Historical Background

Parley P. Pratt was born on 12 April 1807 in Burlington, Otsego County, New York. He married Thankful Halsey on 9 September 1827 at Canaan, New York. Pratt was baptized on 1 September 1830 at Fayette, New York. He was ordained a member of the original Twelve Apostles on 21 February 1835.

Kirtland Temple (South View), Kirtland, Ohio
(Temple construction began in 1833 at a cost
of approximately $50,000)
RLDS Archives—unknown, c. 1890

Kirtland Temple, Kirtland, Ohio
(The first temple built by the Saints and
completed in 1836)
RLDS Archives—W. A. Faze, c1870

KIRTLAND TEMPLE

To visit the Kirtland Temple, proceed to the Kirtland Temple Historic Center operated by the RLDS Church at 9020 Chillicothe Road.

Historical Background

By far the most important building in Kirtland during the Mormon period was the Kirtland Temple. The Saints began construction of this "House of the Lord" in 1833 and dedicated it on 27 March 1836.

During the dedication services, Joseph Smith offered a prayer of dedication.[84] Among the things Joseph said are the following:

> We ask thee, Holy Father, that thy servants may go forth from this house armed with thy power, and that thy name may be upon them, and thy glory be round about them, and thine angels have charge over them; and from this place they may bear exceedingly great and glorious tidings, in truth, unto the ends of the earth, that they make known that this is thy work, and that thou has put forth thy hand, to fulfill that which thou hast spoken by the mouths of thy prophets concerning the last days . . . O Jehovah, have mercy upon this people, and as all men sin forgive the transgressions of thy people, and let them be blotted out forever. Let the anointing of thy ministers be sealed upon them with power from on high. Let it be fulfilled upon them, as upon those on the day of Pentecost; let the gifts of tongues be poured out upon thy people, even cloven tongues as of fire, and the interpretation thereof. And let thy house be filled, as with a rushing mighty wind, with thy glory . . . O hear, O hear, O hear us, O Lord! And answer these petitions, and accept the dedication of this house unto thee, the work of our hands, which we have built unto thy name; and also this church, to put upon it thy name. And help us by the power of thy Spirit, that we may mingle our voices with those bright, shining seraphs around thy throne, with acclamations of praise, singing Hosanna to God and the Lamb! And let these, thine anointed ones, be clothed with salvation, and thy saints shout aloud for joy. Amen, and Amen.[85]

Kirtland Temple (North View), Kirtland, Ohio
(The temple was dedicated in 1836)
LDS Historical Dept.—unknown, before 1920

The dedicatory service was a most memorable event for the Saints. About five hundred Saints were waiting near the temple doors at 7:00 A.M., an hour before they opened. When the doors were opened, several brethren waited to collect donations at the doors. "There were three large tin pans full of gold and silver," recalled Ira Ames.[86] The Saints occupied every available seat, and many had to stand outside during the ceremonies. Because of the number of people who were forced to remain outside, a second service was held on Thursday, 31 March.

Kirtland Temple (Lower Auditorium), Kirtland, Ohio
(Numerous religious meetings held here)
LDS Historical Department—unknown, before 1920

The services began at 9:00 A.M. and lasted until 4:00 P.M., a seven-hour meeting. When Eliza R. Snow recorded her feelings of the dedication, she wrote, "[N]o mortal language [could] describe the heavenly manifestations of that memorable day. [There was a] sweet spirit of love and union . . . a sense of divine presence, [and] each heart was filled with joy inexpressible and full of glory."[87]

Several Church leaders, among them Sidney Rigdon, spoke during the services, while others bore their testimonies of the great latter-day work. M. C. Davis led the choir in hymns written by members of the Church. Members of the Church sustained their leaders, including Joseph Smith as "Prophet and Seer."

The congregation also sang several new hymns from the Saints' first hymnal compiled by Emma Smith and published in 1835.

After a short intermission, the services continued with singing. After making a few remarks, the Prophet presented the names of all the officers of the Church for sustaining. The prayer of dedication was read. Don Carlos Smith then blessed the bread and wine, and the elders passed the sacrament to the congregation. Following remarks by Hyrum Smith and Sidney Rigdon, the congregation sealed the meeting with the sacred hosanna shout, shouting "Hosanna! Hosanna! Hosanna to God and the Lamb," repeating the shout three times and sealing each series of hosannas with three amens.

Brigham Young then arose and spoke in tongues. David W. Patten interpreted and afterwards gave a short discourse in tongues. Finally, Joseph blessed the congregation and concluded the meeting at 4:00 P.M.

Church leaders published their thanks to those who attended the dedication services a few days later in the *Messenger and Advocate*:

> Not only for their demeanor during the whole exercise, which lasted more than eight hours, but for their great liberality in contributing of their earthly substance for the relief of the building committee, who were yet involved. As this was to be a day of sacrifice, as well as of fasting—There was a man placed at each door in the morning to receive the voluntary donations of those who entered. On counting the collection it amounted to nine hundred and sixty three dollars.[88]

Kirtland Temple (Upper Auditorium), Kirtland, Ohio
(School of the Prophets met here in 1836-37)
LDS Historical Department—unknown, before 1920

The unusual outpouring of the Spirit during the services made a great impression on those attending that day. Many individuals sensed a "glorious sensation passing through the house," while others saw visions. It was a day not long forgotten by the Saints. Because of overcrowding, some Saints were unable to attend the services, which made a few Saints disgruntled.

The dedication was not the end of the pentecostal season. Several days later, on 3 April, Joseph Smith and Oliver Cowdery recorded:

> The veil was taken from our minds, and the eyes of our understanding were opened. We saw the Lord standing upon the breastwork of the pulpit, before us; and under his feet was a paved work of pure gold, in color like amber. His eyes were as a flame of fire; the hair of his head was white like the pure snow; his countenance shone above the brightness of the sun; and his voice was as the sound of rushing of great waters, even the voice of Jehovah, saying: I am the first and the last; I am he who liveth, I am he who was slain; I am your advocate with the Father.[89]

Following this vision, Joseph and Oliver said that Moses, Elias, and Elijah also appeared to them in the temple and bestowed on them the keys of the priesthood.

After the departure of the Saints from Kirtland, an arsonist attempted to burn down the temple. The arsonist placed straw, wood shavings, and hot coals in the building; but the bundle failed to ignite, and the temple was saved.[90] For several years following the Saints' exodus, the temple was used as a school.[91] In 1880, the Lake County Common Pleas Court legally settled the debate over ownership of the temple. The court awarded the title of ownership to the RLDS Church, which has retained possession of it and has maintained it to the present day.

KIRTLAND SAFETY SOCIETY SITE

The Kirtland Safety Society site is located on a lot south of the Kirtland Temple on the east side of Chillicothe Road.

Historical Background

The Kirtland Safety Society's inception was in 1836. Several banks were opening in nearby communities; and with the Church under financial pressure, the decision to start a bank was a logical one.

In the last half of 1836, engraving plates were investigated, a safe was purchased, stock shares were sold, the articles of agreement were drafted, and the Ohio legislature was petitioned for a bank charter. In early 1837, the Anti-Bank Company was formed; and the first bills were printed. Wilford Woodruff records his visit to the Safety Society just after it opened:

Kirtland Safety Society Building, Kirtland, Ohio
(Traditionally identified as the Kirtland Safety Society building)
LDS Historical Department—unknown, before 1890

I visited the office of the Kirtland Safety Society and saw the first money that was issued by the Treasurer of Society. It was given to Brother Bump (in exchange for other notes) who was the first to circulate it. I also heard President Joseph Smith Jr. declare . . . that if we would give heed to the commandments the Lord had given this morning all would be well. May the Lord bless Brother Joseph with all the Saints and support the above named institution and Protect it so that every weapon formed against it may be broken and come to nought while the Kirtland Safety Society shall become the greatest of all institutions on EARTH.[92]

However, the Safety Society notes were difficult to circulate from the onset. As Wilford Woodruff indicated,

Mr. B. D. Hart, of Mentor, informs us that he received the first Mormon bill that was located in circulation by this bank. He happened to be in Kirtland the Saturday evening he received it [a ten-dollar note], but the next Monday morning, [found] it impossible to use it for any legitimate commercial ends . . .[93]

Part of the problem was the Church's enemies who refused to honor the notes or who bought the notes at a discount and then presented them at the bank for full payment.

Within a short time of opening, the bank officers suspended payment in hard currency; and after legal maneuvering and difficulties, the bank closed its doors in November 1837.

SIDNEY RIGDON HOME

The Sidney Rigdon home is located across the road from the Kirtland Safety Society site on the west side of Chillicothe Road.

Sidney Rigdon House, Kirtland, Ohio
(Rigdon was a member of the Church's First Presidency)
LDS Historical Department—unknown, before 1910

Historical Background

Sidney Rigdon was born on 19 February 1793 at St. Clair, Allegheny County, Pennsylvania. He married Phebe Brook on 12 June 1820. Rigdon was baptized on 14 November 1830 at Kirtland, Ohio. On 8 March 1832, he became a member of the Church's leading council, the Presidency of the High Priesthood or, as it was known later, the First Presidency.[94]

Sometime after Rigdon moved into this frame home, his wife Phebe became ill. Joseph Smith's diary states,

Thursday the 25th of Feb 1836 attended to my studies as usual, and made some proficiency. In the afternoon I was called upon by President Rigdon to go and visit his wife who was very sick. I did so in company with my scribe, we prayed for and anointed her in the name of the Lord and she began to recover from that very hour—returned home and spent the evening.[95]

WILLIAM MILLER HOME

The William Miller home is located on the north side of Joseph Street between Chillicothe and Cowdery roads.

William Miller Home, Kirtland, Ohio
(Miller was baptized in Kirtland in 1834)
Authors' Collection, Gina Alton, 1991

Historical Background

William Miller was born on 8 February 1814 at Avon, Livingston County, New York. He married Phoebe Scott on 4 May 1834. Miller was baptized in 1834 at Kirtland, Ohio.

WILLIAM MARKS/VINSON KNIGHT HOME

The William Marks/Vinson Knight home is located on the northwest corner of Cowdery and Joseph streets.

William Marks/Vinson Knight Home, Kirtland, Ohio
(Marks and Knight were both prominent leaders in the Church)
RLDS Archives—unknown, unknown

Historical Background

William Marks was born on 15 November 1792 at Rutland, Rutland County, Vermont. He married Rosannah Robinson on 2 May 1813. Marks was baptized shortly before April 1835 at Portage, Allegany County, New York. On 3 September 1837, he was chosen as a member of the Kirtland High Council. He was also elected agent to Bishop Newel K. Whitney.

Vinson Knight was born on 14 March 1804 at Chester, Washington County, New York. He married Martha McBride on 14 March 1826. Knight was baptized in 1834.

HYRUM SMITH HOME

The location of the Hyrum Smith home is disputed by scholars and researchers. One location for the home is on the east side of Chillicothe where Joseph Street intersects with Chillicothe Road. The second location is on the south side of Joseph between Cowdery Street and Chillicothe Road.

Historical Background

Hyrum Smith was born on 9 February 1800 at Tunbridge, Orange County, Vermont. He married Jerusha Barden on 2 November at Manchester, New York.

Hyrum Smith Home, Kirtland, Ohio
(Traditionally identified home located on Chillicothe Road)
LDS Historical Department—George E. Anderson, 1907

Smith was baptized on 29 June 1829. He was one of the eight witnesses of the *Book of Mormon*. He was ordained a high priest on 3 June 1831 and was also a member of Zion's Camp. He was appointed assistant counselor to the First Presidency on 3 September 1837.

Hyrum Smith Home, Kirtland, Ohio
(Traditionally identified home located on Joseph Street)
RLDS Archives—unknown, before 1920

On 24 November 1835, Hyrum hosted a wedding party at his home. His brother, Joseph Smith, recorded the event in his diary as follows:

Tuesday 24th at home, spent the forenoon instructing those that called to inquire concerning to things of God, in the last days. In the afternoon, we translated some of the Egyptian records. I had an invitation to attend a wedding at Brother [Hyrum] Smith's in the evening also to solemnize the matrimonial ceremony, between Newel Knight and Lydia Goldthwaite. I and my wife, went, when we arrived a considerable company, had collected, the bridegroom and bride came in, and took their seats, which gave me to understand that they were ready. I requested them to arise and join hands. I then remarked that marriage was an institution of heaven, instituted in the Garden of Eden, that it was necessary that it should be solemnized by the authority of the everlasting priesthood. Before joining hands however, we attended prayers. I then made the remarks above stated. The ceremony was original with me it was in substance as follows, You covenant to be each others companion through life, and discharge the duties of husband and wife in every respect to which they assented. I then pronounced them husband and wife in the name of God and also the blessings of the Lord conferred upon Adam and Eve in the Garden of Eden, that is to multiply and replenish the earth, with the addition of long life and prosperity. Dismissed them and returned home. The weather is freezing cold, some snow on the ground. [96]

Temple Stone Quarry, Kirtland, Ohio
(The stones to build the Kirtland Temple were quarried here)
RLDS Archives—unknown, unknown

TEMPLE STONE QUARRY

The temple stone quarry is located approximately two miles south of the temple and is situated on the west side of Chillicothe Road. The quarry is presently part of the Chapin Forest Reservation(Park).

Historical Background

When the temple was planned, the brethren desired to construct it out of brick. Soon thereafter, however, the "purpose of building the Temple of brick was abandoned as a stone quarry at easy distance from the temple site was discovered." Heber C. Kimball recalled,

> When we arrived in Kirtland, Joseph said, "Come brethren, let us go into the stone-quarry and work for the Lord." And the Prophet went himself, in his tow frock and tow breeches, and worked at the quarrying stone like the rest of us. Then, every Saturday we brought out every team to draw stone to the Temple, and so we continued until that house was finished.[97]

Joseph Smith's history records, "I acted as foreman in the Temple stone quarry, and when other duties would permit, labored with my own hands."[98]

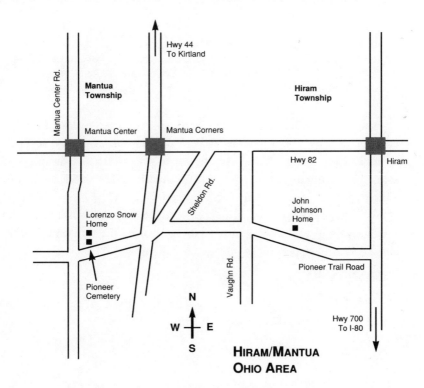

Hwy 44
To Kirtland

Mantua Center Rd.

Mantua Township

Hiram Township

Mantua Center

Mantua Corners

Hwy 82

Hiram

Sheldon Rd.

John Johnson Home

Lorenzo Snow Home

Vaughn Rd.

Pioneer Trail Road

Pioneer Cemetery

N
W + E
S

Hwy 700
To I-80

HIRAM/MANTUA OHIO AREA

Hiram, Portage County, Ohio

Hiram is located approximately thirty-five miles southeast of Kirtland.

Hiram was part of the Western Reserve, which was owned by Daniel Tilden and his partners. In 1799, they met to divide and name their property. Tilden proposed to name this specific area Hiram after the biblical king of Tyre and friend of King David. This name was quickly ratified. Several individuals tried to settle Hiram unsuccessfully in 1803. In 1804, Hiram became a township and was settled by several hopeful farmers.

The Church headquarters were located in Hiram, Portage County, Ohio, for six and one-half months—between mid-September 1831 and the end of March 1832. During this time, Joseph Smith and Sidney Rigdon both lived in the small farming community and held several important Church conferences in the home of John Johnson. Several important revelations were recorded while Joseph and his family lived at the Johnson home.

An unpublished revelation dated 27 February 1832 and given at Hiram emphasized the importance of the "Articles and Covenants," an early statement on Church policy and organization.[99] The revelation states:

> Behold, thus saith the Lord unto you my servants. I have chosen Lincoln [Haskin] to be a servant unto me. Wherefore, verily I say unto you, let him be ordained and receive the Articles and Covenants which I have given unto you and some of the [previously written revelations] that he may go forth and proclaim my Gospel.[100]

Many of these early revelations were organized and copied for inclusion in a proposed book of scripture, known as *A Book of Commandments*. At a special meeting held in Hiram, six men were chosen to prepare the manuscripts for publication. They organized a "literary firm" in the fall of 1831 as a joint stewardship to publish books, newspapers, and periodicals. On 1 November 1831, Joseph Smith recorded "the Lord's Preface" to the new book of scripture that would contain several of the modern revelations. During the following months, more than a dozen revelations were recorded in Hiram.

JOHN JOHNSON FARM

The John Johnson farm is located on Pioneer Trail and is situated about two and one-half miles southwest of present-day Hiram.

John Johnson Farm, Hiram, Ohio
(Joseph and Emma Smith lived here in 1831–32)
Western Reserve Historical Society—unknown, before 1874

Historical Background

During the fall of 1831, Joseph Smith's family made preparations to move to Hiram, Ohio, where they remained for a year. While in Hiram, the Smiths stayed at the home of John Johnson. Sidney Rigdon also moved to Hiram to assist the Prophet on the translation of the scriptures, later known as the Joseph Smith Translation (JST) or Inspired Version.[101]

In October 1831, Joseph Smith received a revelation in Hiram.[102] Many other revelations were canonized in the 1835 *Doctrine and Covenants* published in Kirtland. One of the most memorable for the Saints in Hiram was a vision dated 16 February 1832.[103] Known as "The Vision," this revelation was of major doctrinal importance to the young Church. Philo Dibble, an early member of the Church and a witness to the events in Hiram, indicated that he saw the glory and felt the power but did not see the vision. Referring to the vision, Dibble stated:

> Joseph would, at intervals, say: "What do I see?" Then he would relate what he had seen or what he was looking at. Then Sidney replied, "I see the same." Presently Sidney would say, "What do I see?" and would repeat what he had seen or was seeing, and Joseph would reply, "I see the same." This manner of conversation was

John Johnson Home, Hiram, Ohio
(Joseph Smith was tarred and feathered here in 1832)
Authors' Collection, Milton V. Backman, before 1983

repeated at short intervals to the end of the vision, and during the whole time not a word was spoken by any other person. Not a sound nor motion [was] made by anyone but Joseph and Sidney, and it seemed to me that they never moved a joint or limb during the time I was there, which I think was over an hour, and to the end of the vision. Joseph sat firmly and calmly all the time in the midst of a magnificent glory, but Sidney sat limp and pale, apparently as limber as a rag, observing which Joseph remarked, smilingly, "Sidney is not used to it as I am."[104]

After returning to the John Johnson home in Hiram from a Church conference in Amherst, Joseph and Sidney resumed their work on the translation of the *Bible*.

Mantua, Portage County, Ohio

Mantua is located approximately thirty miles southeast of Kirtland. Mantua is on the Cuyahoga River and was named in honor of Napoleon, who had conquered a town by the same name in Italy. The town was surveyed for settlement in 1798–99.

Main Street, Mantua, Ohio
(Near home of Lorenzo and Eliza Snow)
Village of Mantua—unknown, c1909

When Oliver and Rosetta Snow arrived in Mantua, only ten families lived in the small village. Rosetta Snow and her daughter, Leonora, were baptized in 1831. Another daughter, Eliza Roxey, was baptized in April 1835. Lorenzo attended high school in Ravenna and then attended Oberlin College in the fall of 1835. On his way to school, he met David W. Patten, a Mormon missionary on his way home from Canada. They traveled some twenty-five miles together. This meeting had a profound effect upon Lorenzo; and, after completing a year of studies at Oberlin, Lorenzo was baptized in Kirtland in June 1836.

LORENZO SNOW HOME

The Lorenzo Snow home is located approximately a mile south of Mantua Center and southwest of Mantua Corners and is located on the east side of Mantua Center Road.

Oliver and Rosetta Snow Home, Mantua, Ohio
(Parents of Lorenzo and Eliza Snow)
LDS Historical Department—unknown, unknown

Historical Background

Lorenzo Snow was born on 3 April 1814 at Mantua, Portage County, Ohio. Snow was baptized in June 1836 at Kirtland, Ohio. He was assigned as a missionary in 1837. He became the fifth president of the LDS Church on 13 September 1898 in Salt Lake City, Utah.

The Snow home was a frequent stop of Mormon missionaries during the early 1830s. Among those first visitors was Joseph Smith. Eliza R. Snow later recalled her first visit with him at her parents' home:

> In the winter of 1830 and 31, Joseph Smith called at my father's home. As [Joseph] sat warming himself, I scrutinized his face as closely as I could without attracting his attention, and decided that his was an honest face. My motto, "Prove all things and hold fast to that which is good," prompted me to investigation, as incredulous as I was.[105]

Oberlin, Lorain County, Ohio

Oberlin is located approximately sixty-five miles southwest of Kirtland.

John J. Shipherd, originally of New York, and Philo Penfield Stewart, originally of Connecticut, together desired to open a school for Christian families

in the Western Reserve. The town and school were named after a well-known German pastor, John Frederic Oberlin. Shipherd and Stewart visited an area they desired for their school and obtained that land from the owners in New Haven, Connecticut. The actual foundations of the college and the town began together in 1833.

OBERLIN COLLEGIATE INSTITUTE (OBERLIN COLLEGE)

Oberlin College is located in the center of downtown Oberlin, Ohio.

Historical Background:

Oberlin Collegiate Institute, later called Oberlin College, was established in the spring of 1833. The construction of the first building was begun in the summer of 1833. This building, Oberlin Hall, was a multipurpose building that included a dining hall, boarding rooms, chapel, meeting house, classrooms, offices, and professors' private living quarters. The two-story wooden structure

Main Street, Oberlin, Ohio
(Lorenzo Snow attended school here)
Oberlin Historical Society—unknown, c1878

measured thirty-five by forty feet and constituted the only building on the campus until 1835.

A carpenter's shop was built in the fall of 1835 and was located just west of Oberlin Hall. The shop also was a two-story building—made of wood and painted red. A big tent was donated to Oberlin by friends of Mr. Finney, an early

Tappan Hall and other Oberlin College Buildings, Oberlin, Ohio
(Lorenzo Snow attended Oberlin Collegiate Institute (College) in 1833)
Oberlin College—unknown, c1854

religious educator and popular speaker. The tent could hold three thousand people within its one-hundred-foot diameter and was used for the commencement exercises from 1835 to 1843. Other buildings were added to the campus in 1835, including the First Ladies Hall, Cincinnati Hall, Finney House, Mahan-Morgan House, and Walton Hall.

The Mahan-Morgan House was located on the northwest corner of the intersection of Professor and College streets. The house was a two-story brick building occupied by Oberlin College President Mahan in 1835.

Two other buildings, Colonial Hall and Tappan Hall, were begun in 1835. Tappan Hall was named in honor of Arthur Tappan, an early financial supporter of Oberlin. The hall was located at the center of the college campus. The main walk across the campus passed through this building, as the long central corridor formed a section of the walkway. The first floor consisted of four separate rooms dedicated to recitation purposes. The upper floors contained ninety single rooms for men, each room being eight by sixteen feet with a door at one end and a window at the other.

Lorenzo Snow attended Oberlin before his conversion to Mormonism. His sister, Eliza R. Snow, wrote about his experiences there:

> An unseen hand evidently was guiding him . . . Ever a student, at home as well as in school . . . his book was his constant companion when disengaged from filial duties; and when sought by his associates, *"hid up with his book"* became proverbial . . . [H]e completed his scholastic training in Oberlin College . . . On his way to Oberlin, my brother accidentally fell in company with David W. Patten, an incident to which he frequently refers as one of those seemingly trivial occurrences in human life which leave an indelible trance . . . [I]n Oberlin, clubbed with three or four classmates, alternately cooking their meals and pursuing their studies with combined energies . . . So intimately was my brother associated while in college, with professors and students, that he became thoroughly acquainted with the profession and the practice of the denomination by which that popular institution was controlled; and, although he cherished very friendly regards of the people, he was unfavorably impressed with their system of religion. A short time before leaving Oberlin, he wrote, asking me many questions concerning revealed religion, at the same time saying, "If there is nothing better than is to be found here in Oberlin College, good bye to all religions." I answered his questions, and knowing he intended crowning his studies with a thorough knowledge of Hebrew, invited him to come to Kirtland at the close of this term in Oberlin, as a school was soon to commence [in Kirtland].[106]

Fairport, Geauga County, Ohio

Fairport is located approximately fifteen miles northeast of Kirtland.

The Connecticut Land Company sold the area of Fairport to forty-eight men living in New England. The scholars disagree on when the town was actually laid out; however, the original name was Grandon. In 1836, the town was incorporated; and the name was changed to Fairport. The word "Harbor" was added later. In 1823, the importance of the harbor was rewarded by an appropriation from Congress in the amount of one thousand dollars. The money was used to improve the harbor. In 1825, Jonathan Goldsmith built the first lighthouse.

Main Street, Fairport, Ohio
(Missionaries and Saints used this port extensively in their travels)
Lake County Historical Society—unknown, c1858

FAIRPORT HARBOR AND LIGHTHOUSE

Fairport was an important port for the Saints coming to and leaving Kirtland. The harbor is located on Lake Erie about twelve miles from Kirtland. In his journal entry of 20 October 1834, Oliver Cowdery described an experience that

View of Fairport Harbor, Fairport, Ohio
(New York Saints landed at Fairport and then
traveled to Kirtland)
Lake County Historical Society—
unknown, c1858

he had with Joseph Smith, David Whitmer, F. G. Williams, Hyrum Smith, and A. Orton:

> At 9 in the evening we took passage on board the Steam Boat Monroe at Fairport . . . Fairport is an excellent harbor, and affords a safe moorage for shipping.—Government has expended a considerable amount in extending its pier several rods into the lake, at the end of which a small light house is now being finished to render the ingress of vessels more easy during the dark gales to which this lake is subject. The main light house is situated on a commanding eminence, and is some 60 or 70 feet from its base to its summit. [107]

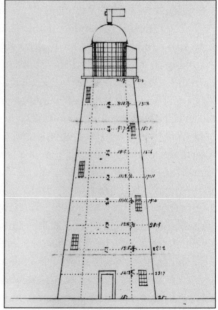

Drawing of First Lighthouse, Fairport, Ohio
(Saints would have viewed lighthouse on their
approach to Fairport)
Lake County Historical Society—
unknown, c1825

Shortly after the first members of the Twelve Apostles were ordained, they were called on a mission to the eastern states. Orson Pratt wrote,

> The next morning [4 May 1835] at half past 2 o'clock we [the Twelve] and two others left Kirtland for Fairport, where we arrived a little after sunrise, and went immediately on board of a steam boat which left the port a few minutes after we got on board . . . Thus the Lord in his mercy provided a boat for us at the very moment we arrived which was according to our prayers. We had a speedy and prosperous voyage.[108]

Water Routes

An early water route used by the Saints was the Erie Canal in New York. The canal took the early missionaries from the Palmyra area to other nearby regions in an effort to spread the news of the restoration; but before those early missionaries began their efforts, the canal brought individuals to the Smith home in Manchester, New York, where they found out about the "marvelous work and a wonder," the *Book of Mormon.*

The Church was barely organized when Joseph Smith announced that the Lord had commanded his little flock to leave New York and "go to the Ohio."[109] As many as two hundred members of the Church followed Joseph Smith to Kirtland, Ohio, as soon as they could.

One of the first group of Saints to leave New York for Ohio departed in early April 1831 under the direction of Newel Knight. They were from the Colesville, New York, area near the Pennsylvania border. From Ithaca, New York, they began their water-route travel on a boat up Cayuga Lake, then on the Cayuga and Seneca Canal for eleven miles, and then to Buffalo on the Erie Canal. The canal took them nearly 160 miles to Buffalo, where they took a steamer for 150 miles southwest to Fairport, Ohio, only fifteen miles from Kirtland where the Saints were gathering. Once they reached Ohio and established a new Church headquarters in Kirtland, the Saints used the water routes available to them in Ohio and Missouri, a combination of canals, rivers, and lakes, to complete their travel.

Since Fairport Harbor was somewhat closer to the Church's headquarters at Kirtland than was the Ohio Canal, most of the Saints' travels remained on Lake Erie and the Ohio River.

A large group of Saints, members of the Colesville Branch and now settled in Thompson, Ohio, were directed to "take [their] journey into the regions westward, unto the land of Missouri, unto the borders of the Lamanites [Mormon

View of Grand River Shipyard from Fairport Lighthouse, Fairport, Ohio
(This was the beginning of one of the river/canal systems)
Lake County Historical Society—unknown, c1858

name for native American Indians]."[110] The members of the branch carried their belongings and provisions in twenty-four wagons. At Wellsville, Ohio, they transferred their goods from the wagons to a steamboat. Their water journey began on the Ohio River and continued to the junction of the Mississippi River. They then traveled up the Mississippi River to St. Louis on the *Chieftain*, a side-wheel paddle steamboat. From St. Louis, the journey continued on a steamboat traveling on the Missouri River to Independence, where they arrived sometime in July.

Water travel, a convenient and comfortable means of travel, was not without dangers and difficulties, including possible drowning. A newspaper in Kirtland published the following account about a young six-year-old boy:

DROWNED in Lake Erie on the 2nd [October 1837] Andrew J. Reader, son of George and Gerusha Reader, aged six years. Brother Reader was formerly a citizen of the State of New York but had resolved to remove to this State with his family and accordingly had taken a passage on board the Steam Boat "Uncle Sam." We are not aware that blame is attached to anyone; he fell overboard when there was none to help, he was seen by his parents when 15 or 20 rods distant, waving his hands and crying for help. There was an exertion made by the crew and small boat to save him, but in vain.[111]

While many groups headed west to the new Mormon Zion in Missouri, other Saints, mainly missionaries, used other water routes to complete their journeys. Brigham Young recorded in his journal many accounts of travel on steamboats on Lake Erie during the Ohio-Missouri period. On the occasion of a return trip from missionary work in the East, Young left Buffalo on the steamboat *Daniel Webster* in 1837 and traveled to Fairport, Ohio. Once the steamboat left the pier, a woman immediately fell into the water. A ship's crew member jumped into the water to save her. She was found about ten feet below the surface, and very quickly the first mate brought her to the surface holding her by the neck. Young noted, "The passengers on board, in a few minutes, made up a purse of $60 to the mate for saving her life. I learned from the lady herself the cause of her falling into the water."[112] She was taking a farewell look at the city, where she had left her family and friends, when she slipped and fell into the water.

On another occasion, 22 November 1839, Young, along with Heber C. Kimball, Reuben Hedlock, John Taylor, Theodore Turley, and George A. Smith, took a steamboat trip on Lake Erie to Buffalo, New York. The journey started at Fairport, Ohio. Young wrote,

> The lake was so rough that no boat came into port until the 26th, when we went on board the steamboat Columbus, at one o'clock, and arrived in Buffalo next morning. We had an excellent time on the lake. The wind rose about one o'clock in the morning. I went up on deck and felt impressed in spirit to pray to the Father . . . for a forgiveness of my sins, and then I felt to command the winds to cease, and let us go safe on our journey. The winds abated . . . The boat stopped at Erie, Pennsylvania. She had no freight and but few passengers, and coming out of the harbor she ran against the pier, which was covered with an immense body of ice. She struck it with such force that she ran right up on the ice out of the water, and remained a short time, and then slid backwards into the water without damage.[113]

W. W. Phelps reported his first of many trips from Kirtland, Ohio, to Independence, Missouri, in a travel narrative published in a local newspaper. Phelps wrote:

> After I left Canadaigua, on the 9th of June, I went on board a canal-boat the same evening for Buffalo, where I arrived on 12th. Started for Cleveland on the 18th. Passed from thence to Newark, 176 miles on the Ohio canal; found it superior to the Erie canal in point of better locks and wider excavation. From thence to Dayton, 101 miles. I passed through Columbus, the capital of the state, an ordinary town about as large as Geneva [New York]; and from thence to Cincinnati, 65 miles by water on the Miami Canal. Cincinnati is a thriving place, as large as Albany [New York], but not so handsome. Took steamboat for Louisville, 165 miles (Deck passage) and was roused in the night by the cry of wood! wood!—the

common practice among southern boats to replenish the stock of fuel. Arrived at Louisville on the 25th. This is a considerable southern city . . . [P]assed down one and half miles to Shippingport (or Shavingport), and tarried three days in wait for a passage to St. Louis. Viewed the Grand Canal round the falls of Ohio—a magnificent display of human skill, which cost $900,000. Three superb locks of hewn stone, the largest of which, for high water, is 60 feet wide, 43 feet deep, and 3000 feet long . . . On the 27th, left for St. Louis in the steamboat, Don Juan. On the 29th I passed the mouth of the Ohio, where three states were in sight, in the 37th degree of north latitude, and the sun nearly over head. 30th I saw mills on the Mississippi propelled by current wheels: constructed like cidermill screws, 100 feet long . . . July lst stopped at Genevieve, saw large quantities of lead and white sand. Arrived at St. Louis same day, quite a city, with the small pox in it.[114]

At St. Louis, Phelps, along with his party, went on foot to Independence.

The water routes used by the Saints in Ohio included Lake Erie, the Ohio River, the Mississippi River, and canals. Sometime in February 1825, Ohio launched a canal-building program that eventually allowed travel from Lake Erie and the Ohio River, thereby connecting the Hudson River (by means of the Erie and Ohio canals) with the Mississippi River and creating America's greatest system of internal waterways. Eventually, the Ohio-Erie Canal, the

Canal boat on the Ohio and Erie Canal
(Began in 1825 and completed in 1832, the canal connected Cleveland with Portsmouth on the Ohio River)
Western Reserve Historical Society—unknown, c1900

Pennsylvania-Ohio Canal, the Sandy-Beaver Canal, the Hocking Canal, and the Miami-Erie Canal were constructed. Travelers could travel from northern Ohio (Toledo) to southern Ohio (Cincinnati) or from Cleveland on the north to Portsmouth or Hockingport on the south by canal.

The original specifications for the construction of the canals were at least twenty-six feet at the bottom and forty feet at the water line and a towpath at least ten feet wide at the top.[115]

The canal barges on the Ohio Canal during the 1830s were some seventy-five feet long and fourteen feet wide. Like those on the Erie Canal, they were towed by mules or horses in teams of two or more and were by law restricted to four miles per hour, or no more than ninety-four miles a day. Traveling by canal boat was less expensive and much more convenient and comfortable than overland travel in the early 1830s. The cabins were usually divided into male and female quarters, with bunk beds as many as four high for a reasonably comfortable sleep. Passengers usually stayed below or sat on the roof of the cabin. They could jump off the barge and walk alongside to stretch their legs. Three meals were served each day during a trip, and additional supplies and refreshments could be purchased from local vendors near the canal. Those who could not afford the fare on a passenger barge traveled on the freight barges that also boarded travelers. Many passengers slept on deck or wherever they could. In many instances, Mormon missionaries using the canal system traveled on freight barges because of the lack of funds.

Joseph Smith's history mentions his first trip from Kirtland to Missouri at the time when the Colesville Saints left Thompson for Missouri. Both groups departed Ohio and traveled separately during the first part of the journey. Joseph's trip used several means of transportation, including the Ohio canal system:

> On the 19th of June [1831], in company with Sidney Rigdon, Martin Harris, Edward Partridge, William W. Phelps, Joseph Coe, Algernon S. Gilbert and his wife, I started from Kirtland, Ohio, for the land of Missouri, agreeable to the commandment before received [LDS D&C 48/RLDS D&C 48], wherein it was promised that if we were faithful, the land of our inheritance, even the place for the city of the New Jerusalem, would be revealed. We went by wagon, canal boats, and stages to Cincinnati, where I had an interview with the Rev. Walter Scott, one of the founders of the Campbellites, or New Light Church . . . We left Cincinnati in a steamer, and landed at Louisville, Kentucky, where we were detained three days in waiting for a steamer to convey us to St. Louis. At St. Louis, myself, Brother Harris, Phelps, Partridge and Coe, went by land on foot to Independence, Jackson County, Missouri, where we arrived about the middle of July, and the rest of the company came by water a few days later.[116]

Although several important ports in Ohio played a significant role in Church history, Cincinnati on the Ohio River and the terminus of the Miami-Erie Canal remained important during the entire Ohio-Missouri period and continued to play a role during the Church's Nauvoo period (1839–46).

Cincinnati, Hamilton County, Ohio

Cincinnati is located in the southwest portion of Ohio and is situated approximately 245 miles from Cleveland.

Cincinnati, one of the chief river ports on the Ohio River, was an important commercial center as long as the primary means of moving goods and people was on river and canal routes. The first dock on the Cincinnati landing was established in 1811, shortly after the advent of steamboats. The opening of the Miami-Erie Canal to Dayton in 1829 (and subsequently to Toledo) enhanced Cincinnati's role as a trade and market center.

Panoramic View of Cincinnati, Ohio
(Cincinnati was the chief river town in Ohio)
Cincinnati Public Library—W. S. Porter, 1848

Cincinnati's population was heterogeneous, including New Englanders, Southerners, foreign immigrants, and a sizable community of freemen (free blacks). Here Joseph Smith and other New England Saints came in contact with a large population of free blacks for the first time. Joseph Smith, who became convinced that blacks were and could be equal in education and occupation with

hite population if given the same opportunities, made the following
~~comm~~ n 1843 (during a period when the term "negro" was still in common use):

> Elder Hyde inquired [about] the situation of the negro. I replied, they came into the world slaves, mentally and physically. Change their situation with the whites, and they would be like them. They have souls, and are subjects of salvation. Go into Cincinnati or any city, and find an educated negro, who rides in his carriage, and you will see a man who has risen by the powers of his own mind to his exalted state of respectability. The slaves in Washington are more refined than many in high places, and the black boys will take the shine off many of those they brush and wait on. Elder Hyde remarked, "Put them on the level, and they will rise above me." I replied, if I raise you to be my equal, and then attempted to oppress you, would you not be indignant and try to rise above me . . . [I]f I had anything to do with [them, I would] put them on a national equalization.[117]

Cincinnati Water Front, Cincinnati, Ohio
(Many Saints and missionaries traveled through Cincinnati)
Cincinnati Public Library—W. S. Porter 1848

A year later, Joseph campaigned for a national policy that would sell federal land and purchase all slaves in the United States from the proceeds so they could be set free. Contact with a variety of peoples and groups, like the free blacks in Cincinnati, allowed the Saints to become educated about an America that was more than a white Protestant New England. Although Cincinnati offered some diversity of cultures and people, it also was the site of several race riots and was the site of a famous abolitionist press that was destroyed in a terrible riot in 1836.

Missionary work in Cincinnati began very early. A revelation to Joseph Smith commanded him and Oliver Cowdery to travel to the city, "and at that place they shall lift up their voices unto God."[118] Shortly thereafter, W. W. Phelps was given instructions to buy a printing press in Cincinnati for the Church's first publication, *The Evening and the Morning Star*, published in Missouri.

Steamboats Docked at Cincinnati, Ohio
(Several business activities with the Kirtland Saints were transacted here)
Cincinnati Public Library—W. S. Porter, 1848

The city continued to play an important role in Mormon publication efforts during the entire 1830s and 1840s. Joseph noted in a letter to Brother Granger, "[W]e expect to have an edition of the Book of Mormon printed by the first of September; it is now being stereotyped in Cincinnati."[119] Elder Orson Hyde revised the *History of the Late Persecution by the State of Missouri* by Parley P. Pratt and had two thousand copies printed in Cincinnati.

Missionary work continued throughout the period; and the population of the branch increased, sometimes through conversions and at other times by visitors. In June 1832, Alpheus Gifford started for Missouri; but he stopped in Cincinnati where he "wintered" with the Saints who had previously been baptized by Lyman Wight. Later, another Church leader, John E. Page, preached "with the manifestations of the Spirit and power in [Cincinnati]," wrote Samuel Bent. Page noted in a letter to Church headquarters that thirteen people had been baptized in the city during his visit.[120] Several Church conferences were held in the city, usually presided over by members of the Twelve Apostles. In the 1840s, such meetings were held in the Temperance Hall.

During the trying days leading to the martyrdom, Joseph Smith advised his brother to take himself and his family to Cincinnati. "Hyrum replied, 'Joseph, I can't leave you.'"[121] Others were warned to flee also, including Joseph's own wife and family. Amasa Lyman, who was visiting Cincinnati when Joseph was killed on 27 June 1844, said he had felt a "depression of spirit" the entire day. Later, he heard that Joseph and Hyrum Smith had been assassinated in Carthage, Illinois.

When the Saints decided to vacate Nauvoo and migrate west to the Rocky Mountains, letters notifying individuals of their intentions were sent, one to Bishop Purcell of the Cincinnati Catholic Church. The letter proposed the sale of property in Nauvoo to the Catholic Church. Within a short time, Bishop Purcell sent a letter and met with an LDS Church leader in an attempt to buy Church property in Nauvoo and to lease the Nauvoo Temple.

Columbus, Franklin County, Ohio

Columbus is located in approximately the center of the state of Ohio. In 1812, Columbus was named the state capital. It was established in 1797 on the

State Capitol, Columbus, Ohio
(Church leaders visited the capitol on political, business, and Church matters)
Columbus Historical Society—unknown, c1850

west bank of the Scioto River and is situated on the banks of both the Scioto and Olentanay rivers. Columbus was connected to the Ohio and Erie Canal in 1831 and the National Road in 1833.

Several Church leaders visited Columbus on Church business and on other related matters, including financial and political concerns. For example, Oliver Cowdery was elected a delegate to the state convention. He relates his visit to Columbus in 1836:

> Sunday the 3rd This morning I left for Columbus, the capital of this State, to attend a Convention to nominate a candidate for Governor, in company with Benj. Adams, Lyman Root and Simeon Wright. I did not like to start a journey on Sunday, but was obliged to do so, or go in the stage: this I could not do for want of means. From the 3rd to the morning of the 8th I was on the road, a part of the way being very muddy. My company used me with perfect respect, and spoke favorably of the cause of truth.
>
> Friday & Saturday, the 8th & 9th Sat in convention in the Theatre: a great many men assembled from different parts of the State. Here the delegation from this section treated me with deference, and appointed me on an important committee in preference to others.
>
> While in Columbus I had several interviews with Mr. John A. [Bryan], the Auditor of State, from whom I received expressions of the most perfect friendship and confidence. My only wish in forming acquaintances with the great men of the nation, is, that I may be of service to my fellow beings and benefit the cause of truth and righteousness. I would that all these were men of God, walking in the path of holiness. While in Columbus I also visited the house of Cyprian Rudd, a member of the Church of Christ: his wife was very low of a fever.
>
> Sunday the 10th Left for home in company with Mr. Root and Wright. On my way I called on Silas Austin, the son of my present mother: he received me with a smile, and wished me to remember him.[122]

Orson Hyde made a similar trip to Columbus in an effort to secure a Kirtland bank charter. The following account in *The Return* explains the results of that trip:

> On the 2nd of November the brethren at Kirtland drew up certain articles of agreement, preparatory to the organization of a banking institution, to be called the "Kirtland Safety Society."
>
> President O. [Oliver Cowdery] was delegated to Philadelphia to procure plates for the institution; and Elder O. [Orson] Hyde, to repair to Columbus, with a petition to the legislature of Ohio, for an act of incorporation, which was presented at an early period of their session, but because we were "Mormons," the legislature raised some frivolous excuse on which they refused to grant us those banking privileges

they so freely granted to others. Thus Elder Hyde was compelled to return without accomplishing the object of his mission, while Elder Cowdery succeeded at a great expense in procuring the plates, and bringing them to Kirtland.[123]

Cleveland, Cuyahoga County, Ohio

Cleveland, on Lake Erie, is located in the northeast triangle of the state known as the Western Reserve, which was part of the vast lands promised to Connecticut by King Charles II in 1662. In 1796, Moses Cleveland, a director of the Connecticut Land Company, and a team of surveyors arrived on the high, forested plain overlooking the east bank of the Cuyahoga River, just beyond the Appalachian foothills. Their mandate was to establish township boundaries in that portion of the Western Reserve east of the Cuyahoga and to lay out townsites that would serve as the center of future settlements in the area.The area now known as Cleveland was originally named Cleaveland. The "a" was inexplicably dropped later.

Cleveland, Ohio
(Terminus of the Ohio and Erie Canal)
Western Reserve Historical Society—unknown, 1832

During the next two decades, Cleveland experienced slow growth. This growth pattern changed when the Ohio-Erie Canal was opened in 1827. Cleveland became a major port and terminus on the waterway. Located near the Mormon headquarters at Kirtland during the 1830s, Cleveland was a place of constant contact with Church leaders and missionaries.

Cuyahoga River Valley, Cleveland, Ohio
(Cleveland, the largest city in the Western Reserve in the 1830s)
Western Reserve Historical Society—unknown, c1870

A local Cleveland newspaper, the *Cleveland Herald*, published an article entitled "The Golden Bible" in 1830. The author admitted that he had not personally read the *Book of Mormon* but had "perused it sufficiently to be convinced" that the book was "one of the earliest impositions" of the time. The author speculated that Joseph Smith's purpose was to make money and that Joseph had sent his "twelve apostles" to sell the book. All this was "new proof that all fools are not dead, and knavery in any garb may yet find votaries [followers]."[124]

Nevertheless, such critical reviews of the Mormon religion did not necessarily equal an endorsement for persecution of the Mormons. During the turbulent period in Missouri, the same newspaper, the *Cleveland Herald*, condemned the actions of Missourians against the Saints.

One of the earliest recorded Church meetings in Cleveland occurred sometime before March 1831 when John Murdock preached in "the Masonic Hall." Several citizens had requested Mormon missionaries to come, but apparently the plan was not to investigate Mormon claims but to harass the elders. According to John Whitmer's history:

Cleveland, Ohio
(The Cleveland Herald, which contained numerous articles on the Mormons, was published here)
Western Reserve Historical Society—unknown, c1890

> Elder Murdock addressed the congregation on the subject of the gospel; and warned the inhabitants of that place to flee the wrath to come. Others followed him, and while they were yet speaking one of the congregation came toward the stand and kneeled down and began to pray, a sign to the bandity to begin their abuse. At this time they began to blow out the candles and throw inkstands and books, etc. at the speaker.[125]

In the summer of 1834, a plague of cholera was sweeping the nation. Cholera, essentially a water-borne disease caused by sewage-contaminated water or food supply, violently gripped the nation beginning in 1832. Cleveland witnessed this epidemic of cholera in August 1834. Frederick G. Williams returned from the city to Kirtland to report to Joseph Smith the nature of the epidemic and its extent. Joseph Smith recorded:

> August 21st 1834 This day Brother Frederick Williams returned from Cleveland and told us concerning the plague, and after much consultation we agreed that Bro. Frederick should go to Cleveland and commence administering to the sick, for the purpose of obtaining blessings for them, and the glory of the Lord. Accordingly we, Joseph, Frederick, and Oliver united in prayer before the Lord for this thing. "Now, O Lord, grant unto us this blessing, in the name of Jesus Christ, and thy name shall have the glory forever; Amen."[126]

During the following months and years, many Church leaders and missionaries traveled to Cleveland, including Joseph Smith on 9 July 1835 to regulate the affairs of the Church in the city.

Shaker Heights (Cleveland), Cuyahoga County, Ohio

Shaker Heights is located approximately seven miles from downtown Cleveland and is considered a suburb of Cleveland.

Panoramic View, North Union (Shaker Heights), Ohio
(Mormon missionaries visited here in 1830)
Shaker Historical Society—unknown, c1890

When Moses Cleveland surveyed and divided the Western Reserve area in 1796 into five-mile townships, he prepared the way for Daniel Warren, who built a log cabin near the intersection of Lee and Kinsman, the first roads in the area. Shaker Heights was first known as Warrenville Township, after Daniel and Margaret Warren. After the arrival of the first members of the United Society of Believers in the Second Coming of Christ (Shakers), the Warrenville Township became known as North Union.

The Shaker community of North Union remained in this location from 1822 to 1889 and eventually occupied nearly fourteen hundred acres of the surrounding area. Ralph Russell, who lived in a log cabin near the present intersection of Shaker Boulevard and Lee Road, became interested in Shakerism during the fall of 1821. He founded the community of North Union in March 1822, and the first public meeting was held later in the fall on 20 September. The community prospered during the next few years, and frame buildings and homes replaced the original log cabins. The first frame home was completed at the Center House, located on the west side of the Lee Road, north of Shaker Boulevard.

Center Family Dwelling, North Union (Shaker Heights), Ohio
(Sidney Rigdon and Parley P. Pratt proselyted here in 1831)
Shaker Historical Society—unknown, c1890

The North Union Shakers were almost continuously engaged in the building of barns, living quarters, mills, and shops to accommodate the growing needs and industries of the community. The membership increased from 89 to 148 by 1841. One member of the Shakers, Leman Copley, left the community and became a Mormon for a brief time. During this period, Mormon missionaries arrived at North Union to preach the "restored gospel" to the Shakers.

NORTH UNION (SHAKER HEIGHTS)

The Shaker village of North Union was located in what is presently Shaker Heights, a suburb of Cleveland. The Shaker Historical Museum is located at 16740 South Park Boulevard. In the vicinity of the museum are "Old Gate Posts" with a plaque and the "Shaker Gate" marking the location of the meetinghouse. At Shaker Square, at the corner of Shaker Boulevard and North Moreland Boulevard, are the "Old Millstone" and "Gate Posts."

Historical Background

Brother Ashbel Kitchell, an elder of the Shaker community at North Union, recorded the following in his "pocket journal":

> Sometime in the year [1830] the new religion, (if so it may be called,) of the Mormons began to make a stir in a town not far from North Union. It created a good deal of excitement among the people. They stated they had received a New Revelation, had seen an angel, and had been instructed into many things in relation to the history of America, that was not known before.

> Late in the fall a number of them came to visit the Believers. One by the name of Oliver [Cowdery], who stated that he had also seen the Angel, and had been commissioned by him to go out and bear testimony, that God would destroy this generation.

> We gave him liberty to bear his testimony in our meeting; but finding he had nothing of us, we treated them kindly, and labored to find out what manner of spirit they were of. They appeared meek and mild; but as for light, or knowledge of the way of God, I considered them very ignorant of Christ or his work; therefore I treated them with the tenderness of children. They tarried with us two nights and one day, and when they were ready to start they proposed to leave some of their Books among us, to which we consented, and they left seven, which we distributed among the people, but they were soon returned as not interesting enough to keep them awake while reading. After some months they called for them and took them away, except one which was given me a present. They appeared to have full faith in the virtue of their Books.[127]

However, this was not the last contact the Shakers had with Mormon missionaries. In March 1831, Joseph Smith received a revelation directing another mission to North Union.[128] Upon learning of the revelation, Leman Copley proposed to share his newly found faith with his friends at the Shaker community. John Whitmer's history records the following:

> Leman Copley one of the disciples, who was formerly a shaker quaker, he was anxious that some of the elders should go to his former brethren and preach the gospel. He also feared to be ordained to preach himself, and desired that the Lord should direct in this and all matters, and thus saith the Lord: Given at Kirtland March 1831.[129]

The revelation commanded Sidney Rigdon and Parley P. Pratt to accompany Leman Copley to North Union to preach the gospel to the Shakers. The John Whitmer record continues:

The above named brethren went and proclaimed according to revelation given to them, but the shakers hearkened not to their words, and received not the gospel that time; for they were bound up in tradition and priestcraft, and thus they are led away with foolish and vain imaginations.[130]

Ashbel Kitchell also mentioned this visit:

We continued on friendly terms in the way of trade and other acts of good neighborship until the spring of 1831, when we were visited on Saturday evening by Sidney Rigdon and Leman Copley, the latter of whom had been among us, but not liking the cross any too well, had taken up with Mormonism as the easier plan and had been appointed by them as one of the missionaries to convert us. They tarried all night, and in the course of the evening, the doctrines of the cross and the Mormon faith were both investigated; and we found that the life of self-denial corresponded better with the life of Christ, than Mormonism . . . Sabbath morning, matters moved on pleasantly . . . They came into meeting and sat quietly until the meeting was through, and the people dismissed; when Sidney Rigdon arose and stated that he had a message from the Lord Jesus Christ to this people; could he have the privilege of delivering it? He was answered, he could. He then said it was in writing; could he read it? He was told he might.[131]

Rigdon then read the full text of LDS D&C 49/RLDS D&C 49. However, the Shakers did not accept it as a revelation from Christ. Although Parley P. Pratt left immediately following the meeting, Sidney stayed for dinner; and Leman Copley remained overnight.

According to Kitchell, "[Copley] felt very bad; was not able to rest and came back to us and begged for union . . . [W]e concluded to give him union, and help him through."[132] In June, Copley broke his promise to the members of the Colesville Branch Church who had settled on his land. As a result, Copley's fellowship in the Church was withdrawn in the summer of 1831 but was re-extended sometime before October 1832. He was disfellowshipped in 1834, made satisfaction on 1 April 1836, but eventually remained in Ohio when the Saints left in 1838.

Painesville, Geauga County, Ohio

Painesville is located approximately twelve miles northeast of Kirtland.

As the population of the Western Reserve was expanding in the early 1800s, numerous villages were established. In 1803, Abraham Skinner and Eleazar Paine laid out a village originally named Champion. However, within a short time, the

Main Street, Painesville, Ohio
(Painesville was the heart of anti-Mormon activity in the 1830s)
Lake County Historical Society—unknown, 1850

village was renamed Painesville in recognition of General Edward Paine. By 1820, Painesville was one of the largest towns in the Western Reserve.[133]

The first Mormon missionaries to the Western Reserve (Cowdery, Pratt, Whitmer, and Peterson) not only visited Kirtland and Mentor but also visited Painesville. When they arrived in Painesville, they called on Edward Partridge at his hatter's shop. Lydian Partridge recorded her husband's reaction:

> He told them he did not believe what they said, but believed them to be imposters. Oliver Cowdery said he was thankful there was a God in heaven who knew the hearts of all men. After the men were gone my husband sent a man to follow them and get one of their books.[134]

Partridge eventually joined the Church and became the Church's first bishop.

Anti-Mormon activity was prevalent in the Kirtland area, but Painesville seemed to be at the heart of the unrest.

E. D. Howe, the publisher of the *Painesville Telegraph*, became one of the most vocal critics of Joseph Smith and the Church. The first article about the Church appeared in the 30 November 1830 issue of his paper. The article quoted the Book of Mormon title page and preface and rejected the book as vile superstitions. Another forty-two articles appeared during the period of 1830–39.

The newspaper noted the arrival of David Whitmer in Painesville and Joseph Smith in nearby Kirtland. On 25 October 1831, the first of Ezra Booth's series of articles on Mormonism appeared.

Howe's attacks in the paper were not sufficient to accomplish his personal goal of seeing the Saints leave the area, so he added "legal persecution" to his methods.

He confided that the anti-Mormons used legal suits to harass the Church leaders. He stated:

> All their vain babblings and pretensions were pretty strongly set forth and noticed . . . [The] surrounding country was becoming somewhat sensitive, and many of our citizens thought it advisable to take all the legal means within their reach to counteract the progress of so dangerous an enemy in their midst, and many law suits ensued.[135]

On several occasions, Joseph Smith and other Church leaders were brought to the Methodist Church in Painesville to stand trial. For example, on 3 June 1837,

Public Square, Painesville, Ohio
(Methodist Church, first building on the left, was the site of a Joseph Smith trial in 1837)
Lake County Historical Society—Henry Howe, 1846

Joseph stood trial in the building for attempting to take the life of Grandison Newell. (Newell filed approximately thirty lawsuits against Joseph Smith.) As a result of this hearing, Joseph was eventually bound over for trial at the county courthouse in Chardon.[136] He was arrested many times and on one occasion several times in one day.

Because Painesville was on the road between Kirtland and Fairport, a number of Church members and missionaries made trips to Painesville. Orson Pratt records such a trip in his journal:

> On the 6th of April [1836] I left Kirtland in company with several brethren. We went to Painesville, hired a team to carry six of us to Erie. There three brethren took the Wersing stage and left us. They were expecting to go to Nova Scotia. The next morning Brother F. Nickerson and P. Pratt and myself took the Stage to Buffalo.[137]

In 1831, Lucy Mack Smith (the Prophet's mother) recorded a visit to Painesville. She states:

> [H]e [Joseph] took them as far as Painesville, where we stopped at the house of Brother Partridge. Here we found a fine supper prepared for the whole company. Soon after partaking of this refreshment, I was taken to Brother Kingsbury's, in his own carriage, where I was treated with great kindness and respect.[138]

Painesville was an important economic center, and the Saints also transacted business there. The following account from Joseph Smith's journal indicates that the Church did some banking in Painesville:

> Friday, 4th [December 1835] Today in company with Vinson Knight we drew three hundred and fifty Dollars out of Painesville Bank on three months credit for which we gave the names of Frederick G. Williams and Company, Newel K. Whitney, John Johnson, and Vinson Knight.[139]

Mentor, Geauga County, Ohio

Mentor is located approximately two miles northeast of Kirtland.

The United States Congress confirmed Connecticut's claim to the Western Reserve on 14 September 1786. Thereafter, Connecticut began to sell off the Western Reserve; and Mentor was one of the first settlements. It was surveyed and divided in 1796 by John Milton Holley and settled by Ebenezer Merry in 1797. By 1800, three families were living in the village.

Mentor Avenue, Mentor, Ohio
(Sidney Rigdon lived and taught as a Campbellite minister here)
Lake County Historical Society—unknown, c1900

Mentor was the residence of Sidney Rigdon in 1830. At that time, Rigdon had associated himself with the Campbellite Church. Orson Hyde relates:

> The Campbellite doctrine began to be preached in Mentor and in Kirtland. Elder S. Rigdon was its chief advocate there. Being forcibly struck with the doctrine of immersion or baptism for the remission of sins, and many other important items of doctrine which were advocated by this new sect, . . . [Hyde] became a convert to this new faith. Feeling that one day I might be called to advocate it, and feeling my great deficiency in learning, I resolved to go to school. Accordingly, I took up my abode in Mentor, in the house of Elder Sidney Rigdon, and began the study of English grammar under his tuition. Elder Rigdon took unwearied pains and care to instruct me in the elementary science. After spending months in this way, studying day and night.[140]

In October 1830, Parley P. Pratt (a friend of Sidney Rigdon) and his three missionary companions arrived in Mentor. Josiah Jones recorded, "These men appeared in the town of Mentor at Elder Sidney Rigdon's on Thursday."[141] After speaking with Rigdon, the missionaries received permission to preach to his Mentor congregation: The *Times and Seasons* states:

> The appointment was accordingly published, and a large and respectable congregation assembled. Oliver Cowdery and Parley P. Pratt severally addressed the meeting. At the conclusion, Elder Rigdon arose and stated to the congregation that the information they had that evening received, was of extraordinary character,

and certainly demanded their most serious consideration: and as the apostle advised his brethren "to prove all things and hold fast that which is good," so he would exhort his brethren to do likewise, and give the matter a careful investigation; and not turn against it, without being fully convinced of its being an imposition, lest they should, possibly, resist the truth.[142]

Sidney Rigdon and a number of his congregation eventually joined the Mormons. The initial response to the gospel in Mentor met with great success; and in 1831, the Saints established a branch of the Church there.

Because of Mentor's proximity to Kirtland and because of Mentor's location on the road to Painesville and Fairport, numerous missionaries and members of the Church visited or traveled through Mentor. Parley P. Pratt relates the following negative experience when he went to Mentor to preach. He took this opportunity to preach while waiting for his missionary companions at Kirtland so they could begin a mission through the eastern states.

Taking an affectionate leave of my family and friends in New Portage, I repaired to Kirtland, ready to accompany my brethren. While they made ready, I paid a visit to an adjoining township called Mentor; and visiting from house to house, I attempted to preach to them; but they were full of lying and prejudice, and would

Branch Tavern, Mentor, Ohio
(Early Mentor business that operated in the 1830s)
Lake County Historical Society—unknown, before 1900

not hear the Word. I then appointed a meeting in the open air, on the steps of a meeting house owned by a people called "Campbellites," one Mr. Alexander Campbell being their leader; they having refused to open the house to me. Some came to hear, and some to disturb the meeting; and one Mr. Newell soon appeared at the head of a mob of some fifty men and a band of music. These formed in order of battle and marched round several times near where I stood, drowning my voice with the noise of their drums and other instruments. I suspended my discourse several times as they passed, and then resumed. At length, finding that no disturbance of this kind would prevent the attempt to discharge my duty, they rushed upon me with one accord at a given signal, every man throwing an egg at my person. My forehead, bosom, and most of my body was completely covered with broken eggs. At this I departed, and walked slowly away, being insulted and followed by this rabble for some distance. I soon arrived in Kirtland, and was assisted by my kind friends in cleansing myself and clothes from the effects of this Christian benevolence.[143]

In 1835, the Prophet Joseph Smith also mentions visiting Mentor on the way to Painesville. He records:

Wednesday, [December] 2nd [1835] A fine morning. I made preparation to ride to Painesville with my wife and family, also my Scribe. We had our sleigh and horses prepared and set out. When we were passing through Mentor Street we overtook a team with two men on the sleigh. I politely asked them to let me pass. They granted my request and as we passed them they bawled out, "Do you get any revelation lately," with an addition of blackguard that I did not understand.

This is a fair sample of the character of Mentor Street inhabitants who are ready to abuse and scandalize men who never laid a straw in their way. In fact those whose faces they never saw and cannot bring an accusation against either of a temporal of spiritual nature, except our firm belief in the fullness of the gospel.

I was led to marvel at the long suffering and condescension of our Heavenly Father in permitting these ungodly wretches to possess this goodly land which is indeed as beautifully situated and its soil as fertile as any in this region of country, its inhabitants wealthy even blessed above measure in temporal things and fain would God bless them with spiritual blessings, even eternal life, were it not for their evil hearts of unbelief.

We are led to mingle our prayers with those Saints that have suffered the like treatment before us.[144]

Chardon, Geauga County, Ohio

Chardon is located approximately ten miles southeast of Kirtland.

In 1808, Chardon was uninhabited. The owner of the area was Peter Chardon

Main Street, Chardon, Ohio
(Several members lived here, including Joseph Smith's two sisters)
Geauga County Historical Society—unknown, before 1868

Brooks, who applied to the county commissioners to have the area named Chardon. Shortly thereafter, the town was platted. However, not until 1811 did Captain Edward Paine of Painesville begin clearing the area. He succeeded in chopping all the timber off the town square. In 1812, Norman Canfield brought his family to Chardon and erected the first building. Later that year, Edward Paine also moved his family to Chardon.

Besides being the site of the county courthouse, Chardon was the residence of several members of the Church, including Joseph Smith's sisters. Joseph Smith's diary indicates the following: "November 29 [1832] this day rode from Kirtland to Chardon to see my sister Sophronia and also called to see my sister Cathrine found them well."[145]

Joseph wrote, "31st [March 1834] Monday. This day [I] came to Chardon to tend the court against Doctor P. Hurlburt etc." While in Chardon, Joseph stayed with a "Brother Riders" and prepared for the trial, which began on 2 April 1834. The court met and decided that Joseph "had ground to fear that . . . Hurlburt would wound, beat or kill him, or destroy his property." Hurlburt was ordered to pay the court costs, to post a bond amounting to two hundred dollars, and "to keep the peace" for six months.[146]

In July 1834, the *Chardon Spectator and Geauga Gazette* erroneously reported the death of Joseph Smith. The report shocked the Kirtland community and Joseph's family, including Emma. The newspaper reported that Joseph had been killed following a skirmish in Jackson County when Zion's Camp entered. Joseph was supposedly wounded in the leg. And although his leg was amputated in an attempt to save his life, Joseph supposedly died of infection three days following the operation.[147] Several days later, another local paper, the *Painesville Telegraph*, reported that the rumors of Joseph's death were without foundation.

The Smith brothers attended court in Chardon on a matter that continually plagued them. The case of George Metcalf, Paymaster of the 1st Brigade, 2nd Regiment, 9th Division, Ohio Militia, vs. Samuel H. Smith came before the court at Chardon on 26 October 1835. Samuel had been fined $1.75 for failing to attend company and regimental musters in 1833. He claimed that he was a minister of the gospel and hence not subject to the military requirement. The Militia Act of 1792 required the enrollment of every free, white male citizen between the ages of eighteen and forty-five to serve in his state militia. Joseph Smith's history states:

> [Joseph] went to attend the County Court, in company with three of his Brothers (viz.) Hyrum, Samuel and Carlos. His Brother Samuel was summoned before this court for not doing Military duty and was fined because they had not their conference minutes with them, for testimony to prove that F. G. Williams was clerk of the conference. This testimony, they would have carried with them, had it not been for the neglect of their Council, or Lawyer, who did not notify them that it was necessary to his success in the suit. This act of the Attorney, he felt as did his

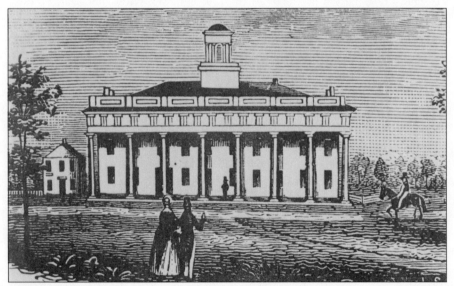

Geauga County Courthouse, Chardon, Ohio
(Joseph Smith attended court here)
Lake County Historical Society—Henry Howe, 1846

brethren, was a want of fidelity to his client, apparent indeed, and an insult practiced upon him on account of his religious faith, that the ungodly might have an unlawful power over him, and trample him and our feelings under their unhallowed feet. In consequence of this omission of duty a fine of twenty dollars including costs, was imposed upon his brother, and to cancel it and the expenses attending the cost he was obliged to sell his cow.[148]

Thompson, Geauga County, Ohio

Thompson is located approximately twenty-five miles northeast of Kirtland.

Thompson was named by and for Mathew Thompson of Suffield, Connecticut. Apparently, he was an early owner of the area. The first public road was established to Thompson in 1798. In 1800, Dr. Isaac Palmer settled there. In 1801, Thompson was incorporated; and in 1809, it was surveyed by Chester Elliot of Hambden. By 1817, the population of Thompson had grown considerably.

LEMAN COPLEY FARM SITE

The Leman Copley farm site's location is somewhat uncertain. However, it is situated north of Thompson.

Historical Background

Leman Copley was born in 1781 in Connecticut. He married his wife, Sally, in Massachusetts. Copley was baptized in March 1831 in Ohio. He was ordained an elder and appointed with Sidney Rigdon and Parley P. Pratt to preach the gospel to the Shaker community at North Union (Cleveland, Ohio).[149] Copley agreed to permit Saints from New York to settle on his property, but he broke that promise by June 1831. He testified against Joseph Smith in the Hurlburt trial in 1833 and was disfellowshipped. He was reinstated on 1 April 1836. He remained in Kirtland after the exodus of the Saints.

Upon the arrival of the Colesville Saints in Kirtland in May 1831, "it was advised that the Colesville branch remain together, and go to a neighboring town called Thompson, as a man by the name of Copley had a considerable tract of land there which he offered to let the Saints occupy."[150] Joseph Knight, Jr., recounts what happened next:

> We went to Kirtland, Ohio [then to Thompson, Ohio], and commenced preparing houses on a brother's land who had a thousand acres, my folks came on, they were called the Colesville church; we planted and sowed a great deal; the man was turned out of the church for bad conduct; his name was Leman Copley, he then

began to persecute us and we had to leave his farm and pay sixty dollars damage for fitting up his house and planting his ground.[151]

Joseph Smith dictated a revelation regarding this situation sometime before 19 June 1831.[152] The revelation instructed the Saints to "flee the land" and journey to Missouri. About sixty members left Ohio as commanded and arrived in Independence on 25 July. The *Painesville Telegraph* reported the following:

> We mentioned two weeks since that the Mormons . . . were about to take up a line of march for Missouri. The leaders have already departed. Before Jo left, he had a special command for all those of his followers who had located themselves in the township of Thompson, to depart forthwith for Missouri . . . There were in that township about twenty families, the most of whom started last week for the Ohio River, leaving their spring crops all upon the ground.[153]

Willoughby, Cuyahoga County, Ohio

Willoughby is located approximately five miles northwest of Kirtland at the mouth of the Chagrin River. In 1750, Willoughby was a French fur-trading post known as Charlton. In 1797, David Abbot, a Yale-educated lawyer, became the first permanent white settler. He built the first grist mill in the Western Reserve,

Erie Street, Willoughby, Ohio
(Site of the infamous medical school)
Willoughby Historical Society—unknown, 1894

Public Buildings, Willoughby, Ohio
(College building is in the center of the drawing)
Lake County Historical—Henry Howe, 1846

and the mill encouraged settlement of the area.

Willoughby, known as Chargrin before 1834, was a frequent stop for the Saints living in Kirtland. Other members, Shadrack Roundy, for example, lived in the Willoughby area. Joseph Smith "rode to Willoughby in company with his wife, to purchase goods at W. Lyon's Store" on 12 October 1835.[154]

Willoughby was the location of the Willoughby Medical College. In November 1835, Joseph Smith, Sidney Rigdon, Oliver Cowdery, and F. G. Williams left Kirtland for the short trip to the college. They "went to Willoughby to hear Doctor [Peixott] deliver a lecture on the theory and practice of Physics." The Church leaders' visit began when they called upon Mr. Cushman: "[They] had their horses put in the stable, took dinner, attended the lecture and [were] treated with marked respect, throughout."[155]

Orange, Cuyahoga County, Ohio

Orange is located twenty miles south of Kirtland, Ohio. The Orange area was first settled by Surenus and Jane Burnett in 1815. They paid $2.50 an acre for one hundred acres. In 1820, the township of Orange was named and organized. The village of Orange gained prominence when the state legislature passed an act establishing a road (Kinsman Road) from Cleveland through Orange to the town of Kinsman (located on the eastern border of the state). In the early 1820s, a stage line was established in the Western Reserve including along the Kinsman Road, with a daily stage to Orange.

Large numbers of individuals were baptized as members of the Church in the area, and as many as sixty-five members constituted the Orange Branch by the end of 1830. Among those who were baptized was the John Murdock family. Following the death of Joseph and Emma's twins, Sister Murdock died and left a set of twins motherless. These twins, whom Joseph and Emma named Joseph and Julia, were given to Emma to raise just nine days following their birth in Orange on 30 April 1831. Within a few months, an important Church conference was held at the home of Irenus Burnett, on 25–26 October 1831. Joseph Smith's history states:

> At the conference on the 25th [October], at Orange, twelve High Priests, seventeen Elders, four Priests, three Teachers, and four Deacons, together with a large congregation attended. Much business was done, and the four remaining members of the committee, authorized by the conference at Hiram on the 11th, were appointed, and consisted of Simeon Carter, Orson Hyde, Hyrum Smith, and Emer Harris.[156]

The entire minutes of this conference were recorded in the *Far West Record*,[157] including a revelation that was recorded for William McClellan.[158] The conference was an important priesthood meeting where those who attended bore strong testimonies of the divinity of the latter-day work. McClellan said, "he had the greatest reason to rejoice of any present and that he also would be subject to the will of God even unto death."[159]

The first high priests ordained in the Church were selected and ordained at a conference on 3 June 1831 in Ohio. The second such ordinations occurred during this conference at Orange, when seventeen men were ordained by Oliver Cowdery.

Hudson, Summit County, Ohio

Hudson, located some forty-five miles southwest from Kirtland, is the oldest community in Summit County.

On 10 October 1795, David Hudson of Goshen, Connecticut, acquired three thousand acres in the Western Reserve. In 1799, Hudson, his ten-year-old son, Ira, and a number of hired men traveled from Connecticut to Hudson's property in the Western Reserve. A year later, the passage of the Quieting Act rectified numerous deed and title problems in the Western Reserve. As a result, settlement of the area increased substantially. In 1802, the Trumball County commissioners voted that the settlement of Hudson be made a township.

The community established the Western Reserve College in 1826 and modeled it after Yale. The school was eventually moved to Cleveland in 1882,

Main Street, Hudson, Ohio
(Site of the Western Reserve College)
Western Reserve Academy—unknown, c1849

Western Reserve College
(Orson Hyde and William McClellan were sent here to retain Joshua Seixas to teach
Hebrew in Kirtland)
Western Reserve Academy—unknown, c1867

but the facility was purchased for use as a private preparatory school, Western Reserve Academy. The academy is located at 115 College Street, and many buildings from the 1830s remain standing.

Joseph Smith sent Orson Hyde and William McClellan to Western Reserve College (Western Reserve Academy) to hire Joshua Seixas to teach Hebrew in Kirtland. Earlier, Oliver Cowdery was sent to New York City to purchase Hebrew texts (Hebrew Bible, lexicon, and grammar) for the Hebrew school that was scheduled to be held during the 1835–36 winter.[160]

An earlier attempt to hire Dr. Daniel Piexotto, a professor at the Willoughby Medical College, failed. Joseph Smith was determined to start a Hebrew school during the upcoming winter. Apparently, Seixas taught Hebrew to Lorenzo Snow at Oberlin College; and through Lorenzo's sister, Eliza R. Snow, Seixas' abilities became known to Joseph Smith. Joseph's history reports on 6 January 1836:

> Elder [McClellan] returned from Hudson, and reported to the school that he had hired a teacher to teach us the term of seven weeks, for three hundred and twenty dollars; that is, forty scholars for that amount; to commence in about fifteen days. He is highly celebrated as a Hebrew scholar, and proposes to give us sufficient knowledge during the above term to start us in reading and translating the language.[161]

Seixas was well educated and taught at two institutions in Ohio before arriving in Kirtland. He began teaching classes at Oberlin College in 1835 but soon left there and began teaching at the Western Reserve College in Hudson. Following his contacts with the Church, he made arrangements to leave the Western Reserve College to spend the winter in Kirtland. He arrived in Kirtland on 26 March 1836 and began teaching soon thereafter. His teaching program was rigorous, with four classes being held along with private lessons. Classes were held from 10:00 to 11:00 A.M. and from 2:00 to 3:00 P.M. each day, but members often met before and after class to read to each other. Joseph Smith wrote in his history, "My soul delights in reading the word of the Lord in the original."[162]

New Portage (Barberton), Medina County, Ohio

New Portage (Barberton) is located fifty-five miles southwest of Kirtland.

New Portage is on the Tuscarawas River and eventually was part of the Ohio Canal. Apparently, New Portage was first settled in 1812; and a village was established in 1816. In 1819, William Laird built flatboats to send produce and goods as far away as New Orleans. The community of New Portage has been absorbed into Barberton's north side.

While the Saints began to establish themselves in their new Church headquarters at Kirtland, missionaries continued their work to proselytize the nation. Missionary activity in Ohio continued to be successful; and sometime in 1831, Ezra Booth "preached at the 'Bates Corners' in Norton" some fifty miles southwest of Kirtland.[163]

Soon other Mormon elders arrived in the New Portage area, including Reynolds Cahoon, Lyman Johnson, Thomas Marsh, and David Whitmer. The first preaching was fruitful when Milton Stow arrived and a number of individuals in New Portage were baptized, including Ambrose Palmer, who later became the Presiding Elder of the Church for the New Portage area. By 1833, a branch of more than sixteen individuals met with Sidney Rigdon, who arrived in the area to conduct Church business. By the end of 1834, another forty individuals joined the small, but growing, branch.

Rigdon returned to New Portage in the spring of 1834 to counter anti-Mormon claims that he had been involved with the writing of the *Book of Mormon*. A large group of people met in the home of Samuel Baker. Many stood in the doorway to hear the Mormon leader review his association with the Church and express his denial that he had anything to do with the coming forth of the *Book of Mormon*. The Church in New Portage was well known to the elders. As Oliver Cowdery reported, they "always manifested a cheerfulness in entertaining their brethren from a distance."[164]

New Portage served as the staging ground for Zion's Camp, a volunteer group who marched to Missouri to assist Church members following their expulsion from Jackson County in 1833. Orson Pratt, a Church leader, was sent from Kirtland on 1 May 1834 to make advance arrangements for the arrival of Zion's Camp. Joseph Smith's history notes:

> On the 6th [May 1834] we arrived at New Portage, about fifty miles distance from Kirtland, and joined our brethren who had gone before . . . On the 7th we made preparation for traveling, gathered all the moneys of every individual of the company, and appointed Frederick G. Williams paymaster to disburse the funds thus collected; and Zerubbabel Snow was chosen commissary general. The whole company now consisted of more than one hundred and thirty men, accompanied by twenty baggage wagons . . . Through the remainder of this day I continued to organize the company, appoint such other officers as were required, and gave much instructions as were necessary for the discipline, order, comfort and safety of all concerned. I also divided the whole band into companies of twelve, leaving each company to elect its own captain, who assigned each man in his respective

company his post and duty, generally in the following order: Two cooks, two firemen; two tent men, two watermen, one runner, two wagoners and horsemen, and one commissary.[165]

**JOURNEY OF
ZION'S CAMP
OHIO–MISSOURI**

The New Portage Branch remained an important facet of the Church in Ohio. The Church community continued to experience growth through local missionary activities. In addition to New Portage's missionary growth, it became a temporary gathering place for other Saints. Parley P. Pratt arrived in New Portage in October 1834 with his nearly destitute family. They were returning from Missouri following the severe persecution of 1833. Pratt notes:

> After a journey of near one thousand miles, we arrived at New Portage . . . early in the winter, and finding a large society of the Saints who welcomed us among them, we stopped for the winter.[166]

Pratt continued his missionary activity in the area; and upon returning home from one such journey, he was called again by Joseph Smith to leave his family. Pratt later recalled,

[I] began to make preparation for my mission, but the state of my affairs was such that it seemed almost impossible for me to leave home; my wife was sick, my aged mother had come to live with me, and looked to me for supportage and infirmity having rendered my father unable to do for himself or family. I was also engaged in building a house, and in other business, while at the same time I was somewhat in debt, and in want of most of the necessaries of live.[167]

Unsettled by the prospect of leaving his family in such a situation, Pratt was called to New Portage to attend a sick brother who had requested a blessing. While he was praying with the man, Pratt's prayer was interrupted by the cry of "fire! fire! fire!" Pratt wrote,

We sprang from our knees and ran towards my house, which was all in a blaze, being an unfinished two story frame building, open to the fresh breeze and full of shavings, lumber, shingles, etc. while a family occupied a small apartment of the same, and no water near. Our utmost exertions barely accomplished the removal of the family and their goods; the building, tools, boards, shingles, building materials, all consumed in a few moments. Thus closed all my hesitation; my works of that nature were now all completed, and myself ready to fill my mission. One gave me a coat; another a hat; a third, house room; a fourth, provisions;, while a fifth forgave me the debt due them; and a sixth bade me God speed to hasten my mission. Taking an affectionate leave of my family and friend in New Portage, I repaired to Kirtland, ready to accompany my brethren.[168]

Soon thereafter, members of the Church began to sell their holdings to gather with the Saints in Clay County, Missouri. Ambrose Palmer, the presiding elder, deeded to Norton Township (New Portage) trustees a piece of the Saints' property in a gesture of gratitude for the friendship to the community. The deed of conveyance included the phrase "We do convey [this land] for the consideration of the love we owe to the people [New Portage]."[169] Although several leading Church families left New Portage, the branch continued to number about one hundred members in 1837. New Portage played another important role in Church history the following year.

Following severe internal strife and external persecution, Church leaders in Kirtland were forced to abandon Church headquarters in Ohio and to flee to Missouri. Joseph Smith's history reports that on the evening of 12 January 1838 at "about 10 o'clock we [Elder Rigdon and Joseph] left Kirtland, on horseback, to escape mob violence, which was about to burst upon us."[170] Joseph and Sidney continued their flight until they arrived at New Portage the next morning at 8:00 A.M. They remained in New Portage for the next thirty-six hours until their families arrived from Kirtland. From there, they traveled to Far West, Missouri, the new Church headquarters. During the next few days and months, the New Portage area township served as a place of refuge for Smith family members seeking asylum from mobs in Kirtland. Joseph Smith, Sr. and Don Carlos Smith arrived a few days following Joseph and Sidney's flight. In May, Lucy Smith arrived from Kirtland; and on the 7th of May, she started her trip to Missouri with a company of Saints.

Amherst, Lorain County, Ohio

Amherst, Ohio, is located about fifty-five miles west of Kirtland.

Main Street, Amherst, Ohio
(Parley P. Pratt lived here before his conversion)
Amherst Historical Society—unknown, before 1900

"Amherst" is derived from two old-English words—"ham," meaning village or town, and "herst," meaning in the woods. The area was surveyed by Colonel Manfield in 1802 and was first settled by Jacob Shupe. In 1811, Shupe settled approximately one and a half miles north of the present city.

Parley P. Pratt was an early settler of Amherst in 1826 following his departure from New York. "I travelled by land till I came to a small settlement about thirty miles west of Cleveland, in the State of Ohio," he recalled.[171] Pratt procured an axe, a gun, and some food stuffs and retired two miles from the settlement into "a dense forest and prepared a small hut, or cabin, for the winter." He was alone for the entire winter:

Some leaves and straw in my cabin served for my lodging, and a good fire kept me warm. A stream near my door quenched my thirst; and fat venison, with a little bread from the settlement, sustained me for food . . . [In] my little cabin the fire blazed pleasantly, and the Holy Scriptures and a few other books occupied my hours of solitude.[172]

When spring arrived, Pratt returned to New York and married Thankful Halsey. Following their marriage on 9 September 1827, Parley and Thankful returned to Amherst, Ohio, to begin their life together.

The Pratts returned to the small clearing in the woods of Ohio where Parley had spent a winter in solitude. Soon a comfortable log cabin was constructed. Later, this cabin was replaced by a small frame home, along with a flower garden, a fruit orchard, and grain fields. The entire community and surrounding area changed during this period.

Sidney Rigdon, a preacher, came into the area and converted Parley to the restoration movement. Soon those converted in Amherst were organized into a society and began to meet in public worship meetings. Parley felt compelled to leave his home to begin a mission that led him to Manchester, New York, and the Smith family.

One year later, in 1831, Parley Pratt, now a Mormon missionary, returned to Amherst to preach the restored gospel. The members of the community were divided in their reaction to Parley's new message. He recounts:

We had stopped for the night at the house of Simeon Carter, by whom we were kindly received, and were in the act of reading to him and explaining the Book of Mormon, when there came a knock at the door, and an officer entered with a warrant from a magistrate by the name of Byington, to arrest me on a very frivolous charge. I dropped the Book of Mormon in Carter's house, and went with him some two miles, in a dark, muddy road; one of the brethren accompanied me.[173]

Parley noted that a late-night trial was held, where false witnesses brought charges against the missionaries. The judge himself seems to have been interested in testing their religious "powers." As a result, Pratt said nothing and made no defense, "but treated the whole matter with contempt." He continues,

I was soon ordered to prison, or to pay a sum of money which I had not in the world. It was now a late hour, and I was still retained in court, tantalized, abused and urged to settle the matter, to all of which I made no reply for some time. This greatly exhausted their patience. It was near midnight. I now called on brother Petersen to sing a hymn in the court. We sung, "O how happy are they." This exasperated them still more.[174]

Pressed by the judge to settle the matter by paying the fine, Pratt said, "May it please the court, I have one proposal to make for a final settlement of the things which seem to trouble you." Pratt's solution was that the witnesses and the judge should repent. If they would repent, Pratt indicated he would kneel down and pray that "God might forgive you in these matters." Both the witnesses and the judge responded in sarcastic tones and urged Pratt to settle the matter, but Pratt remained silent.

Soon thereafter, the court adjourned; and the prisoner was sent to a "public house" and secured until morning, when they planned to take him to a local prison some distance away. Pratt remembered,

> In the morning the officer appeared and took me to breakfast; this over, we sat waiting in the inn for all things to be ready to conduct me to prison . . . After sitting awhile by the fire in charge of the officer, I requested to step out. I walked out into the public square accompanied by him. Said I, "Mr. Peabody, are you good at a race?" "No," said he, "but my big bull dog is, and he has been trained to assist me in my office these several years; he will take any man down at my bidding." "Well, Mr. Peabody, you compelled me to go a mile, I have gone with you two miles. You have given me an opportunity to preach, sing, and have also entertained me with lodging and breakfast. I must now go on my journey; if you are good at a race you can accompany me. I thank you for all your kindness—good day, sir."[175]

Soon Pratt was on his way, while the officer stood in amazement, unable to move or to take a step forward in pursuit. Seeing this, Pratt "halted, turned to him and again invited him to a race. He still stood amazed," Pratt wrote. Parley did not wait long before he was off again. "I then renewed my exertions," he recalled; and he soon increased his speed to "something like that of a deer. The officer did not respond until Pratt had gained two hundred yards. Pratt had already leaped a fence and was well on his way through a field toward the forest before Peabody began his pursuit. Pratt enthusiastically recalled,

> He now came hallowing after me, and shouting to his dog to seize me. The dog, being one of the largest I ever saw, came close on my footsteps with all his fury; the officer behind still in pursuit, clapping his hands and hallowing, "stu-boy, stu-boy— take him—watch—lay hold of him, I say—down with him," and pointing his finger in the direction I was running. The dog was fast overtaking me, and in the act of leaping upon me, when, quick as lightning, the thought struck me, to assist the officer, in sending the dog with all fury to the forest a little distance before me. I pointed my finger in that direction, clapped my hands, and shouted in imitation of the officer. The dog hastened past me with redoubled speed towards the forest; being urged by the officer and myself, and both of us running in the same direction. Gaining the forest, I soon lost sight of the officer and dog, and have not seen them since.[176]

Pratt came back around and crossed a bridge over the Vermilion River and began his journey to another place to preach. The legal authorities were unable to imprison Pratt and halt the spread of the restoration message. Simeon Carter was converted and baptized. Within a short time, a branch of the Church was organized in Amherst.

The Amherst congregation grew sufficiently that a Church conference was held in Amherst on 25 January 1832. This was an important conference at which considerable business was done, and a number of elders were called by revelation to the ministry and appointed to take missions to various parts of the United States.[177] Also at that conference, Joseph Smith was by unanimous vote sustained as President of the High Priesthood and ordained. The following March, he learned that the office of President of the High Priesthood is vested with the authority to preside, with the assistance of counselors, over all Church concerns.

The March unpublished revelation states in part,

> I give unto you a commandment, that you continue in this ministry and presidency and when you have finished the translation of the prophets [Old Testament], you shall from thence forth preside over the affairs of the Church and the School and from time to time as shall be manifested by the Comforter, [you shall] receive revelations to unfold the mysteries of the Kingdom and set in order the church.[178]

As a result of the Amherst Conference and the 8 March revelation, Joseph selected and ordained Jesse Gause and Sidney Rigdon as counselors in the new Presidency of the High Priesthood, later known as the First Presidency. The "Kirtland Revelation Book" for 8 March 1832 states, "Chose this day and ordained Brother Jesse Gause and Brother Sidney [Rigdon] to be my counselors of the ministry of the Presidency of the High Priesthood." Shortly thereafter, Gause denied the faith; and Frederick G. Williams was called to replace him.

The Amherst conference allowed Joseph and the other brethren present to perform missionary work in the local area. A few weeks following these proceedings, Wesley Perkins, a cynical non-Mormon in the area, described the Mormon presence in the city to a relative in Vermont:

> As it respects religion in this town there is considerable stir at present. The Mormon religion excites the greatest curiosity at present. Joseph Smith and Sidney Rigdon [are] the head men in this business. Their god is the Devil. None but the simple will embrace their doctrine . . . I understood that Jared Carter [an Amherst neighbor] was in Benson [Vermont] and had baptized a number and would start for the promised land [Missouri] in the spring. It is nothing more than I should expect of the Carters and some others in that part of [the] town of Benson. Whoever joins

them will become a priest, prophet or a prophetess. I would send you a paper that contains a letter written by the Rev. Ezra Booth [an anti-Mormon]. I will send you the letters and you may read them and satisfy yourself.[179]

For several years following the 25 January 1832 priesthood conference, the Amherst Branch was an important base for some of the missionaries laboring in Ohio.

3

THE KIRTLAND TEMPLE,
A Photographic Essay

One of the earliest and most complete architectural descriptions of the Kirtland Temple was made as part of a federal government project in 1935.

The National Park Service, the American Institute of Architects, and the Library of Congress joined together in 1933 to create the Historic American Building Survey (HABS) as part of President Franklin D. Roosevelt's response to the Great Depression. This program provided work for teams of unemployed architects, historians, and others in documenting outstanding historic buildings throughout the nation. The HABS was one of many "New Deal" programs that made lasting contributions, including the improvement of the national parks, vast public works construction projects, and creative efforts as various as the Federal Writers' Program, the Federal Theater Project, and the HABS.

The HABS was an attempt to preserve the national architectural heritage through graphic and written records of American buildings. Thomas C. Vint directed the work, which began in late 1933. The program received its legislative mandate through the Historic Sites, Building, and Antiquities Act of 1935. The photographs, measured drawings, and written histories of buildings made for the HABS are located in the United States Library of Congress.

The HABS collection was created by the founders of the HABS with the intent that the collection would be made available to the public and reproduced at a minimum cost to patrons. Shortly after the HABS completed its work in Kirtland, an article published in the *Architectural Forum* printed most of the photographs and drawings of the Kirtland Temple.[1] The HABS Kirtland Temple project was under the direction of William A. Bohnard, who directed the work in northern Ohio. The building was the twenty-fifth structure surveyed by the

135

HABS in the northern Ohio district.

The following description of the Kirtland Temple is part of the HABS file on the temple, is located in the Library of Congress, and is reproduced in the *Architectural Forum* article published in 1936.

> The Temple is 59 x 79 ft. in size, contains a partly excavated basement, two full stories and an attic. The long axis of the building lies east and west with the front facing east. The exterior walls up to the cornice line are of stone, covered, except for the exposed stone foundation, stone quoins at the corners and the stone frieze of the cornice, with stuccoed plaster which contains bits of broken glass, china, etc., collected according to tradition, by the women of the church (a tradition not supported by contemporary records), and used to produce a sparkle on the wall surfaces. The gables, dormers and tower are of frame construction. The original roof was covered with hand-made wood shingles. The exterior trim around the door and window openings is of stone in long lengths neatly and accurately tooled. The interior framing construction is of hewn and sawed material following the usual heavy construction of that period. The interior trim, stairs, pews, pulpits, doors, etc., are of native woods hand molded, carved and painted.

> The first story is the apostolic floor, the second the church floor, and the attic the school and quorum floor. The first and second stories each contain two groups of nine pulpits, that at the east end being for the Aaronic order and the opposite one for the Melchizedek order. The pulpits are raised in tiers above the main floors. The seating arrangements in these two stories consist of stalls with doors and movable pews in each stall making possible the use of the entire auditorium from either pulpit. The second story auditorium and the school room story were originally used for instruction purposes in connection with preparation for the ministry, priesthood and missionary work. The workmanship, moldings, carvings, etc., show unusual skill in execution. Many motifs are used in the various parts, varying in outline, contour and design, but blended harmoniously. This phase of the work indicated facility in adapting the design to meet varying conditions, as for instance the change in outline of moldings and in design and size of carving on the spiral stairs. It is not probable that all of the workmen engaged on the building were skilled artisans and yet the result is so harmonious as to raise the question if they may not have been inspired as were the builders of the cathedrals of old.[2]

Several important architectural studies have been written on the Kirtland Temple, including Laurel B. Andrew, "Temple-Building Begins," *The Early Temples of the Mormons: The Architecture of the Millennial Kingdom in the American West* (Albany: State University of New York Press, 1978), 29-53; Nancy J. Brack, "A Mormon Temple in the American Rural Tradition," *Lake County Historical Quarterly* 31 (September 1989): 17-16; Roger D. Launius, "The

Architecture of the Kirtland Temple," *An Illustrated History of the Kirtland Temple* (Independence: Herald Publishing House, 1986), 21-25; Ray W. Luce, "Building the Kingdom of God: Mormon Architecture before 1847," *BYU Studies* 30 (Spring 1990): 33-45; and Henry C. Smith, "An Architectural Appreciation of the Kirtland Temple," *Autumn Leaves* 40 (April 1927): 185–88.

The Kirtland Temple "is a notable example of vernacular American architecture."[3] The temple architecture is a blend of many styles and forms, including Federal, Georgian, Gothic, and Greek elements. The building incorporates many features and styles common to the period and to the Western Reserve Reserve area where it was built. Evidence suggests that many features were copied from the carpenters' handbooks of the day; these pattern books contained woodcuts and engravings of architectural details and were a very important source for builders in Ohio, especially during the Greek Revival period (1820-1860).

The Kirtland Temple, nevertheless, has several striking features that emphasize the unique uses of the building and that also may have been incorporated in an effort to emphasize the Saints' belief that the Church was distinguished from all other sects as the "only true Church of God."

Several architectural historians who have written about the temple suggest that the Saints incorporated many features unique to the building. The first striking feature is the two courts in the temple (upper and lower). The second is the pulpits (Aaronic and Melchizedek) found at both ends of the lower and upper assembly floors. The third is the use of curtains or "veils" that were supported on rollers in the ceiling and that could be lowered to create small classrooms and chambers. These design features distinguish the temple from other ecclesiastical buildings of the day and were incorporated into the plans of the temple because of the building's unique uses.

The photographs and architectural drawings that follow are reproduced with permission from the LIbrary of Congress Print and Photographs Department. The photographs and drawings illustrate many of the unique design features that the Saints incorporated into the Kirtland Temple.

No. 1–Exterior of Temple from the Southeast

Built between 1834 and 1836, the Kirtland Temple was the first major structure erected by the Church. It was a remarkably monumental and substantial building, illustrating the devoted labor and sacrifice of the first few thousand church members. Although some other religious groups in northern Ohio also built sturdy and well-crafted meetinghouses during this period, most local churches were modest, wood-frame structures. In contrast, the Kirtland Temple was unusually large and substantial. Its walls were constructed of stone covered with plaster, in harmony with Joseph Smith's 1833 plan for the City of Zion calling for buildings of solid masonry construction. The expectation that their first meetinghouse would be a "temple," a sacred structure reminiscent of the biblical temples where divine revelations were received, inspired the early Saints to create an impressive symbol of their faith.

No. 2—Exterior of Temple from the Northeast

In its general shape, the Kirtland Temple followed a simple American meetinghouse tradition—a rectangular structure covered by a gabled roof with a bell tower. The details of the building are a mixture of several styles. The quoins (exposed stone blocks on the corners) and dormer windows in the attic are survivals of the eighteenth-century Georgian style. The elliptical arches over the doors, the central windows above them, the large elliptical window in the gable, and the general form of the domed tower are typical of the early twentieth-century Federal style. The pointed arches of the other windows around the building and on the tower show the influence of the popular Gothic Revival. Despite the stylistic diversity of its parts, the design of the temple achieves a kind of provincial elegance and unity.

No. 3–East Facade

The east end of the Kirtland Temple is the main entrance facade. An ornamental cornice decorates the eaves of the roof and makes the gable end into a triangular pediment, like the front of a Greek temple. The two entrance doors correspond to the two aisles in the building as the "House of the Lord" and proclaim the ownership of the Reorganized Church of Jesus Christ of Latter Day Saints, which has preserved, restored, and displayed the building to the public for over a century. Originally, the inscription may have read, "HOUSE OF THE LORD Built by the Church of the Latter Day Saints A.D. 1834." The inscription was subsequently changed several times during the next decades until its present form.

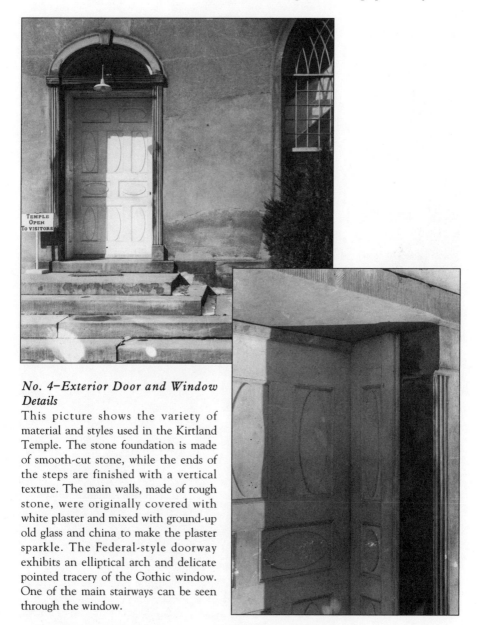

No. 4–Exterior Door and Window Details

This picture shows the variety of material and styles used in the Kirtland Temple. The stone foundation is made of smooth-cut stone, while the ends of the steps are finished with a vertical texture. The main walls, made of rough stone, were originally covered with white plaster and mixed with ground-up old glass and china to make the plaster sparkle. The Federal-style doorway exhibits an elliptical arch and delicate pointed tracery of the Gothic window. One of the main stairways can be seen through the window.

No. 5–Detail of Main Doorway

This close-up view shows the fine workmanship of the stone threshold and door casing. The beautiful door and side panel are decorated with recessed panels framing flat elliptical medallions typical of a simplified Federal style.

No. 6–Entrance Foyer

The two entrance doors open onto a wide symmetrical foyer with light-colored plaster walls and a plank floor. The large interior window allows the natural light in the foyer to continue on into the main meeting room beyond. The doorways have moldings decorated with precisely cut geometric patterns in the fashionable Greek Revival style. The rope connects to the bell in the tower high above.

No. 7–Stair Detail

Skillful craftsmanship is also evidenced in the smoothly curving handrails and fine decorations on the ends of the stairs.

No. 8–Upstairs Foyer

In an unusual innovation, the Kirtland Temple's builders illuminated both upstairs and downstairs foyers with a single arched window in the building's facade, bridged around on the second floor with a curbed balcony. The stairs in the background continue up to the attic story, while the large interior window, like the window one floor below, passes light on into an upper meeting room.

No. 9–Lower Assembly Room, Looking East

The interior arrangement of the Kirtland Temple is more distinctive that the exterior. Unlike the typical one-room meetinghouses of the time, the temple was divided into two large meeting rooms, one above the other. Two rows of square columns divide the central space with its elliptically arched ceiling from the lower side sections. Seating was in traditional box pews, each entered through its own door. Natural light from the foyer can be seen through the window above the pulpits.

No. 10–West End of Lower Assembly Room

Elaborate pulpits are the principal feature of both ends of the assembly rooms providing seats of honor for leaders of the Church's two priesthoods. Each end of the room has three levels of triple pulpits behind a drop-leaf sacrament table. Moveable benches allowed the listeners in the box pews to face either direction, depending on which leaders were conducting the meeting. Choir seats were provided in each corner.

No. 11–West End of Lower Assembly Room from Choir Seats

The doors of the box pews can be seen clearly in this picture. The raised seating on several levels expressed the complex hierarchy of the Church's organizational structure.

No. 12–Detail of West Pulpits, Lower Assembly Room

These pulpits and the window behind displayed the most extraordinary decorative details inside the Kirtland Temple. Curved pulpits framed by fluted plasters bore the initials of the appropriate priesthood office. At the highest level, the Prophet and President of the Church could sit, flanked by his two counselors, and surrounded by a halo of light from the exquisitely decorated window behind. Some doubt exists as to what initials were originally placed on the pulpits.[4]

No. 13–Upper Assembly Room, Looking West from East Pulpits

The upper meeting room that was sometimes used for instruction for missionaries and other leaders was similar to the one below, but with less-elaborate decorations.

No.14–West End of Upper Assembly Room

Rollers in the ceiling of the room originally held curtains that could be let down to divide the room into smaller areas. Spaces between the box pews allowed the curtains to hang to the floor. Similar rollers and curtains were also used in the lower room.

No. 15–Upper Assembly Room Pulpit Details

The upstairs pulpits bear the same initials of priesthood offices as the ones on the lower floor, although the upstairs pulpits are simpler, are less highly elevated, and lack a sacrament table. Like the room below, this space is handsome and is filled with light

No. 16–Rear View of Temple from the Southwest
The arrangement of window on the rear of the Kirtland Temple reflects its complicated interior arrangement. The two rows of pointed windows line up with those on the sides to illuminate the two main meeting rooms, The two arched windows stepping up between the pointed ones show the higher level of the pulpits. Rectangular windows in the gable and the dormers provide light for the smaller offices and meeting rooms in the attic story.

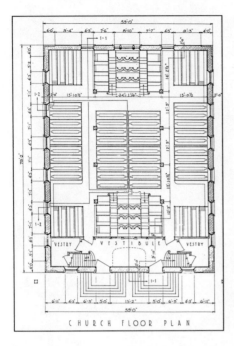

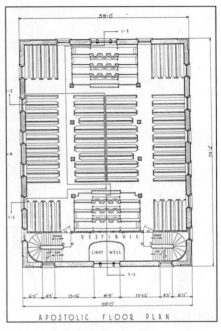

No. 1. This drawing shows the floor plans of the two major levels of the building, with the lower assembly room or "Church Floor" on the left and the upper assembly rom or "Apostolic Floor" on the right. The two plans illustrate the differences between the two major rooms, including the downstairs boxed pews, raised choir enclosures in the corners, and stairways flanking the pulpits–all features not present on the upper floor. The graceful curving stairways at either side of the entrance foyer ("Vestibule") and the light well are also shown.

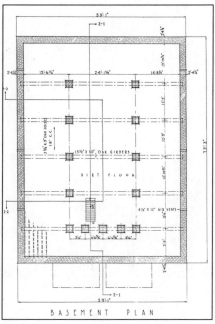

BASEMENT PLAN

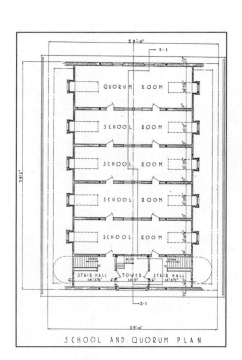

SCHOOL AND QUORUM PLAN

No. 2. This drawing shows the floor plan of the attic and basement levels. The "School and Quorum Plan" shows the attic divided into a series of narrow rooms that were used for priesthood quorum instructions, organizational meetings, and offices. Since no corridor was planned, the inner rooms could be entered only by passing through the outer ones or by ducking through the low attic space to either side.

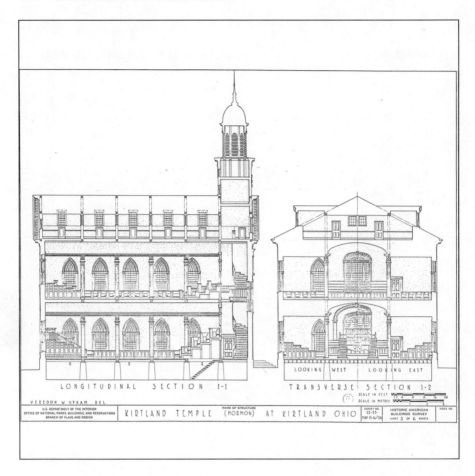

LONGITUDINAL   SECTION   1-1   TRANSVERSE   SECTION   1-2

VEREDON W UPHAM DEL.

| U.S. DEPARTMENT OF THE INTERIOR OFFICE OF NATIONAL PARKS, BUILDINGS, AND RESERVATIONS BRANCH OF PLANS AND DESIGN | KIRTLAND TEMPLE (MORMON) AT KIRTLAND OHIO | SURVEY NO. -22-25 HABS 13-16-734 | HISTORIC AMERICAN BUILDINGS SURVEY SHEET 3 OF 6 SHEETS | INDEX NO. |

No. 3. This drawing shows cutaway views of the building looking north and west. The section at the left shows that the assembly room windows are not centered on the columns as one might expect, suggesting that the exterior and interior design of the building may have been done separately, without complete resolution. The other section drawing shows the west end decorations to the left of the center line and the east end to the right. Notice the greater elaboration of the west end of the lower room, suggesting the greater importance of the Melchizedek Priesthood pulpits over the Aaronic.

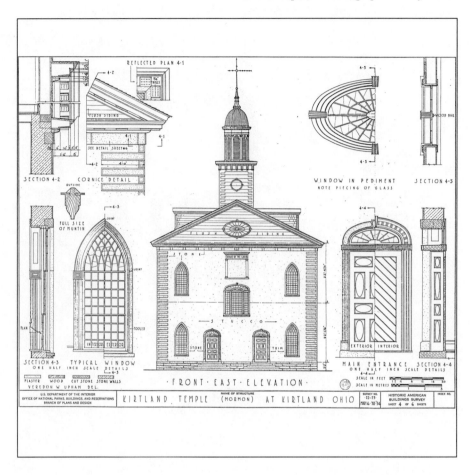

No. 4. This drawing shows the main facade of the temple and the details of doors, windows, and cornice. The detailed drawing of the elliptical "window in pediment" shows how its shape is enhanced by an elegantly tapered molding, wider at the sides than at the top and bottom. Because window glass was available only in small panes, the large glass panels in the elliptical and pointed windows were pieced together from several smaller panes.

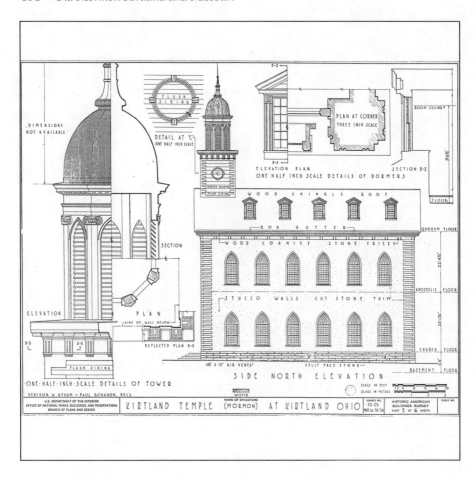

No. 5. This drawing shows the north side of the temple and a larger-scale view of the tower. Notice the combination of Gothic and Greek architectural elements on the tower with pointed-arched windows framed by Ionic pilasters, a remarkably graceful mixing of architectutal styles.

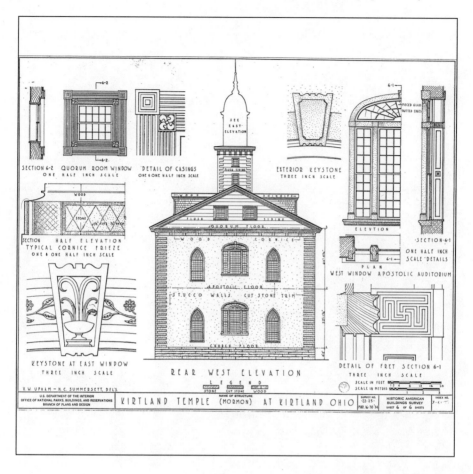

No. 6. This drawing shows the rear or west end of the temple with window and cornice details. The larger-scale drawings in the lower left and right corners show contrasting styles in different portions of the woodwork of the upper assembly room. The "fret Section" of the main west window, shown on the right, has a delicate but precise geometric pattern, while the keystone and arch of the east window shown at the left have a beautidul curvilinear floral pattern.

4

THE CHURCH IN MISSOURI

Almost a thousand years before the white population arrived, a sedentary prehistoric people inhabited the area now known as Missouri. These native American tribes, broadly categorized as the Mississippian and Woodland Indians, farmed, gathered, hunted, and actively engaged in commerce and trade. They lived along the major waterways, which provided them with protein-rich fish, productive soils for farming, and a convenient means of travel. These people suddenly and mysteriously disappeared around 1400 A.D.

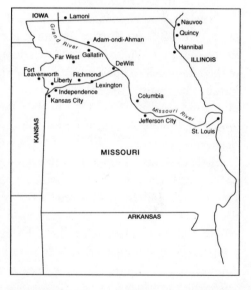

When the first French explorers visited Missouri in the late seventeenth century, they encountered semi-nomadic tribes that were recent migrants to the area themselves. The Sauk, Mesquakie (Fox), and Illinois, all of Algonquian linguistic stock, occupied the northeastern section of the state. The Oto, Ioway, Missouri, and Osage tribes inhabited the rest of Missouri. By the 1730s, the Osage tribe dominated all other groups and itself eventually divided into two major bands—the Great Osage, who frequented the territory around the Osage River, and the Little Osage, who lived in the land near the Missouri River.

Both Indian bands waned in power and influence with the white expansion stimulated by the Louisiana Purchase. In 1808 and again in 1825, the Osage signed treaties relinquishing their land claims in present-day Missouri and parts of Arkansas.

In the late eighteenth century, allied tribes of the Shawnee and Delaware, who had been pushed westward by white settlement, began to regroup in southeastern Missouri. The Spanish provided land grants to these Indians, grateful for the buffer the Indians provided against American expansion.

The U.S. Government forced the Shawnee and Delaware to sell their land grants in 1825. The Shawnee and Delaware made a brief stop in the eastern portion of present-day Kansas on their way to their final destinations of Oklahoma and Canada. The last Indian claims in Missouri ended in 1837 with the Platte Purchase, in which the Sauk, Mesquakie, and other tribes ceded their lands in northwestern Missouri.

French culture and language played a dominant role in the white settlement of eastern Missouri during the early period. The events of the American Revolution proved far more disruptive than the ceding of France's holdings west of the Mississippi to Spain in 1762. The Missouri side of the river was attractive because of Spain's liberal land-grant policy and because slavery was not prohibited as it was after 1787 in the Northwest Territory. Daniel Boone was among the many Americans who chose to move across the Mississippi into Spanish territory.

In 1800, Spain returned the vast expanse of Louisiana to France in the Treaty of San Ildefonso. The United States obtained the area of the present state of Louisiana as well as an ill-defined tract of land lying between the Mississippi River and the Rocky Mountains soon thereafter for $15 million.

The flurry of Indian skirmishes brought on by the War of 1812 served to temporarily discourage white settlement west of the Mississippi. After the Americans won the war and signed peace treaties with the Indians in 1815 and 1816, the one obstacle to expansion was the thick tangle of wilderness that covered much of the land.

Having achieved territorial status in 1816, Missouri applied for statehood in 1818. Because Missouri's entry into the union could have potentially upset the balance of power between slave and free states, at this time the smoldering debate over slavery came to a head in Congress and across the nation. Congress ultimately drafted the Missouri Compromise in 1820—granting Missouri's entry into the union as a slave state but admitting Maine, formerly a part of Massachusetts, as a free state.

Two factors clouded Missouri's entrance into the union—first, political controversy, and second, the financial instability that swept the state shortly after its admission. In 1821, both the Bank of Missouri and the Bank of St. Louis failed. These economic setbacks proved only temporary, however, because soon thereafter the explorer and trader William Becknell established a lucrative trade with Mexican Indians. Although his nine-hundred-mile journey to the Mexican village of Santa Fe was not easy, he found the Mexicans eager to trade their silver for the trading goods he brought. Becknell returned to Santa Fe in 1822, reportedly turning a profit of two thousand percent. Becknell's trading success opened up the Santa Fe Trail.

By the 1830s, many Missouri traders, outfitters, and merchants were benefiting from commerce on the Santa Fe Trail. The Missouri River in the northwestern edge of the state provided convenient stopping places, and here the traders founded the towns of Independence and later Westport, which became part of Kansas City. The opening of the Oregon Trail in 1843 and the advent of the California gold rush in 1849 also served to guarantee the futures of these outposts. The Saints viewed Missouri as a new land of promise.

The Saints were told in June 1831 that the land of their inheritance would be revealed to them as soon as their leaders went to Missouri:

> If ye are faithful, ye shall assemble yourselves together to rejoice upon the land of Missouri, which is the land of your inheritance . . . But, behold, I, the Lord, will hasten the [New Jerusalem] in its time, and will crown the faithful with joy and with rejoicing.[1]

The desire to build Zion—the ideal community mentioned in ancient Biblical and modern Mormon scriptures—permeated the lives of the Saints during their early history. Within ten years, the Saints had sought to establish three major Church centers in Missouri: Jackson County, 1831–33; in the adjoining counties, including Clay and Ray counties, 1833–36; and in the northern counties of Caldwell, Carroll, and Daviess counties, 1836–39.

Soon after the revelation that commanded Church leaders to go to Missouri, three groups prepared to leave the Church headquarters at Kirtland, Ohio. These included the missionaries to the Lamanites (the Mormon name for native American Indians), Joseph Smith's party, and the Colesville, New York, Saints who had temporarily settled in Thompson, Ohio.

About the middle of July, Joseph Smith, Jr. and his companions arrived at Independence, Missouri. W. W. Phelps, a companion, preached at the first sabbath meeting following their arrival. About ten days later, the Colesville

Saints also arrived in the area. The location of the New Jerusalem was revealed to the Saints during this visit.[2] Another revelation dated 1 August explained to the Saints how to locate in the land of Zion.[3] On the following day, the Saints erected a log cabin in Kaw Township, twelve miles southwest of Independence. On this occasion, Sidney Rigdon dedicated the land of Missouri (Zion) as a gathering place of the faithful.

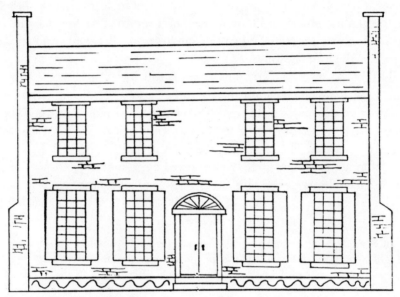

Courthouse, Independence, Missouri
(Sidney Rigdon preached here in 1832)
Jackson County Historical Society—Pauline S. Fowler, unknown

The temple site at Independence was dedicated on 3 August 1831 when Joseph Smith, Sidney Rigdon, Edward Partridge, W. W. Phelps, Oliver Cowdery, Martin Harris, and Joseph Coe met a short distance west of the courthouse in Independence. On the following day, the first conference of the Church in Missouri was held at the home of Joshua Lewis, in Kaw Township. On Sunday, 7 August, Joseph Smith recorded a revelation about the sabbath day.[4]

As a result of another revelation given in Missouri, some of the elders began a return trip to Ohio.[5] At McIlwaine's Bend on the Missouri River, W. W. Phelps saw "in open vision, by daylight, the Destroyer in his most horrible power ride upon the face of the water; others heard the noise, but saw no vision." The following day, Joseph Smith dictated a revelation concerning the "cursing of the waters in the last days."[6]

On 13 August 1831, Joseph Smith met several elders of the Church on their way to the land of Zion and received a revelation for their instruction.[7] A few days later, after touring the land of Missouri, Joseph and those traveling with him eventually arrived in Ohio. In Kirtland, late in August, Joseph recorded another revelation concerning Zion.[8]

The newspapers of the day noted the presence of Mormon activity in Missouri. In September 1831, the *Missouri Intelligencer & Boon's Lick Advertiser* (published at Columbia, Missouri) printed a story from an Ohio newspaper and added its own information:

> THE MORMONITES.—We learn from the Plainsville Gazette, that this infatuated people are again in motion. In their own cant phrase, "they are going to inherit the promise of God to Abraham and his seed." Their destination is some indefinite spot on the Missouri river, they say about 1500 miles distant. About eighty of them have recently been ordained, and some of them have gone; others are about going, two and two, part by the western rivers and part by land, to their distant retreat, far away from the cheering voice of civilized man . . . They still persist in their power to work miracles. They say they have often seen them done—the sick are healed and the lame walk, devils are cast out—and these assertions are made by men heretofore considered rational men, and men of truth. The Gazette expresses the opinion that although the leaders of the sect are gross impostors, a great portion of its members are sincere and honest.
>
> Some of the leaders of this sect, we are told, passed through this place [Columbia, Missouri] two or three weeks since, on their return to Ohio. We understand, that they have determined to migrate to Jackson County, on the extreme edge of this State; for which purpose they have purchased a sufficiency of land whereupon to locate the whole of the believers of Mormonism. We have some hope that the latter part of the paragraph may not be true; as in any other event, we should not rejoice much in the acquisition of so many deluded, insane enthusiasts.[9]

After Jackson County had been revealed as the center place for Zion, Church leaders and missionaries worked tirelessly to spread the word. A Boston newspaper reported missionary activity in New England, saying, "There has been in this town [Lyman, New Hampshire] and vicinity, for about a week, two young men from the westward, who are Mormonites." The missionaries were reported to have said, "that all who do not embrace their faith and mode of worship, forsake their friends, houses, and lands, and go with them to a place of safety, which is in the state of Missouri, where they are about building a city, will be destroyed by the sword, famine, pestilence, earthquakes." The only recourse for the people, according to the report, was "a speedy removal to their city of refuge."[10]

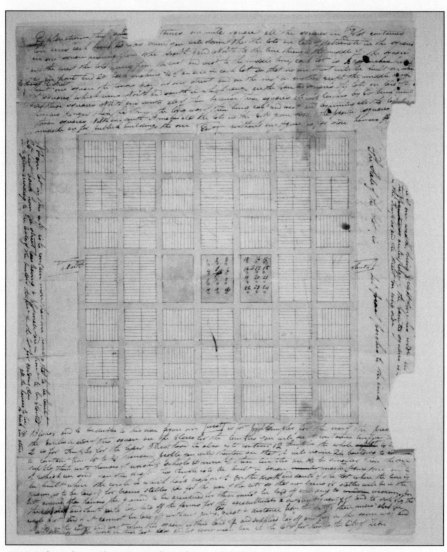

1833 Independence Plat Map, Independence, Missouri
(The plat is one mile square, with each square representing ten acres)
LDS Historical Department—Joseph Smith, 1833

During a Church conference in September 1831, W. W. Phelps was instructed to purchase a printing press and type and to establish a Church newspaper, called *The Evening and the Morning Star*, at Independence, Missouri. Commonly known as the *Star*, it was dedicated to building the faith of the Saints and to assisting in spreading the restored gospel. In the early part of November, Oliver Cowdery was called to take the written revelations that Joseph Smith had received up to that time and to have them printed in Zion. The revelation known as the "Preface" was given at this meeting.[11] Two days following this conference, Joseph Smith received the "Appendix" to the Book of Commandments.[12] John Whitmer, called by revelation, accompanied Oliver Cowdery with the *Book of Commandments* manuscript to Missouri.[13]

Joseph Smith left Hiram, Ohio, for his second visit to Missouri in the spring of 1832. Newel K. Whitney, Peter Whitmer, Jr. and Jessee Gause accompanied Joseph on this journey that took nearly twenty-five days. Two days following their arrival, Church leaders held a council in Independence at which Joseph Smith was "acknowledged by the High Priests in the land of Zion to be President of the High Priesthood, according to commandment and ordination in Ohio, at the Conference held in Amherst, January 25, 1832."[14]

The Church received a revelation at the conference "showing the order given to Enoch and the Church in his day."[15] This was one among many revelations and instructions dealing with the Mormon economic order, known as the Law of Consecration. On the following day, 30 April 1832, the issue concerning the rights of women and children in the Church was addressed in a revelation received by Joseph Smith.[16]

These revelations received by Joseph were to be printed in a book entitled *A Book of Commandments*.[17] At a Church conference held in Missouri on 1 May, conference attendees proposed that three thousand copies be printed by W. W. Phelps. In the meantime, the first edition of the *Star* was published in June. Phelps also published another newspaper in Independence, *The Upper Missouri Advertizer*, dedicated to secular and business news. These two newspapers were the first newspapers printed in western Missouri.

Even after Joseph Smith returned to Ohio, he continued to keep in close contact with the Saints who were now gathering to Zion. In one communication, he included a written revelation answering questions of those living in Zion, particularly concerning the keeping of records.[18]

At a special Church meeting on 13 July 1832 (held at the home of Joseph Knight in Kaw Township), the elders decided to divide the Church in Zion "into branches for the better convenience of holding meetings and organizing the Church etc."[19] Thus, Kaw Township was divided into small geographical units beginning with "Branch No. 1." Blue Township was "considered a [single] branch."

At the beginning of 1833, difficulties between the Saints and the non-Mormon residents of Jackson County increased. By April of that year, old settlers concerned about the Mormon presence in the county met to discuss plans for the removal of the Saints.

In the meantime, the Saints in Jackson County convened at the ferry on the Big Blue River to celebrate the third anniversary of the founding of the Church. Phelps reported,

> On the 6th of April, between seventy and eighty ordained members, representing more than five hundred members of the Church of Christ, met for instruction, serving God, &c. in the land of Zion, and spent the day, from ten till four o'clock, very agreeably.

> It affords us much pleasure to record this little fact. When the foundations of this earth were laid, the morning stars sang together, and all the sons of God shouted for joy: the Passover was kept solemnly by the children of Israel, and so let the solemnities of eternity rest upon our minds, since the Lord has been so merciful as to reestablish his Church for the last time, in these last days.[20]

The Saints were excited about the future possibilities as Zion grew. Joseph Smith prepared the plat for the city of Zion and an explanation and sent them to Church leaders in Missouri on 25 June 1833. By this time, nearly twelve hundred Saints, including children, had migrated to Missouri from the eastern states. The spirit of excitement and anticipation of the future were short lived, however, as anti-Mormon hostility rapidly increased.

On 20 July 1833, the destruction of the Church's printing office constituted the first major mob action against the Saints in Missouri. Bishop Edward Partridge and Brother Charles Allen were captured by the mob and tarred and feathered. Within three days, the Jackson County Saints signed a treaty with mob leaders indicating the Saints' willingness to leave the area. Oliver Cowdery left immediately for Ohio to inform the Church leaders of the precarious situation in Missouri.

Feelings of distrust and misunderstanding between the Saints and their neighbors in Jackson County had been simmering for a long period. In October 1832, a local Baptist clergyman from Independence wrote a letter to the editor of the *Christian Watchman*. He expressed the sentiment that "The very materials of which the society is composed must at length produce an explosion." One of the explosive factors he pointed to was the Mormon teaching of inheritances with its corollary "law of consecration and stewardship":

> Sir,—Dwelling as I do among a people called Mormonites, and on the very land which they sometimes call Mount Zion, at other times the New Jerusalem—and where, at no distant period, they expect the reappearing of the Lord Jesus to live and reign with them on earth a thousand years—I have thought perhaps it

might be a part of duty to inform those who may feel interested in relation to this subject . . . four or five hundred Mormonites in all—men, women and children—arrived at this place . . . The very materials of which the society is composed must at length produce an explosion. Yet judging from the past, and from what our Savior has told us of the future, that there should be false Christs and false Prophets, showing signs and wonders so as to deceive, if it were possible, the very elect, we may well look on this new sect as ominous and to give good heed to the word of our Savior, where he says, "Go ye not after them, nor follow them." Yours, &c. Independence, Jackson Co. Mo. Oct. 12, 1832. B. Pixley.[21]

September, 1833, brought several important decisions regarding the Church in Missouri. Edward Partridge was acknowledged as the presiding authority of the Church in Missouri, and ten high priests were called to preside temporarily over the ten branches of the Church located in Missouri. To replace the *Star*, the Saints organized a newspaper at the Mormon headquarters in Ohio.

During the next few weeks, Church leaders in Missouri worked to alert state officials, including the governor, Daniel Dunklin, of the Saints' plight. Dunklin acknowledged the Saints' rights to their lands in Jackson County and promised to enforce these rights in protection of the Saints. On 31 October 1833, the Saints were again victims of mob action, as the Mormon settlement west of the Big Blue was attacked. The mob destroyed ten homes and brutalized several of the Saints.

This mob activity continued the following day, when a group of anti-Mormons partially destroyed the Gilbert and Whitney store, operated by Algernon S. Gilbert, and several other private Mormon dwellings in Independence. During the next few days, more attacks occurred at the Big Blue settlements. On 4 November, a skirmish between the Saints and Missourians resulted in the death of Andrew Barber, a Mormon, and of a non-Mormon.

Between 6–8 November, a significant number of Saints in Jackson County were driven from their homes. The vast majority fled across the Missouri River and into Clay County. Approximately a dozen ferries operated between Jackson and Clay counties, and a principal landing site was Independence Landing, known later as the Wayne City Landing. Despite the difficult circumstances, the Saints made their journey to the river; and apparently no one was molested along the Missouri River bottoms. The inhabitants there assisted the Saints as they crossed the river to refuge. Many citizens treated the Mormons fairly and even hired some to cut wood, construct buildings, teach school, and work on nearby farms. Many Mormon refugees encamped on the banks of the Missouri River,

Big Blue River, Missouri
(Site of a battle with anti-Mormons in 1833)
LDS Historical Department—George E. Anderson, 1907

where they spent the winter in rough huts, tents, abandoned slave quarters, and other shanties. Emily Austin, camping on the Missouri River bottoms during this period, recalled, "We lived in tents until winter set in, and did our cooking out in the wind and storms. Log heaps were our parlor stoves, and the cold, wet ground our velvet carpets, and the crying of little children our piano forte."[22] Far from finding the refuge they were seeking, the Saints who fled to Van Buren County were met with continued persecution.

A conference of scattered Saints in Clay County resulted in a decision to send Lyman Wight and Parley P. Pratt as special messengers to the Church leaders in Ohio.

In Ohio, Church leaders received information regarding the redemption of Zion.[23] This revelation included raising an armed group of men to help the Saints in Jackson County regain their holdings. Soon thereafter, Joseph Smith left Kirtland to gather volunteers for the redemption of Zion. This expedition to Missouri was called "Zion's Camp."[24] This operation had its origins in the divine injunctions to redeem Zion and was a central part in Joseph Smith's mission of establishing the latter-day kingdom of God in Missouri.[25] Zion's Camp was a defensive operation that relied on the promises of the governor of Missouri to support Mormon property claims in Jackson County.

The Missouri state attorney general wrote the following:

> I believe I am warranted in saying to you, and through you to the Mormons, that if they desire to be replaced in possession of their property, that is, their houses in Jackson county, an adequate force will be sent forthwith to effect that object . . . If the Mormons will organize themselves into regular companies, or a regular company of militia, either volunteers or otherwise, they will, I have no doubt, be supplied with public arms.[26]

While Joseph Smith garnered support for Zion's Camp, mobs in Jackson County burned almost one hundred fifty of the homes abandoned by the Saints in their flight to safety. In May, nearly twenty-five men in wagons left Kirtland for New Portage, Ohio, in anticipation of the march to Missouri with Zion's Camp. Soon, Joseph Smith also arrived at New Portage to begin the trip.

By 8 May 1834, Zion's Camp was organized and traveled nearly twelve miles. In June, they crossed the Mississippi River into Missouri. Another group, led by Hyrum Smith, combined with the main body of Zion's Camp shortly thereafter. Zion's Camp arrived near Independence on 19 June and camped between two branches of the Fishing River. A large mob, intent on attacking the camp, was prevented from doing so by a summer rain storm. Joseph Smith, who sought shelter in a log Baptist chapel nearby, stated, "God is in this storm."[27]

Fishing River, Missouri
(Site of Fishing River revelation in 1834)
LDS Historical Department—George E. Anderson, 1907

On 22 June, Joseph Smith recorded a revelation given at Fishing River.[28] This revelation informed the members of Zion's Camp that the time to redeem Zion "was not yet." The camp arrived at Church member George Burkett's farm on Rush Creek the following day and met in council. The *Far West Record* states:

Clay County, June 23 [1834]—A council of High Priests met according to revelation [LDS D&C 105/RLDS D&C 102] in order to choose some of the first Elders to receive their endowments [at the Kirtland Temple in Ohio]. [They] being appointed by the voice of the Spirit through Brother Joseph Smith, jr. President of the Church of Christ.[29]

A terrible cholera outbreak occurred in camp on the following day, June 24. Thirteen members of the Camp ultimately died, including Algernon S. Gilbert.

Joseph Smith and a few others visited Jackson County secretly on 1 July 1834. Two days later, Joseph organized a council of twelve high priests in Clay County at the farm of Colonel Michael Arthur, a sympathetic non-Mormon. Colonel Arthur had hired several Saints, including Lyman Wight and Wilford Woodruff, to build a grist mill and a large brick home southwest of Liberty. At the time of the organization of the high council, several Saints resided in the area, including Wight and Woodruff who lived on Arthur's property in a log cabin.

Joseph Smith arrived at Arthur's home to complete the work of establishing the Church in Missouri on the foundation already established in Ohio. David Whitmer was chosen president, with W. W. Phelps and John Whitmer as counselors. Christian Whitmer, Newel Knight, Lyman Wight, Calvin Bebee, William E. McClellan, Solomon Hancock, Thomas B. Marsh, Simeon Carter, Parley P. Pratt, Orson Pratt, John Murdock, and Levi Jackman were sustained as council members. This was the first high council organized in Missouri and the second organized in the Church. Within five days, Joseph Smith began his trip back to Ohio.

Following a policy adopted by the Missouri High Council on 12 July 1834, Church leaders for a time discouraged public Church meetings in Clay County, a policy that demonstrated the tense situation of the Church during this time. Missionaries were also counseled not to preach in Jackson and Clay counties; and by November 1834, the Saints were counseled only to administer the "sacrament if they see convenient opportunity."[30]

Church leaders in Missouri were summoned to a special meeting in Kirtland, Ohio, on 14 February 1835. At this important weekly meeting, the original three witnesses to the *Book of Mormon* chose the first twelve apostles. Members of the Quorum of the Seventy were chosen and ordained the same day, all of whom

Arthur Home, Liberty, Missouri
(Missouri High Council organized here in 1834)
Max H. Parkin—unknown, c1960

were members of Zion's Camp. Missouri Church leaders were summoned to Kirtland, Ohio, again in March 1836 to attend the Church's first temple dedication.

During this period, Saints continued to gather to Missouri. One early convert wrote, "My fourth child was born in November 1835 and we called her name Rebecca." Drusilla Hendricks and her husband sold their home during the winter and "settled all our finances [to be] ready to start for Missouri in the Spring of 1836." With their preparations completed, the Hendricks began their journey on 1 May 1836. While enroute, Drusilla wrote,

> In Illinois we were under the necessity of buying a yoke of cattle. We stopped at "Knight Prairie." Our men went to a little town and found where they could buy the cattle and they also found some Latter-day Saints. They were as glad as we were and they came back with our men and stayed two nights. It was a Brother Clark and wife and a Brother Lane and wife. We had never met them before but were so glad to see a Latter-day Saint. We sang, prayed and praised God for the light we had received. We had a good time but had to part, but in hopes that we should meet again. We went on until we came to a little river . . . [H]ere the fish were so plentiful at times that the surface of the water was covered. It was decided to stop and fish and lay in a supply. We went on our way rejoicing until we reached Clay County.[31]

Like other Mormon emigrants, the Hendricks bought land and began planting to prepare for the summer harvest. "We soon bought fifty acres of land there," Drusilla recalled. Although being in Missouri fulfilled a dream of these early Saints, the dream of the "center place—Jackson County" remained a focus of their beliefs. In Clay County, the Hendricks met a number of Saints "that had been driven from Jackson County and we had great time in talking of their trials in that County."

Although the Saints were not allowed back into Jackson County, the Hendricks had an unusual opportunity to visit Independence. "It was not a week until my husband's father, brother and wife and sister came to see us," Drusilla wrote. Her in-laws, who came from Jackson County, invited them to visit their home there.

The Hendricks accompanied them back, "partly to satisfy the old gentlemen and partly to satisfy our own curiosity to see Independence where the center Stake of Zion should be."

After they returned to their home in Clay County, the Hendricks "began to live as we supposed the saints should live, to make their own clothing. We bought some sheep and prepared to sustain ourselves." In late June 1836, however, a large group of citizens in Clay County, Missouri, met at Liberty and passed a resolution to expel the Saints from Clay County. On 1 July 1836, the Saints agreed to leave Clay County to avoid trouble similar to that which they had experienced previously in Jackson County. Alexander Doniphan, their non-Mormon lawyer, sponsored a bill in the state legislature recognizing Caldwell and Daviess counties as places for Mormon settlement. The new governor, Lilburn W. Boggs, signed the bill on 29 December 1836 in Jefferson City.

The Saints began their preparations to leave Clay County beginning in September 1836—several months before Governor Boggs signed the bill. A newly selected location near Shoal Creek, later known as Far West, became a Church gathering place. Although almost completely uninhabited at the time of their arrival, this area was soon organized into a new county called Caldwell.

In April 1837, a city plat map for Far West was surveyed. W. W. Phelps, John Whitmer, and Edward Partridge were put in charge of lot sales. Jacob Whitmer, Elisha H. Groves, and George M. Hinkle were appointed to organize a building committee for the erection of a house of the Lord at Far West. The groundbreaking ceremony for the temple took place on 3 July 1837 at Far West.

In September, Joseph Smith and Sidney Rigdon left Kirtland, Ohio, to visit Missouri in an effort to establish other settlements for the Saints who were

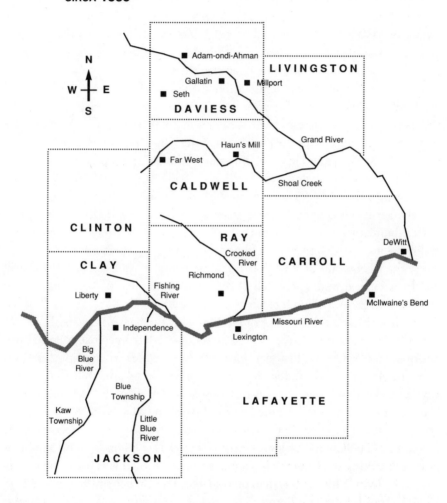

WESTERN MISSOURI
CIRCA 1838

arriving in Missouri almost daily. The Saints held an important Church conference at Far West on 7 November 1837. Joseph Smith's counselor, Frederick G. Williams, was rejected; and Hyrum Smith replaced him. David Whitmer, John Whitmer, and W. W. Phelps were sustained as the presidency at Far West, with a high council consisting of John Murdock, Solomon Hancock, Elias Higbee, Calvin Bebee, John M. Hinkle, Thomas Grover, Simeon Carter, Lyman Wight, Newel Knight, George M. Hinkle, Levi Jackman, and Elisha H. Groves.

When Joseph Smith returned to Kirtland, several of the leading brethren, including Warren Parrish, John F. Boynton, Luke S. Johnson, and Joseph Coe, opposed Joseph's leadership there. The dissension in Ohio was echoed among the Saints in Missouri. The internal conflict became as serious as the external persecution of the Church. Joseph Smith and Sidney Rigdon left Kirtland on 12 January 1838 to escape mob violence against them.

Fresh from the apostasy and disruption at Kirtland, Joseph and Sidney arrived in Missouri to find that the Far West stake presidency was no longer supported by the local Church members. David Whitmer, John Whitmer, and W. W. Phelps were ultimately rejected as the presidency of the Church in Missouri. In the same month, W. W. Phelps and John Whitmer were "cut off" from the Church.

At an important meeting on 15 March 1838, "the High Council of Zion, together with the Bishopric met in Far West . . . President Joseph Smith, Jr. took the charge of the council." Joseph also opened and closed the meeting with prayer, indicating both the importance he placed upon this meeting and his ability to gain control of local priesthood quorums and Church meetings.

At the celebration of the Church's founding on 6 April 1838, John Corrill and Elias Higbee were appointed as historians; and George W. Robinson was appointed as general Church recorder and clerk to the First Presidency. Thomas B. Marsh was sustained as president *pro tem*, with Brigham Young and David W. Patten as assistant presidents. The Church's quarterly conference followed this meeting. Former Church historian John Whitmer refused to give up his records to the newly appointed Church clerk and recorder. Other Church leaders, Oliver Cowdery, David Whitmer, Lyman E. Johnson, and William E. McClellan, were excommunicated during the difficult days of April and May 1838.

In the latter part of April, the Church's name was changed by revelation to its final form, "The Church of Jesus Christ of Latter Day Saints."[32] The ambitious project of writing the Church's history was begun during this period. The history written by John Whitmer was then unavailable. The Church's history in the LDS Church's fourth book of scripture, *The Pearl of Great Price*, was a product of this project.

Sidney Rigdon delivered a fiery oration at Far West on 9 June 1838, now known as the "salt sermon." With this discourse, Rigdon hoped to weaken any attempt by dissenters to undermine Joseph Smith's leadership. This discourse led to further conflict between the Saints, the dissenters, and their non-Mormon neighbors. Despite these problems, new members of the Church arrived at an ever-quickening pace.

Church leaders visited the north side of the Grand River, about twenty-five miles north of Far West, an area called Spring Hill, in an effort to establish other Mormon settlements. Joseph Smith revealed that it was a holy place and would be of great importance to the Saints in the future.[33]

Within forty days, a stake of Zion called Adam-ondi-Ahman (also known as Diahman during this period) was organized in Daviess County, with John Smith as president and Reynolds Cahoon and Lyman Wight as his counselors. The high council organized at this time included John Lemon, Daniel Stanton, Mayhew Hillman, Daniel Carter, Isaac Perry, Henry Harrison Sagers, Allanson Brown, Thomas Gordon, Lorenzo D. Barnes, George A. Smith, Harvey Olmstead, and Ezra Thayer.

Between Diahman and Far West was another important Mormon location known as "Littlefield's Half-way House," situated half way between the two Mormon settlements. Joseph Smith noted in his journal, "The First Presidency [with] Judge Higbee (as surveyor) started this morning for the halfway house (as it is called) kept [by] Brother Littlefield, some 14 or 15 miles from Far West directly north."[34]

The Church's public activity continued unabated during this period. The *Elders' Journal*, formerly a Kirtland Church newspaper, began publication at Far West in July 1838; and the corner stones of the House of the Lord were laid on the public square in the city on 4 July.

Following the excommunication of several Church leaders in Missouri, John Taylor, John E. Page, Wilford Woodruff, and Willard Richards were called to positions in the Quorum of Twelve "to fill the places of those who had fallen."[35]

During this period, the daily life of the Saints was difficult but full. Daily challenges, like farming and child rearing, demanded long hours and tedious labor. Levi Hancock recalled his circumstances of sixty acres, including a city lot, in Far West. "I had cows, hogs, and one good mare," he wrote, "sheep and hens a plenty and [it] was a good way to live, with plenty to eat."[36]

The pioneers frequently sought ways to divert themselves from their daily routine. Hancock said that when he got weary he took his babe and little boy on his lap and sang songs to them. One of these songs is recorded in his history:

> Here far in the realm of Missouri
> I'll sit and sing and tell a story
> How many trials I have passed over
> Before I found this dwelling in peace
>
> Oh here, here beside the fire
> I have my sweet babe and little Mosiah

And here is mother, I'll set me down beside her
And sing, I've found a dwelling peace.

Here in this grove while water I'm bringing
My ears are charmed to hear the birds singing
With songs so sweet they keep the grace ringing
While here at home I live and have peace

Oh here, here we've butter and honey
And many will hire and pay me the money
And nothing I owe, and no man to dun me
And here at home I live and have peace

My cows go oft and come in the morning
And also at night I see them returning,
To give us cream and keep us churning
While here at home we live and have peace

Here in my field all things are growing
And on the prairie I have men mowing
That I may have feed to keep the stock growing
While here at home I live and have peace

My ground is covered with strawberries
And in the grove I've plums and I've cherries
And I will thank my God and be merry
For giving me this dwelling in peace

May we love Him forever and ever
For peace bestowed upon the believer
And turn from Him O never O never
But always love the spirit of peace.[37]

Levi Hancock's peaceful world did not exist very long. Following initial mob violence at Gallatin, Daviess County, Missouri, in August 1838 mob action occurred against the Saints at DeWitt, Carroll County Missouri, (location of a port settlement on the Missouri River). Albert Rockwell noted:

The attack was made on DeWitt by taking Elder Humphrey's family and burning his house. He lived about one and half miles from the landing which is head quarters, several scattering shots were made at the brethren during three or four of the first days, no damage save making holes in their clothing. One heavy charge was received from the mob when the brethren returned the fire and killed four Missourians. The campaign lasted about a week when a treaty [of peace] was made with the mob the brethren have left the place. DeWitt was not an appointed stake of Zion, but was designed as a Port of Landing on the Missouri River.[38]

The Mormons abandoned DeWitt in the fall after a violent confrontation. The persecution reached a new level with a fierce battle when several non-Mormon residents opposed the voting of the Saints at Gallatin, Daviess County, on 6 August 1838. This action's repercussions spread to the other counties. In addition to mob raids on Mormon settlements, in which men were beaten, cattle killed or driven off, and homes and farm buildings burned, the following months brought about several major confrontations.

As a result of the actions of the people in the northern counties during the preceding weeks, Missouri Governor Lilburn W. Boggs ordered the state militia to quell the civil disturbances in Caldwell, Daviess, and Carroll counties.

On 7 August 1838, Joseph Smith and Lyman Wight appeared before Judge Austin A. King in Daviess County. They and several other Church members were accused of threatening Adam Black's life on their visit to his home in August following the Gallatin skirmish. State militia units under the direction of Generals Atchison, Doniphan, and Parks succeeded in restoring temporary peace in Daviess County. During this period, James Aldrich wrote a letter to his brother, Daniel, in Littleton, New Hampshire:

[30 Sept. 1838] Brother Daniel, it is about two years since I have written you; I have not received any letter from you since I left the Ohio . . . We are about nineteen-hundred miles apart yet the same sun shines on you that does on me . . . I am in a fertile country and am well suited with it. It is a healthy country yet there is sickly places but in general it is healthy, there is some few cases of the fever ague and of the chills and fever. I am on about the 39th degree north latitude and I am two hundred and fifty miles west of St. Louis . . .

Mother urges me to have you write immediately, and she also sends her respects to you both and the children. Crops are very good this year there is corn in abundance it is worth from 20 to 25 cts. per bushel. Money is plenty considering the times. I have got along as well as could be expected considering the distance that I have moved with my large family. We have got five children. We have enjoyed good health, better than we could expect considering our coming from such a cold country to one that is so warm for there is a great difference. Our aged mother is in as good health . . . Myself and Almira have not been sick since we left New Hampshire. We are all well at present . . . Mormonism so-called has not come to naught . . . notwithstanding the many prophesies of its coming to naught. But it is like the stone that Daniel saw that was cut out of the mountain without hands that filled the whole earth. We have been threatened with a mob to drive the Mormons from certain counties but did not undertake it.[39]

The Kirtland Camp, made up of several hundred Mormons from Ohio, arrived at Daviess during this very tense period. Pressure increased in northern Missouri until it finally erupted into a "civil war." By 3 October 1838, Saints from smaller settlements were fleeing to Far West for safety as the mobs increased in numbers.

Eventually, Mormon units of the army of Israel burned a few homes in Gallatin and Millport in a defensive measure. These actions increased mob fears.

Most Saints had already born persecution patiently but now had to defend themselves by forming military units. Eventually, the "Danites" Society was formed, an organization named after the Old Testament prophet Daniel. Albert Rockwood wrote that during this period many men were armed and "determined to maintain their rights even at the expense of life."[40] Some of the Mormons who were also Danites carried out countermeasures against Missouri mobbers under the direction of Samson Avard. These activities intensified non-Mormon sentiment against the Saints.

Parley P. Pratt wrote his family at the end of the court of inquiry following his arrest: "They accuse us of things that never entered into our hearts." Joseph Smith, writing from Liberty Jail in December 1838, added:

> We have learned also since we have been in prison that many false and pernicious things which were calculated to lead the saints far astray and to do great injury have been taught by Dr. Avard as coming from the Presidency . . . which the presidency never knew of being taught in the church by any body until after they were made prisoners . . . the presidency were ignorant as well as innocent of these things.[41]

Avard's activities in northern Missouri eventually caused fears and misunderstandings that were directed from the "old settlers" toward the Mormons.[42]

The "Battle of Crooked River" in Ray County occurred on 25 October between the Mormons and Missouri state militia soldiers. Gideon Carter was killed and eleven others wounded. Among those wounded were David W. Patten and Patrick O'Bannion, both of whom died soon afterwards.

The exaggerated reports about the confrontation at Crooked River alarmed Governor Boggs and was the final report that caused him to issue his famous "extermination order." This order authorized General John B. Clark of the state militia to drive the Saints from the state or to exterminate them. That was on 27 October 1838. Three days later, an unauthorized militia mob under the command of Colonel Thomas Jennings of Livingston County killed eighteen Mormons, including children, at Haun's Mill, Caldwell County. In Mormon history, this attack has become known as the "Haun's Mill Massacre."

At the end of October 1838, as the Saints prepared to defend themselves against attack, approximately two thousand militia men arrived near Far West. Joseph Smith, Sidney Rigdon, Parley P. Pratt, Lyman Wight, and George W. Robinson were arrested during negotiations between Church leaders and state representatives outside of Far West. The following day, Hyrum Smith and Amasa Lyman were also arrested and detained with the others. A court martial was held, and the prisoners were sentenced by Samuel D. Lucas, the militia leader, to be shot the following morning. Colonel Alexander Doniphan who was given the order to execute, protested by saying, "It is cold blooded murder. I will not obey your order." His intervention saved the lives of these Church leaders.[43]

The town of Far West capitulated to the superior state militia force on 1 November 1838. Church leaders, now prisoners, were taken to see their families in Far West and then were moved to Independence, where they arrived on 7 November. They eventually arrived at Richmond on 9 November, where they were put in chains and abused by the guards. A trial for nearly sixty Mormon men commenced at Richmond and lasted sixteen days. The Church leaders were charged with treason, murder, burglary, arson, robbery, and larceny. Of those charged, twenty-three were discharged at Richmond. The remaining prisoners in Richmond were released, or admitted to bail, except two groups: (1) Joseph Smith, Lyman Wight, Caleb Baldwin, Hyrum Smith, Alexander McRae, and Sidney Rigdon, who were sent to jail in Liberty, Clay County, and (2) Parley P. Pratt, Morris Phelps, Luman Gibbs, King Follett, Darwin Chase, and Norman Shearer, who were retained in custody in Richmond Jail to stand trial on similar charges.

While in Liberty Jail, following a failed escape attempt and languishing in his miserable surroundings, Joseph Smith pled to the Lord, "O God! where art thou? And where is the pavilion that covereth thy hiding place? How long shall thy hand be stayed, and thine eye, yea thy pure eye, behold from the eternal heavens, the wrongs of thy people, and of thy servants, and thine ear be penetrated with their cries?" In answer to this plea, Joseph received a reply from the Lord, since incorporated into the canon of LDS scripture in D&C 121–123.[44] Alexander McRae recorded the revelation as it came from Joseph's mouth:

> My son, peace be unto thy soul; thine adversity and thine afflictions shall be but a small moment; and then, if thou endure it well, God shall exalt thee on high; thou shalt triumph over all thy foes; thy friends do stand by thee, and they shall hail thee again, with warm hearts and friendly hands; thou are not yet as Job; thy friends do not contend against thee, neither charge thee with transgression, as they did Job . . . Thou art called to pass through tribulations . . . and . . . if the

Liberty Jail, Liberty, Missouri
(Church leaders incarcerated here in 1838–39)
LDS Historical Department—unknown, 1888

> very jaws of hell shall gape open the mouth wide after thee, known thou, my son, that all these things shall give thee experience, and shall be for thy good. The Son of Man hath descended below them all; art thou greater than he?[45]

While these Church leaders were incarcerated, those Church leaders still free continued to conduct Church business in Far West in preparation for their exodus from Missouri. John Taylor and John E. Page were ordained apostles at Far West. In December, a petition from the Mormons in Caldwell County and signed by several leaders of the Church was presented to the Missouri State Legislature:

> To the Honorable Legislature of the State of Missouri, in Senate and House of Representatives, convened.—

> We the undersigned petitioners, inhabitants of Caldwell County, Missouri, in consequence of the late calamity that has come upon us, taken in connection with former afflictions, feel it a duty we owe to ourselves and our country, to lay our case before your Honorable Body for consideration.

> It is a well known fact, that a Society of our people commenced settling in Jackson County, Missouri in the summer of [1831], where they according to their ability purchased lands and settled upon them, with the intention and expectation of becoming permanent citizens in common with others.

Soon after the settlement began, persecution began, and as the society increased, persecution also increased; until the society at last was compelled to leave the county . . .

The society made their escape to Clay County, as fast as they possibly could . . . The society remained in Clay County, nearly three years, when, at the suggestion of the people there, they removed to that section of country, now known as Caldwell County. Here the people purchased out most of the former inhabitants and also entered much of the wild lands . . . Here we were permitted to enjoy peace for a season; but as our society increased in numbers and settlements were made in Daviess and Carroll Counties, the mob spirit showed itself again . . . [T]he mob went towards Daviess County and whilst on their way there, they took two of our men prisoners, and made them ride upon the cannon, and told them, that they would drive the Mormons from Daviess to Caldwell, and from Caldwell to *HELL*; and that they would give them no quarters, only at the cannon's mouth . . .

When Gen. Lucas arrived near Far West, and presented the Governor order, we were greatly surprised, yet we felt willing to submit, to the Authorities of the State.—We gave up our arms without reluctance, we were then made prisoners and confined to the limits of the town . . . Much property was destroyed by the troops in town, during their stay there; such as burning house-logs, rails, corncribs, boards, and the using of corn and hay, the plundering of horses; the killing of cattle, sheep and hogs, and also the taking of horses not their own . . .

In the meantime men were abused, women insulted and ravished by the troops; and all this, while we were kept prisoners . . .

In laying our case before your honorable Body, we say that we are willing and ever have been to conform to the Constitution and laws of the United States and of this State. We ask, in common with others, the protection of the laws. We ask for the privileges guaranteed to all free citizens of the United States and of this State, to be extended to us; we may be permitted to settle and live where we please, and worship God according to the dictates of our own consciences, without molestation;—And whilst we ask for ourselves this privilege, we are willing all others should enjoy the same.

We now lay our case at the feet of our Legislature and ask your Honorable Body to consider it, and do for us after mature deliberation, that which your wisdom, patriotism and Philanthropy may dictate—And as duty bound will ever pray.[46]

John Corrill presented the memorial to the state legislature on 19 December 1838, but it was rejected. On 4 May 1840, long after the Saints had left Missouri, the appointed committee assigned to investigate the matter announced that the Mormons could not be helped by the legislature.

In January 1839, plans were established to assist the poorest Saints to move from Missouri. In February, Brigham Young, now president of the Twelve Apostles, left Missouri for Illinois and Iowa with his family and a group of Saints. Drusilla Hendricks recalled this moment:

> We were compelled to stay at Far West until after the surrender when we went home. The mob had robbed the house of my bedding and in fact everything but my beds. My husband could not yet move hand or foot. Then we had to settle our business matters and fix to get out of the state. I went to work and sold what I could and gave our land for money to buy two yoke of cattle. Finally, we had to leave everything, only what we could put into a little wagon. About the middle of January, Father Joseph Smith and Father Morley, with five or six others came and anointed and administered to my husband. They stood him on his feet and he stood by them holding to each arm. He began to work his shoulders. I continued to rub him with strong vinegar and salt and liniments. The brethren were leaving the State as fast as they could.[47]

The brethren were leaving the state because their lives were in immediate danger. Charles C. Rich left immediately following an attempt on his life at Far West by Missouri militia personnel. His wife, Sarah Rich, was left behind and forced to make her way east from Far West to Illinois without his help. When the group reached the Mississippi River, the ice had broken up on the west side of the river and was running, so the ferry boat could not cross. Having traveled so far and now being only a few hundred yards from safety, Sarah and another woman felt very downhearted. The knowledge that their husbands were on the opposite side in Quincy (Illinois) waiting for them worsened the emotional strain of the situation. Because the ferry was not in operation, the only way they could cross was by using a skiff or a canoe to maneuver through the ice to the island and from there to walk on the ice to Quincy on the east side.

While Sarah waited on the river bank, a male member of their group, George D. Grant, told her to cheer up because he would go over and tell Brother Rich where she was. In his attempt to cross, George fell through the ice and was barely saved by two other men. "So when we heard this news we went back to our wagons clearly discouraged," Sarah recalled. "I went into the wagon to cry," she continued, "while Sister Stout and my dear father . . . prepared dinner."

Not much time elapsed before Sarah's husband learned that she was there, and he made the crossing himself with another Latter-day Saint. "Great was our joy to meet with our dear companions," she enthusiastically remembered, "who were compelled to part with us three months before and flee for their lives from a howling mob." On the following day, both husbands decided to take their wives across the river to better shelter and security. Because Sarah was pregnant and near delivery, she agreed to cross over immediately, as she did not know when she would have the baby.

They got into a canoe, and the men rowed them across the river to the point where they could cross the remainder of the way on the ice. Sarah left her aged father on the shore so she could take care of the teams and wagons until the ferry boat could cross. She remembered that the old man "stood with tears in his eyes watching us, not knowing whether we could reach shore or not."[48]

Many other Saints crossed at the same location during this dangerous season to avoid the consequences of the "extermination order." In Illinois, they found safe refuge for a season.

During this period of confusion and mass migration, Joseph Smith kept in contact with Church leaders through letters and the Church leaders' visits to the jail. During the month of March, Joseph wrote several epistles to the Saints at Quincy, Illinois, and to those scattered abroad, one dated 20 March 1839.[49] In April 1839 Joseph and his fellow prisoners were allowed to escape and arrived in Illinois on 22 April 1839. Parley P. Pratt records that "One of the guards who allowed the Church leaders to escape was ridden through Gallatin on a steel bar and died as the result of the brutal experience."[50]

Joseph and his associates were not the last Mormons in Missouri. Several other brethren still remained in prison. Parley P. Pratt, who ironically could have escaped much earlier, was one of the last Mormon prisoners. He remained incarcerated at Columbia, Missouri, because of a change of venue order from Ray County (Richmond) to Boone County (Columbia) on the grounds of prejudice.

The transfer from Richmond to Columbia took nine days. Parley P. Pratt and Morris Phelps were handcuffed together. They traveled in a carriage guarded by the Ray County sheriff and four others.

The prison at Columbia was situated on the north edge of the town in the square with the court house. The prison consisted of a block house, two stories high, with two rooms below and two above. Upon their arrival in Columbia, Morris Phelps immediately felt by the spirit that they would soon be released.

When their release did not occur as anticipated, he went to the Lord in prayer. He records the following:

> I went . . . upon my knees and said, O Lord and My God thou hast told me that I might go home to my family and friends and I believe what thou hast said. Now O Lord tell me what I must do to get out of these walls and I will do as thou wilt direct me.[51]

Broadway Street, Columbia, Missouri
(Parley P. Pratt and others were incarcerated here in 1838-39)
Boone County Historical Society—unknown, 1864

As soon as he stopped speaking, a vision apparently occurred; and he viewed his complete escape. The prisoners then decided to escape and conceived their plan. Parley noted in his autobiography:

> No sooner was the key turned [to the prison door by the jailer] than the door was seized by Mr. Follett with both hands; and with his foot placed against the wall, he soon opened a passage, which was in the same instant filled by Mr. Phelps, and followed by myself and Mr. Follett. The old jailer strode across the way, and stretched out his arms like Bunyan's Apollion, or like the giant Despair in Doubting Castle, but all to no purpose. One or two leaps brought us to the bottom of the stairs, carrying the old gentleman with us headlong, helter skelter, while old Luman sat and laughed in his corner of the prison . . . [I]n another instant . . . we were all three scampering off through the fields towards the thicket. By this time the town was all in motion. The quietness of the evening was suddenly changed into noise and bustle, and it was soon evident that the thrilling scenes of the great drama of the 4th of July, and the Columbian celebration of liberty were yet to be enacted. The streets on both sides of the fields where we were running were soon thronged with soldiers in uniform, mounted riflemen, footmen with fence stakes, clubs, or with whatever came to hand, and with boys, dogs, etc, all running, rushing, screaming, swearing, shouting, bawling and looking, while clouds of dust rose behind them.[52]

Soon the escapees found their friends waiting with horses in the thicket, not far from the prison. Only King Follett was unable to escape, as he was captured shortly after he mounted his horse.

Parley P. Pratt describes his joy after reaching the Missouri-Illinois border and crossing safely:

> I then descended from the height and entered the town . . . I examined the shore and soon convinced myself that no public ferry was kept there. I was extremely glad to learn this fact—being fully aware that by this time all the ferries would be watched . . . We soon landed in the woods in a low bottom, with no sign of inhabitants, although while crossing I had seen some houses on the shore a mile or two below. I now paid the boy his dollar, and he pushed off and commenced his way back exceedingly well pleased. I immediately stepped a few paces into the woods, and kneeling down kissed the ground as a land of liberty, and then poured out my soul in thanks to God.[53]

Follett was returned to jail, while his fellow prisoners made their way to freedom. He was finally acquitted and set free in September.

Though the incarcerated Church leaders' flight from Missouri ended when they were reunited with their families and the Church in Quincy, the escape was not the end of the Saints' involvement in Missouri. Legal actions and conflict continued between Church members and the state of Missouri for several years. Years later, Missouri officials attempted to extradite Joseph Smith back to Missouri to stand trial.

Although terrible experiences are part of the Mormon legacy in Missouri, some "fair-minded gentiles" sympathized with and in many cases defended the Saints' rights. For those Mormons who wrote down their story years later, Missouri was both a place of happiness and sorrow. Some personal histories are long and painfully rehearse the wrongs suffered in Missouri, while others are short, although just as poignant. Milo Andrus wrote about his arrival in Missouri and the subsequent expulsion in just a few lines:

> Early in the spring of 1837, we started for Missouri, and arrived in Caldwell County in time to put in a crop. In 1838, we were mobbed out of the county. We had one child born in Missouri, a girl, namely: Sarah Ann. We went to Illinois in the winter of 1838 and the next summer we lost our little girl born in Missouri.[54]

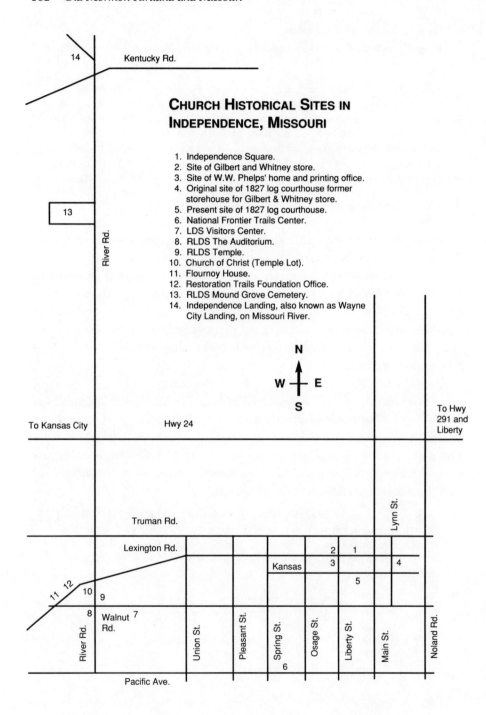

CHURCH HISTORICAL SITES IN INDEPENDENCE, MISSOURI

1. Independence Square.
2. Site of Gilbert and Whitney store.
3. Site of W.W. Phelps' home and printing office.
4. Original site of 1827 log courthouse former storehouse for Gilbert & Whitney store.
5. Present site of 1827 log courthouse.
6. National Frontier Trails Center.
7. LDS Visitors Center.
8. RLDS The Auditorium.
9. RLDS Temple.
10. Church of Christ (Temple Lot).
11. Flournoy House.
12. Restoration Trails Foundation Office.
13. RLDS Mound Grove Cemetery.
14. Independence Landing, also known as Wayne City Landing, on Missouri River.

Independence, Jackson County, Missouri

Independence, Missouri, is located nine miles southeast of Kansas City, Missouri. Geographical considerations made it a departure point of emigrants and traders during the early period. Each spring, traders gathered at Independence, a town founded in 1827 after the town of Franklin was washed away by a shift in the Missouri River's channel. For a month, all was bustle in the tiny community—steamboats unloading, wagons rumbling through the dirt streets, and traders haggling with local merchants over the price of goods. As soon as the grass turned green, heavy Conestoga wagons began pulling out of Independence for the southern traders' frontier—Santa Fe. The trade of all the Far West centered in Missouri. By 1830, eastern Missouri was filling up; and settlements reached along the Big Muddy to the border.

Independence, Missouri
(Site of the future city of Zion)
RLDS Archives—unknown, unknown

Following the Mormon period (1830–33), Independence remained an important staging ground for westward migration. Both the Oregon and Santa Fe trails were two days' journey from Independence. Forty miles out, a signboard pointed the way to the "Road to Oregon."

Independence was the county seat for Jackson County, which was named in 1826 for General Andrew Jackson, who became President of the United States two years later. The area was known as Blue County and was often called the "Blue" by early trappers, because of the two clear streams, "Little Blue" and "Big Blue," that flowed through the area. Mormons began to visit this land in 1831.

Just before the Saints began to arrive in Jackson County, a Protestant missionary wrote to his friends in the East about the conditions he found in this area. He wrote:

> The prospects for our evangelical work appear less likely here than any place I have seen in my westward journeyings. Such a godless place, filled with so many profane swearers, would be difficult to imagine . . . There are many suspicious characters who headquarter here, but when intelligence arrives that a federal marshall is approaching this country, there is a hurried scurrying of many of this element to the Indian territory on the west side of Missouri. As soon as the marshall returns down stream, this element is back in the saloons and other centers of sin . . . Christian Sabbath observance here appears to be unknown. It is a day for merchandising, jollity, drinking, gambling, and general anti-Christian conduct . . . There appears to be an over abundance of females here practicing the world's oldest profession . . . Gouging and more serious forms of violence are common.[55]

Obedient to the direction given them by revelation, several pairs of missionaries started for Independence, Missouri, in 1831.[56] Joseph Smith left Kirtland, Ohio, in company with several others on 19 June 1831. The trip to Independence consisted of travel by wagon, canal boat, stage, steamer, and finally by foot. At Independence, missionaries to the Lamanites, including Oliver Cowdery and a few Missouri converts, greeted Joseph Smith's party. Joseph said that this "meeting of our brethren, who had long awaited our arrival, was a glorious one, and moistened with many tears."[57]

Following a tour of the surrounding area, Joseph received a revelation designating "the very spot upon which [the Lord] designed to commence the work of gathering, and the building up of a 'holy city,' even the New Jerusalem."[58] A few days later, on 2 August 1831, about twelve miles west of Independence, Church leaders consecrated and dedicated the land of Missouri for the gathering of the Saints.

The revelation clarified that "the place which is now called Independence is the center place; and a spot for the temple is lying westward, upon a lot which is not far from the court-house."[59] Joseph Smith dedicated this "spot," which was located approximately one-half mile west of the newly erected brick courthouse.

The Saints were instructed by revelation to move to Missouri and to consecrate their properties to the bishop in Zion. Martin Harris, an early convert

Independence, Missouri
(View looking at the temple lot from the courthouse on Independence Square)
BYU Harold B. Lee Library—Edward Stevenson, 1895

and a witness to the *Book of Mormon*, was to set the example. Orson Pratt recalled,

> [Martin Harris] was among the favored few who went up from the State of Ohio in the summer of 1831, and journeyed nearly a thousand miles to the western part of Missouri, to Jackson County. [Joseph Smith] went at the same time . . . Martin Harris was the first man that the Lord called by name to consecrate his money, and lay the same at the feet of the Bishop in Jackson County, Mo., according to the order of consecration. He willingly did it; he knew the work to be true; he knew that the word of the Lord through the Prophet Joseph was just as sacred as any word that ever came from the mouth of any Prophet from the foundation of the world. He consecrated his money and his substance, according to the word of the Lord. What for? As the revelation [60] states, as an example to the rest of the Church.[61]

Shortly thereafter, the Colesville Branch of the Church arrived in Jackson County on 25 July 1831. Among the sixty members of the branch was Polly Knight, who died 6 August 1831 and was buried on 7 August. She was the first member of the Church to die in Zion. Her husband, Joseph Knight, Sr., recalled:

> There was one Joshua Lewis that had come into the Church the winter before, he and his wife. And they were faithful and good to us and took us into their house, my wife being sick as before stated. She died on the seventh day of August and Joseph and Sidney attended her funeral on the eighth. She was buried in the woods a spot chosen by ourselves. I was alone by where she was buried a few days after and I found the pigs had begun to root where she was buried. I being very unwell, but I took my ax the next day and built a pen around it. It was the last [thing] I done for her.[62]

Church elders returning from "the land of Zion" visited Sanford Porter and his family and told them about Jackson County. Nathan Porter, Sanford's son, recalled their arrival in Independence following a three-month journey from Illinois during the worst part of winter:

> Arriving at the settlement of our brethren at Independence, Jackson County on the first of March 1832 . . . [w]e were now on the consecrated land . . . We felt that our pilgrimage was over, that our abiding was here until the coming of the Son of Man, and through his reign of a thousand years, yea unto the consumption of all things spoken of by the mouth of all the Holy Prophets, were shown the lot that was selected by revelation through the Prophet Joseph Smith for the Temple, called the Temple Block; it was now in its wild state; being covered with a heavy growth of timber, a portion of which; the brethren had already begun to remove for their present use, at the same time prepare it to some extent for that magnificent temple, soon to stand upon it, for to use it appeared nigh at hand.[63]

The early Church meetings in Zion were held in the homes of various members, including Edward Partridge:

> Zion, July 3, 1832—Minutes of a special council held at the dwelling house of Edward Partridge (Bishop). [The] Conference opened in prayer by William W. Phelps. [Several present] Resolved that the mode and manner of regulating the Church of Christ take effect from this time, according to a Revelation received in Hiram, Portage County, Ohio [on] Nov. 11, 1831 [LDS D&C 68/RLDS D&C 68]. Adjourned for one hour, Prayer by Elder Calvin Bebee. Convened, Prayer by the Bishop. A letter from Brother Patten from Indiana was exhibited and discussed. [It was] advised that he come to this land and also agree by the conference that an epistle be written to the Church scattered abroad. Prayer by Isaac Morley—John Whitmer Clerk of conference.[64]

The original Missouri settlers saw Jackson County fill up with northern emigrants, many of whom were poor. These old inhabitants were afraid that the Saints would soon become a majority and control the political, social, religious, and economic spheres in the area. Exasperated by the conflicts that began to appear, these settlers found voice in extremists like Reverend Finis Ewing, head of the Cumberland Presbyterians. "The 'Mormons' are the common enemies of mankind and ought to be destroyed," he argued.[65]

During the same period, the Saints were plagued with their own troubles. A dissenter sued Bishop Partridge for fifty dollars. As a member, the dissenter had sent money from Ohio to purchase an inheritance for himself and the saints of God in Zion in these last days, only to find that the bishop had drawn the deed in his own name. The *Star* explained this as common practice; the bishop held

Temple Area, Independence, Missouri
(In 1831, Joseph Smith dedicated this area for a temple.)
RLDS Archives—unknown, unknown

the property for the Church. The fifty dollars had been a consecration, a deed of gift no more returnable than donations to missionary societies or colleges in other churches. But the Missouri court found for the plaintiff, who, lamented the *Star*, "shortly after denied the faith and ran away on Sunday," to spread a further bad opinion about the Mormons. Other dissenters likewise withdrew, vexing the Church with lawsuits.

Meanwhile, the conflicts escalated between the Saints and the old settlers. As early as 1832, homes had been stoned and shot at, a haystack burned, and families insulted. In April 1833, nearly three hundred Jackson County residents met at Independence to decide on a course of action against the Saints. The meeting ended in drunken disagreement, a typical "Missouri row." On 4 July 1833, this citizens committee circulated a set of resolutions called the "Secret Constitution," setting forth their grievances against the Saints. Sixteen days later, they met at the county courthouse to issue their ultimatum. A committee waited upon the Church leaders and asked them to close all their workshops, their store, and the *Star* office and to agree to leave the county. Local leaders needed time to respond. Given only fifteen minutes, they refused to comply with the proposals.

The refusal was announced at the courthouse, where the assembly voted to demolish the printing office, which they did forthwith, tarring and feathering Bishop Edward Partridge and Charles Allen. Three days later, several hundred mobsters continued the work of destruction of Mormon properties in and around Jackson County.

The Saints, under the pressure of constant persecution, finally agreed to leave the county. Most left in the winter of 1833, and the rest left in the spring of 1834. For a short period, the mobs were appeased.

The Saints believed that this agreement was illegal and therefore not binding. They prepared petitions to be presented to state officials in the hopes of preventing the Saints' forced removal from their lands in Jackson County.

State Governor Daniel Dunklin's response was less than comforting. He told them that they must appeal to the courts, the civil officers. The judge of the county court, the justices of the peace, the constable and his deputies, and local lawyers were all signers of the agreement seeking to drive the Saints out.

Unable to find anyone to take their case in Jackson County, the Saints retained four attorneys from neighboring Clay County. "Here let me remark," wrote John Corrill, "that up to this time the Mormons had not so much as lifted a finger, even in their own defence, so tenacious were they for the precepts of the gospel—'turn the other cheek.'"[66]

Incensed that the Mormons should attempt to remain in the county, the mobs took to night depredations, pulling down homes of the Saints and whipping those they found alone. A final confrontation between the two groups occurred on 4 November 1833 in a skirmish during which three or four were killed on both sides and several others were wounded. A little after dark, the news reached Independence where several Saints were undergoing a sham trial. So great was the excitement that the court had to keep the prisoners in jail for their protection.

The Saints were forced to leave during the winter. Some went to Van Buren County for a brief period of time; others back trailed east. Most of them crowded the Missouri River bottoms in wretched privation and crossed the river north into Clay County, where they were hospitably received. They were not permitted to return to Jackson County, even to settle business. The old settlers burned down almost one hundred fifty empty Mormon homes in the spring to finish their winter's work.

Even after the Mormons were expelled from Jackson County, the old settlers still exhibited hard feelings for the Mormons. Mormon missionary Wilford Woodruff passed through Jackson County very carefully during a trip in 1835. Woodruff walked in the rain for seventy-two miles without anything to eat. The missionaries preached "from house to house" as they journeyed, "but no one offered them dining or food." They came to the home of a Mr. Connor, who was a Jackson County resident at the time of the Mormon expulsion in 1833; and he invited them for breakfast. Woodruff recalled,

He knew we were "Mormons," and as soon as we began to eat he began to swear about the "Mormons." He had a large platter of bacon and eggs, and plenty of bread on the table, and his swearing did not hinder our eating, for the harder he swore the harder we ate, until we got our stomachs full; then we arose from the table, took our hats, and thanked him for our breakfast, and the last we heard of him he was still swearing. I trust the Lord will reward him for our breakfast.[67]

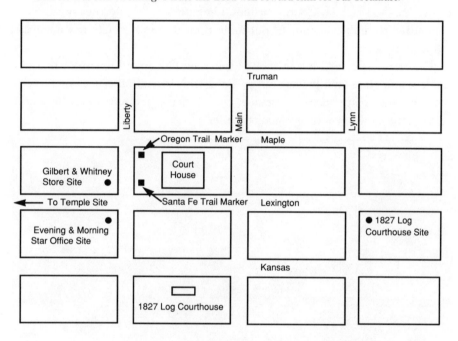

INDEPENDENCE SQUARE, INDEPENDENCE

INDEPENDENCE SQUARE

Independence Square is located at the center of Independence and is bounded by Liberty, Maple, Main, and Lexington streets. The square is situated approximately one-half mile east of the LDS Visitors Center and RLDS Auditorium/Temple.

Historical Background

Much of the action in this rough-and-tumble town centered on Independence Square. Here wagon trains lined up for their westward departure, an event that often required a full day of assembly. In the ante-bellum days, some of the area's largest slave auctions took place on the square. Dominating Independence

Square is the Jackson County Courthouse, a building containing structural elements of successive construction dating from 1839. An earlier brick building was standing when Joseph Smith and other Church leaders visited Independence for the first time in 1831.

During the summer of 1833, the square was the site of a meeting of some four or five hundred Jackson County citizens. On Saturday, 20 July, they organized a committee to draft a document outlining their demands of Church members living in the area.

The group included Missouri State Lieutenant Governor Lilburn W. Boggs, a resident and large land holder. Boggs, along with several other leading citizens including the county judge, constables, county clerks, and justices of the peace, agitated the crowd in anti-Mormon activities.

Independence Square, Independence, Missouri
(The Gilbert and Whitney store and Church printing office were across the street from the square)
Jackson County Historical Society—unknown, c1850

A committee of twelve presented their ultimatum to Church leaders, who were given fifteen minutes to respond. When they returned to the court house, the group of disgruntled citizens became a mob and left the court house to surround the Church's printing establishment, where they commenced ransacking Phelps' home and destroying the printing press and office.

*1827 Courthouse, Independence, Missouri
(This structure was used as the Gilbert and
Whitney storehouse in the early 1830s)
RLDS Archives—unknown, unknown*

1827 COURTHOUSE

The 1827 log courthouse is located about two blocks south of Independence Square. It was moved to its present location (107 West Kansas Street) in 1916 from the original location at the corner of East Lexington and Lynn streets (presently a parking lot), where a sign is now located.

*Lilburn Boggs' Home, Independence, Missouri
(Governor of Missouri who issued the
"extermination order")
RLDS Archives—unknown, unknown*

Historical Background

The 1827 courthouse served as temporary government quarters for Jackson County and subsequently was used for a variety of mercantile, religious, and philanthropic purposes. Daniel P. Lewis began construction of the building in September 1827 and completed the structure in February 1828 for $150, as contracted. The building measured thirty-six feet long by eighteen feet wide, with twelve light windows and, at each end, a fireplace.

The log building served as a courthouse only temporarily. It was then sold to Smallwood Noland, along with an acre and a half of land, and was used as a saddle shop by Samuel Burk. Smallwood Noland sold the building and land for $371 to the firm of Algernon S. Gilbert and Newel K. Whitney on 20 February 1832. Gilbert was one of the newly arrived Mormon settlers in Jackson County.

THE EVENING AND THE MORNING STAR OFFICE SITE

The Evening and the Morning Star office site was located southwest of Independence Square and was situated on the west side of Liberty Street between Lexington and Kansas streets.

Historical Background

While in Ohio, W. W. Phelps received the assignment to purchase a press on his way to the Mormon Zion in Missouri so the Saints could publish a monthly newspaper in Jackson County. The printing operation was located in a two-story

The Evening and The Morning Star Office Site, Independence, Missouri
(Site of the Church's printing establishment and mob action in 1833)
RLDS Archives—unknown, before 1920

brick building on Liberty Street on a lot purchased by Bishop Partridge. The building was constructed by Levi Hancock. Hancock reported, "[I] told them I was just the man to build the printing works. I told them if they knew how they wanted it done, I could do it. Oliver [Cowdery] gave me the plans and I began to work on it and was soon finished."[68]

Oliver Cowdery's arrival in Jackson County from Ohio on 5 January 1832 with the manuscript copies of the revelations added a sense of urgency to Phelps' printing projects. The building was finally completed and dedicated on 29 May 1832. The "Far West Record Book" states,

> Minutes of a Conference held at the office of the *Evening & Mormon Star* on Tuesday 29th day of May 1832 for the purpose of dedicating to the Lord in conformity to certain Revelations given concern the Printing Establishment . . . The conference opened by prayer by John Whitmer. Several appropriate commandments read by br. John Whitmer, after which some explanatory remarks were made by brs. Phelps, Oliver [Cowdery] and others in relation to rules and regulation of the office and the important duties devolving upon those who the Lord has designated to spread his truths and revelations in these last days to the inhabitants of the earth. After which the Bishop [Partridge] proceeded solemnly to dedicate the building for printing and all materials appertaining thereto unto the Lord. This meeting concluded in prayer by brother William W. Phelps—Sidney Gilbert, Clerk of Meeting.[69]

Soon thereafter, the June 1832 issue of the *Star* came off the press. Following its completion, Phelps installed the press in one of the upper rooms and used the main floor for his family's living quarters.

A little over a year later, the printing establishment became the focus of the first major mob action against the Saints in Jackson County. On a hot Saturday in July 1833, a large group of men assembled at the county courthouse to discuss what actions should be taken against the Mormons.

Following a tense discussion between mob and Church leaders, the mob decided to destroy the printing office. The men at the courthouse headed down Liberty Street, just a block south, to W. W. Phelps' home. Led by a minister carrying a red flag, a mob of about five hundred men approached Phelps' home and began demolishing the press and throwing Phelps' personal belongings into the street.

During the one-hour demonstration, a few associated with the Church approached the building in an attempt to collect some of the printed copies of the Book of Commandments. Mary Elizabeth Rollins and her younger sister Caroline watched the men carry out a pile of large sheets of printed paper. They decided to recover some. Mary Rollins later recalled,

They [the mob] brought out some large sheets of paper, and said, "Here are the Mormon Commandments." My sister Caroline and myself were in a corner of a fence watching them; when they spoke of the commandments I was determined to have some of them. Sister said if I went to get any of them she would go too, but said "they will kill us." While their backs were turned, prying out the gable end of the house, we went, and got our arms full, and were turning away, when some of the mob saw us and called on us to stop, but we ran as fast as we could. Two of them started after us. Seeing a gap in a fence, we entered into a large cornfield, laid the papers on the ground, and hid them with our persons. The corn was from five to six feet high, and very thick; they hunted around considerable, and came very near us but did not find us. After we satisfied ourselves that they had given up the search for us, we tried to find our way out of the field, the corn was so high we could not see where to go . . . Soon we came to an old log stable which looked as though it had not been used for years. Sister Phelps and children were carrying in brush and piling it up at one side of the barn to lay her beds on. She asked me what I had. I told her. She then took them from us, which made us feel very bad. They got them bound in small books and sent me one, which I prized very highly.[70]

NATIONAL FRONTIER TRAILS CENTER

The National Frontier Trails Center is located at 318 West Pacific Avenue (between Spring and Osage streets). The center stands on the site of the spring where wagon trains topped off their water kegs, an important finale before the wagon trains left Independence on one of the west-bound trails. The Trails Center contains exhibits and archives dealing with the history of the Santa Fe, Oregon, and California trails. A movie shown periodically throughout the day tells the story of migrations westward, including the Mormon exodus from Nauvoo, Illinois, to the Great Basin.

LDS CHURCH VISITORS CENTER

The Church of Jesus Christ of Latter-day Saints operates the "Independence Visitors Center" at 937 West Walnut. Built upon a twenty-acre section of the original temple lot, the visitors center features two main sections. The entry floor exhibits paintings and displays that explain LDS beliefs and practices. The bottom floor houses an excellent display dealing with the Mormons in Missouri during the 1830–1839 period.

Additional property contiguous to the visitors center is the site of the LDS Church's Independence Stake Center, Independence Missouri Mission headquarters, and LDS Church Educational System Offices.

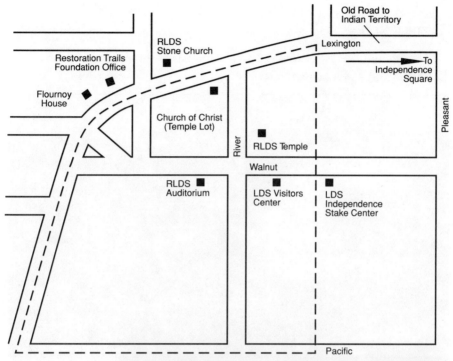

Old Road to
Indian Territory

RLDS
Stone Church

Lexington

Restoration Trails
Foundation Office

To
Independence
Square

Flournoy
House

Church of Christ
(Temple Lot)

River

RLDS Temple

Pleasant

Walnut

RLDS
Auditorium

LDS Visitors
Center

LDS
Independence
Stake Center

Pacific

INDEPENDENCE TEMPLE LOT
(TEMPLE PROPERTY 63 ACRES)

Aerial View of Independence, Missouri
(RLDS Auditorium, LDS Visitors Center, and early Church of
Christ Building)

TEMPLE SITE

The temple site is located on part of the sixty-three acres east of where Lexington and Walnut streets intersect.

Temple Site, Independence, Missouri
(Temple lot includes two and one-half acres of the original 63 acres purchased by Bishop Partridge)
LDS Historical Department—George E. Anderson, 1907

Historical Background

Joseph Smith dedicated a spot in Independence on 3 August 1831. On 19 December 1831, Bishop Edward Partridge purchased sixty-three acres of land, which included the temple site, for $130 from Jones H. Flournoy. While several homes stood on the temple site during the Mormon period (1831–1833), no temple was begun.

During the expulsion, fifteen-year-old Rebecca Cordilia died from exposure, improper food, and exhaustion. According to Horace B. Owens' short account, "Brother John, died [in 1833] and was buried on the Temple lot. Sister Cordilia died and was buried by the side of Brother John."[71]

A 1929 excavation by the Hedrickite Church revealed several stones purportedly marking the northeast and southeast corners. These stones with their markings are displayed in the visitors center of the Church of Christ (Temple Lot). One stone marked "S E C T 1831" supposedly means "south-east corner, temple."

The American Revolution Bicentennial Commission of Independence erected a marker at the temple site in 1976. The marker states:

> TEMPLE SITE—August 3, 1831, Joseph Smith, Jr., Prophet and Founder of the Church of Christ, with seven other Church leaders, dedicated this site for the Temple in the City of Zion, where this Church believes the Lord will come to His people in the Last Days.

On 25 June 1833, Joseph Smith explained the plat of the City of Zion, including the "painted public squares in the middle":[72]

Temple Site Survey Stone, Independence, Missouri
(Traditionally identified as original survey stone)
LDS Historical Department—George E. Anderson, 1907

> [They] are for public buildings. The one without any figures is for store-houses for the Bishop, and to be devoted to his use. Figure first is for the temples for the use of the presidency; the circles inside of the squares, are the places of the temples . . .
>
> The names of the temples to be built on the painted squares as represented on the plot of the city of Zion, which is now about to be forwarded thither:—numbers 10, 11, and 12, are to be called, House of the Lord, for the Presidency of the High and Most Holy Priesthood, after the order of Melchizedek, which is after the order of the Son of God, upon Mount Zion, City of the New Jerusalem. Numbers 7, 8, and 9, the Sacred Apostolic Repository, for the use of the Bishop. Numbers 4, 5, and 6, the Holy Evangelical House for the High Priesthood of the Holy Order of God. Numbers 1, 2, and 3, the House of the Lord, for the Elders of Zion, an Ensign to the Nations. Numbers 22, 23, and 24, House of the Lord for the Presidency of the High Priesthood, after the order of Aaron, a Standard for the People. Numbers 19, 20, and 21, House of the Lord, the Law of the Kingdom of Heaven, and Messenger to the People; for the Highest Priesthood after the Order of Aaron. Numbers 16, 17, and 18, House of the Lord for the Teachers in Zion, Messengers to the Church. Numbers 13, 14, and 15, House of the Lord for the Deacons in Zion, Helps in Government. Underneath must be written on each house—HOLINESS TO THE LORD.[73]

THE CHURCH OF CHRIST (TEMPLE LOT)

The Church of Christ (Temple Lot) is located on two and a half acres of the original temple lot on the southwest corner of Lexington and Walnut streets. The address is 937 West Walnut. An earlier, well-known white frame building burned down by an arsonist has been replaced by a new structure.

Church of Christ Building on the Temple Site, Independence, Missouri
(Former Granville Hedrick's faction returned to Independence in 1870s)
LDS Historical Department—George E. Anderson, 1907

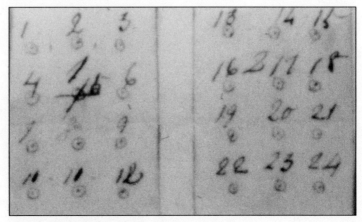

Temple Blocks, Independence, Missouri
(Joseph's 1833 plat map showing 24 "temples")
LDS Historical Department—Joseph Smith, 1833

Historical Background

On 16 August 1863, Granville Hedrick, a leader of six branches of the Church in Illinois following the death of Joseph Smith in 1844, began instructing his followers that the time to begin a return to Zion (Independence) was near at hand. In 1867, under his direction, they began to gather to Missouri and purchased the temple lot, where tradition indicated that it was dedicated by Church leaders in 1831.

RLDS Auditorium/Temple

The Reorganized Church of Jesus Christ of Latter Day Saints Auditorium is located on Walnut Street between Grand and River streets at 1001 West Walnut. The RLDS Temple is located northeast of the Auditorium just across Walnut Street.

The RLDS Church, organized on 8 April 1853 after the death of Joseph Smith in 1844, began to return to Independence in the 1860s. On 25 May 1873, the RLDS Church organized its first branch in the city. Construction of a brick church building on East Lexington Street was begun in 1879. The Stone Church, located nearby the Auditorium, was built in 1888–92.

The RLDS Auditorium is situated on a twenty-five-acre portion of the original temple lot. The building was begun in 1926; however, work was

The Flournoy House, Independence, Missouri
(In this house, Bishop Partridge purchased the 63-acres temple lot from Jones Flournoy in 1831)
RLDS Church—unknown, unknown

discontinued during the depression of the 1930s. The famous organ was installed in 1959, and formal dedication occurred in 1962. The main conference chamber seats nearly six thousand people. The Heritage Hall Museum is in the Auditorium and contains displays of historical material. These displays will be relocated to the temple complex following its completion.

THE FLOURNOY HOUSE

The Flournoy house is located on Lexington Street just northwest of the temple lot.

Historical Background

Jones H. Flournoy built his brick home in Jackson County in 1826. The original site of the home was located on the west side of Pleasant Street where Kansas Street now intersects Pleasant Street. Flournoy's slaves dug the basement and used the clay from the excavation to manufacture the bricks. Joseph Smith and Edward Partridge met in this home and may have made the arrangements there to purchase the 63 acres known as the "temple lot" in 1831.

Later, Flournoy participated in the anti-Mormon activity in Jackson County in 1833. The home was moved to the present location and was reconstructed to its original appearance. It is part of Heritage Plaza, which is operated by Restoration Trails Foundation (RTF), administrator of RLDS Church historical sites. The RTF office is located at 1034 West Lexington.

RLDS MOUND GROVE CEMETERY

The RLDS Mound Grove Cemetery is located north on River Road approximately two miles and is situated on the west side of River Road at 1818 North River.

Historical Background

Several Saints are buried in the Mound Grove Cemetery, including Joseph Smith, Jr.'s son, Joseph Smith III. Other RLDS leaders and members are buried at this cemetery. The cholera victims of Zion's Camp were reinterred there on 25 March 1976, where RLDS and LDS Church leaders met at the cemetery and conducted a reburial service together. RLDS Patriarch Lynn E. Smith conducted and opened the meeting with prayer. RLDS Church Historian Richard Howard gave the scripture reading, and the LDS Church Liberty Missouri Ward Choir sang a hymn. Vivian Graybille, an RLDS member from Jackson County, read a historical sketch and tribute to the deceased. A representative of the LDS

Church , Wayne Lewis, dedicated the grave; and Bishop Verdes Reed, agent for the Missouri Historic Sites of the LDS Church, gave the benediction.

INDEPENDENCE LANDING

Independence Landing, Wayne City, Missouri
(Saints used this landing to cross to Clay County by ferry)
RLDS Archives, unknown, unknown

A historical marker for Independence Landing is located on North River Boulevard just north of Kentucky Road and halfway down the road on the bluff overlooking the Mississippi River.

Historical Background

A dozen ferries operated between Jackson and Clay counties during the 1830s. Independence Landing, a major crossing, became known as "Wayne City Landing" in 1847. Steamboats arrived there in early 1830. The old rock road of broken limestone leading to the landing from Independence is traditionally attributed to the Saints' efforts and may be the first hard-surfaced road in Missouri.

The landing was the site of unusual activity in 1833 when the Mormons fled their homes to Clay County via the ferries in the area. The marker states:

> 1847 Wayne City Upper Independence Landing. Start of the California-Oregon-Santa Fe Trails. Marked August 19, 1983 by the Citizens of Sugar Creek and Independence Pioneer Chapter, Daughters of the American Revolution.

Kansas City, Missouri
(The Colesville Branch and other early Missouri branches were actually located in modern Kansas City)
Kansas City Missouri Public Library—unknown, 1871

Kansas City, Jackson County, Missouri

Kansas City, Missouri, is located nine miles northwest of Independence. Native Americans, the Kansas Indians, lived at the confluence of the Kansas and Missouri rivers until approximately 1820. They left this area to comply with government treaties. Shortly thereafter, Francois Chouteau established a trading post along the river. Eventually, the American Trading Company moved to this area. In 1838, a group of investors purchased the Chouteau trading post property and renamed the settlement the town of Kansas.

SCHOOL IN ZION MONUMENT

The School in Zion Monument is located in Kansas City's Troost Park at the corner of Paseo and Lake streets (just south of 27th Street).

Historical Background

Following the arrival of the Colesville Branch (New York) from Ohio in July 1831, the Saints settled in Kaw Township above the Big Blue River, about twelve miles west of Independence. Joseph Smith's history states:

School of Zion Monument, Troost Park, Kansas City, Missouri
(The marker commemorates the first school in Kansas City, established by the Saints in 1831)
LDS Church Historical Department—unknown, c1964

On the second day of August [1831], I assisted the Colesville Branch of the Church, (which numbered about sixty members) lay the first log, for a house, as a foundation in Zion in Kaw township . . . The log was carried and placed by twelve men, in honor of the twelve tribes of Israel. At the same time, through prayer, the land of Zion was consecrated and dedicated by Elder Sydney Rigdon for the gathering of the Saints.[74]

Sometime later, Joseph Smith received a revelation regarding the school and Parley P. Pratt's position there.[75] "Inasmuch," the revelation states, "as he continueth to abide in me he shall continue to preside over the school in the land of Zion until I shall give unto him other commandments."

In 1963, the dedication of a monument to commemorate this event was held at Troost Park in Kansas City. Extracts from the plaque state:

> This house, a place of worship, was also used as a school and was the first school to be erected within the present boundaries of Kansas City, Missouri. Unveiling and Dedication September 14, 1963 By President Joseph Fielding Smith, The Church of Jesus Christ of Latter-day Saints.

Indian Territory (Kansas)

While the white settlers began to spread across the entire state, another group of migrants from across the Mississippi moved into the area just west of Missouri. These immigrants were not driven by the hope of economic gain but by the bayonets of federal troops. They were eastern native American Indians who, uprooted from their tribal lands, were forced to settle on unwanted vacant lands far outside of white settlement areas. They were driven westward by the federal government between 1825 and 1840 to establish a "permanent" Indian frontier beyond the 95th meridian.

Indian Territory, Western Missouri
(Looking northeast toward Missouri from Fort Leavenworth)
Kansas State Historical Society—unknown, 1872

The notion of a "Permanent Indian Frontier" germinated in the minds of governmental officials soon after the Louisiana Purchase and steadily gained support following the War of 1812. Although the greed of land-hungry farmers was the main and certainly the most significant factor in establishing this policy, the policy also was thought to benefit the eastern Indian nations. Such a removal would eliminate friction between the two cultures, and the natives could be protected from the diseases of the white man. The plan was conceived by John C. Calhoun, President Monroe's secretary of war, in 1824.

The "Permanent Indian Frontier" plan was presented to Congress on 27 January 1825. The plan forced the Osage and Kansas tribes to surrender all of Kansas and northern Oklahoma, except two reservations. During the next fifteen years, the work of "persuading" eastern tribes to accept their new home was pursued. The effort usually followed a pattern. Indian agents bribed a corrupt chief to sign a removal treaty and then forced the entire tribe to move.

The Shawnee of Ohio arrived to a twenty-five-mile-wide strip south of the Kansas River, where they were joined in 1829 by the Delawares, who accepted a reservation on the north bank of the stream together with an outlet to the buffalo country. In quick succession, the Kickappo, Saulk, Fox, Chippewa, Iowa, Potawatomi, Ottawa, Peoria, and Miami were crowded into small reserves just west of the 95th meridian or, in a few instances, onto lands in western Iowa. Other Indians from the south came, including the Choctaw, Chickasaw, Cherokee, Creeks, and Seminole.

The "Permanent Indian Frontier" was planned along the 95th meridian from the Red River to the Great Bend of the Missouri. In their reservations and on the Great Plains just beyond, the Indians were, in theory, to spend the rest of time, free from white molestation and settlement. During this time, the New York Saints' attention became focused on the Indian nations just west of Independence, Missouri.

When the *Book of Mormon* was published in 1830, the Saints became aware that the native American Indians were to play an important role in the establishment of the New Jerusalem and the Second Coming of Christ. Church leader Oliver Cowdery was called to preach to the Lamanites (Mormon name for native American Indians) just six months following the organization of the Church.[76] Subsequently, Ziba Peterson, Parley P. Pratt, and Peter Whitmer, Jr. were assigned to assist Cowdery.[77]

The missionaries were to travel to "the borders by the Lamanites."[78] Joseph Smith understood that the phrase, "borders of the Lamanites," referred to the line between Missouri and the "Permanent Indian Frontier."

When preparations were completed, the missionaries departed on their fifteen-hundred-mile journey on 18 October 1831. The missionaries proclaimed their messages along the way, including to a group of Seneca Indians on the Cattaraugus Reservation near Buffalo, New York. So far as is known, these were the first Indians to have the gospel introduced to them. The Wyandot Indians at Sandusky, Ohio, were the next tribe to be visited by the missionaries to the Lamanites. Pratt wrote, "They rejoiced in the tidings, bid us God speed, and desired us to write to them in relation to our success among the tribes further west."[79]

Missionary work was not exclusively among the native American Indians. Along the way, the missionaries preached and left copies of the *Book of Mormon* with interested individuals. Many persons were baptized in the Western Reserve area of Ohio, including Dr. Frederick G. Williams, who helped the missionaries on their journey by giving them cash and a horse and by accompanying them. Now numbering five, the missionaries proceeded to the "borders of the Lamanites."

Winter was fast approaching, known as "the winter of deep snows"; and the missionaries moved farther west. By the end of December, "bitter cold, a blinding, swirling blur of snow, and leaden, lowering skies, combined to make this storm a thing to paralyze that prairie country. It seems to have continued for days, unabated—a wonder, at first, then a terror, a benumbing horror as it became a menace to [the] life of men and animals."[80]

The elders boarded a steamboat at Cincinnati just five days before Christmas and headed for St. Louis, Missouri. The Ohio River was closed by ice flows; the steamboat disembarked its passengers at Cairo, Illinois. "We halted for a few days," Pratt wrote, "on account of a dreadful storm of rain and snow, which lasted for a week or more, during which the snow fell in some places near three feet."[81]

The missionaries were treated well and preached in several congregations during the time they spent in Cairo. When the weather broke, they continued their trek by foot to St. Louis and St. Charles. From these destinations, they traveled another three hundred miles "through vast prairies and through trackless wilds of snow—no beaten road; houses few and far between; and the bleak northwest wind always blowing in our faces with a keenness which would almost take the skin off the face."[82]

Pratt vividly recalled that portion of their trip:

> We travelled for whole days, from morning till night, without a house or fire,

wading in snow to the knees at every step, and the cold so intense that the snow did not melt on the south side of the houses, even in the mid-day sun, for nearly six weeks. We carried on our backs our changes of clothing, several books, and corn bread and raw pork. We often ate our frozen bread and pork by the way, when the bread would be so frozen that we could not bite or penetrate any part of it but the outside crust. After much fatigue and some suffering we all arrived in Independence, in the county of Jackson, on the extreme western frontiers of Missouri, and of the United States.[83]

They finally arrived at their destination on 13 January 1831 at the "borders of the Lamanites."

Sometime in early February, Oliver Cowdery, Parley P. Pratt, and Frederick G. Williams crossed the 95th meridian to the Indian lands to begin their mission in earnest. The three missionaries spent one night with the Shawnee Indians before reaching the Kansas River. The missionaries entered the land of the Delawares on the next day and sought an interview with the leading chief of the Delaware nation. Some twenty members of the council met at Chief Anderson's lodge. Following a long discourse, Cowdery gave Anderson a *Book of Mormon*.

Chief Anderson thanked Cowdery for the *Book of Mormon* and said,

We feel truly thankful to our white friends who have come so far, and been at such pains to tell us good news, and especially this new news concerning the Book of our forefathers; it makes us glad in here—placing his hand on his heart. It is now winter, we are new settlers in this place; the snow is deep, our cattle and horses are dying, our wigwams are poor; we have much to do in the spring—to build houses, and fence and make farms; but we will build a council house, and meet together, and you shall read to us and teach us more concerning the Book of our fathers and the will of the Great Spirit.[84]

Pratt noted that the missionaries continued to meet with the Delaware leaders for several days. The Indians' interest had been aroused in the story Cowdery had delivered "until at length nearly the whole tribe began to feel a spirit of inquiry and excitement on the subject."[85] Soon, local Indian agents interceded and forced the missionaries to leave the area because the missionaries did not have proper government documents to allow them to meet with the Indians.

Somewhat disappointed, the missionaries returned to Independence where Cowdery prepared a letter for William Clark, a government Indian official in St. Louis, for such permission. Although the missionaries certainly were in violation of the law, Pratt speculated that when the news of their success reached the frontier settlements in Missouri, "it stirred up the jealousy and envy of the Indian agents and sectarian missionaries to that degree that we were soon ordered out of the Indian country as disturbers of the peace; and even threatened with the military [from Fort Leavenworth] in case of noncompliance."[86]

Pratt himself was chosen to return east to report the missionaries' activities to Joseph Smith on 14 February 1831. On 7 May 1831, Oliver Cowdery wrote a letter from Missouri explaining their work, success, and trials among the Indians and the other people in the area. Joseph left Kirtland for Missouri on 19 June 1831 with a group of Church leaders, arriving at Independence soon thereafter. The first Sunday after their arrival, W. W. Phelps preached at the western boundary of the United States to a group of all races, including a group of native American Indians.

Joseph Smith eventually returned to Kirtland, Ohio, following the dedication of the land of Missouri for the gathering of the Saints and the identification of the site of the New Jerusalem Temple, a temple that would be built by both the Saints and the Lamanites.

During the entire Missouri period, the Saints' beliefs and attitudes toward the Indians were distorted and used as a weapon to cause suspicion against the Mormons. In setting forth their apprehensions regarding the Mormons, the Clay County residents wrote:

> They are charged, as they have hitherto been, with keeping up a constant communication with our Indian tribes on our frontier, with declaring, even from the pulpit, that the Indians are a part of God's chosen people, destined by heaven to inherit this land in common with themselves.[87]

Although the Saints in truth regarded the Lamanites as part of God's chosen people and although the Indians had a right to their lands and would eventually assist in building the New Jerusalem, the Saints nevertheless were not intent upon agitating the Indians to open insurrection or warfare against white settlements in Missouri.

Fort Leavenworth, Leavenworth County, Kansas

Colonel Henry Leavenworth established a military fort on the banks of the Missouri River to protect traffic on the Santa Fe Trail and to play a peace-keeping role among the native American Indians in 1827. Besides the soldiers, a few missionaries, trappers, and farmers lived in the area. In the 1830s, the region was declared an Indian territory; and the Kickappo and Delaware migrated into the traditional homeland of the Kaw Indians.

Local Missouri counties, including Jackson and Clay, supplied the Fort Leavenworth garrison a large amount of goods, including agricultural items. Civilian laborers also obtained short-term jobs and small contracts with the government at Fort Leavenworth. Following the Saints' expulsion from Jackson County in 1833, the Saints began to realize the economic importance of Fort Leavenworth. At first, in an unorganized manner, Latter-day Saint men arrived at the fort to obtain work. Usually, the work was typically low-pay, manual-labor jobs such as cutting and hauling wood. A few exceptions existed—for instance, Newel Knight obtained a government contract to build a small mill for the Indians near the fort in the summer of 1838.[88]

Main Entrance to Fort Leavenworth, Kansas
(Shows barracks built in 1838 during Mormon period)
Kansas State Historical Society—unknown, 1872

Following the Saints' relocation from Clay County to Caldwell County, an organized attempt to exploit Fort Leavenworth's location was incorporated into the Saints' general economic plan. The first organized attempt was the formation of "agricultural firms" designed to compete in both agricultural and nonagricultural enterprises with local Missourians. By the end of August 1838, three agricultural companies were organized: the "Western Agricultural Company," the "Eastern Agricultural Company," and the "Southern Agricultural Company." The formation of these companies was well underway several months earlier.

The Church authorities noted the agricultural business advantages in Caldwell County:

Hundreds of acres of corn have been planted already, in our immediate neighborhood; and hundreds of acres more are now being planted. (This is the fourth day of May.) The crops of wheat are very promising, and the prospect is that we will have an abundant harvest. The vast quantities of provisions purchased, in this upper country by the United States, for the use of the Garrison, and also for the Indians, have made all kinds of provisions dear, and somewhat scarce.[89]

The second organized way the Saints planned to use the fort to help stabilize their poor economy was the establishment of an economical and practical trade route between Far West and Fort Leavenworth to deliver goods to the garrison. They hoped that a transportation network could be established between Far West (land route on a "good wagon road") to Adam-ondi-Ahman and then to DeWitt (water route on the Grand River) to Fort Leavenworth (water route on the Missouri River). This system would allow the Saints to avoid the costly fees levied at the landing at Liberty, Missouri.

Before the Saints were able to organize themselves sufficiently to vie for government contracts in a significant way, the 1838 Mormon War ended the Saints' presence in and around Fort Leavenworth for several years.[90]

Seven years following the Saints' expulsion from Missouri, the Mormon Battalion (a group of nearly six hundred Saints) traveled from Council Bluffs, Iowa, to San Diego, California, during the Mexican War. What has been called the longest infantry march in American history began on 20 July 1846. Within a few days, the battalion entered Missouri, marched to the Missouri River, and crossed to Fort Leavenworth. From this time and during the next decade, many Mormon immigrants stopped or passed by Fort Leavenworth on their way to Utah.

A marker commemorating the Mormon Battalion's visit to the area is located on Kearny Avenue just west of the Grant statue. Erected by the Kansas State Historical Society, the Oklahoma State Historical Society, and the LDS Church, the marker states in part:

THE MORMON BATTALION AT FORT LEAVENWORTH. The Mormon Battalion garrisoned here from 1 to 13 August 1846. The battalion received arms, training, supplies, and equipment here before departing on a 2,000 mile march to California via Santa Fe, New Mexico, and Tucson, Arizona.

Panoramic View, Richmond, Missouri
(Church leaders' trials held here in 1839)
LDS Historical Department—George E. Anderson, 1907

Richmond, Ray County, Missouri

Richmond, Missouri, is located approximately twenty-seven miles from the LDS Visitors Center and RLDS Auditorium/Temple. The Ray County Historical Museum is located at 809 West Royal. The museum devotes one room to the

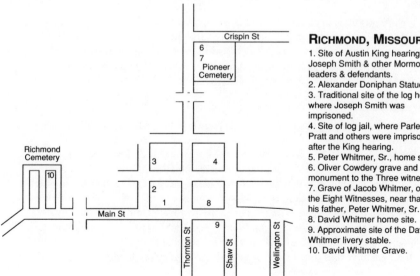

RICHMOND, MISSOURI

1. Site of Austin King hearing for Joseph Smith & other Mormon leaders & defendants.
2. Alexander Doniphan Statue.
3. Traditional site of the log house where Joseph Smith was imprisoned.
4. Site of log jail, where Parley P. Pratt and others were imprisoned after the King hearing.
5. Peter Whitmer, Sr., home site.
6. Oliver Cowdery grave and monument to the Three witnesses.
7. Grave of Jacob Whitmer, one of the Eight Witnesses, near that of his father, Peter Whitmer, Sr.
8. David Whitmer home site.
9. Approximate site of the David Whitmer livery stable.
10. David Whitmer Grave.

Church and its Missouri history, including information on the three witnesses and the coming forth of the *Book of Mormon*.

The Richmond area was originally settled by Southerners in 1814–15. It is situated on lands ceded by the Sac and Fox Indian tribes. Richmond was actually founded in 1827 and is now the county seat of Ray County. The region is extremely fertile. The county was organized in 1820 and is one of the original counties of Missouri.

The conflict between the Saints and the old settlers in Missouri was rooted in economic, political, religious, and social differences between both groups. This confrontation reached its climax in 1838 when Missouri State Governor Boggs issued the "extermination order." At the end of October 1838, a large force of state militia confronted the Saints' largest community in northwestern Missouri at Far West. Joseph Smith and several other Church leaders entered the militia camp under a white flag, hoping to defuse the tense situation. Instead of allowing a discussion of the problems, Church leaders were arrested and incarcerated. This arrest began a five-month imprisonment for Joseph Smith.

Early in November, the prisoners were taken briefly to Independence and then to Richmond. The laxness that had characterized the trip into Jackson County ceased when they arrived on the outskirts of Richmond on 9 November and were met by a contingent of John B. Clark's soldiers.

The prisoners were thrown into an "old log house" and chained together at two-foot intervals with three trace chains and seven padlocks. Joseph Smith wrote,

> We are prisoners in chains and under strong guard, for Christ's sake . . . Brother Robinson is chained next to me. He has a true heart and a firm mind; Brother [Lyman] Wight is next, Br. [Sidney] Rigdon next, Hyrum [Smith] next, Parley [P. Pratt] next, Amasa [Lyman] next, and thus we are bound together in chains as well as the cords of everlasting love.[91]

Joseph Smith's letter continues:

> There have been things that were unbeknown to us, and altogether beyond our control, that might seem, to the mob to be a pretext, for them to persecute us, but on examination, I think that the authorities, will discover our innocence, and set us free, but if this blessing cannot be obtained, I have this consolation that I am an innocent man, let what will befall me, I received your letter which I read over and over again, it was a sweet morsel to me. Oh God, grant that I may have the privilege of seeing once more my lovely family, in the enjoyment, of the sweets of liberty, and social life, to press them to my bosom and kiss their lovely cheeks would fill my heart with unspeakable gratitude, tell the children that I am alive and trust I shall come and see them before long.[92]

While incarcerated in Richmond Jail, Parley P. Pratt wrote of a "tedious night" when the prisoners laid awake until shortly after midnight. For several hours, Pratt explained, they had listened to "obscene jests, the horrid oaths, the dreadful blasphemies and filthy language of our guards." The guards taunted the prisoners with tales of robbery, rape, and murder against the Mormons. "I had listened," Pratt recalled, "till I became so disgusted, shocked, horrified, and so filled with the spirit of indignant justice that I could scarcely refrain from rising upon my feet and rebuking the guards; but had said nothing to Joseph . . . although I lay next to him and knew he was awake."

Pratt continued:

> On a sudden he arose to his feet, and spoke in a voice of thunder, or as the roaring lion, uttering, as near as I can recollect, the following words: "Silence, ye fiends of the infernal pit. In the name of Jesus Christ I rebuke you, and command you to be still; I will not live another minute and hear such language. Cease such talk, or you or I die this instant!" He ceased speaking. He stood erect in terrible majesty. Chained, and without a weapon; calm, unruffled and dignified as an angel, he looked upon the quailing guards, whose weapons were lowered or dropped to the ground; whose knees smote together, and who, shrinking into a corner, or crouching at his feet, begged his pardon, and remained quiet till a change of guards.[93]

This experience deeply moved Pratt. He wrote that he had seen the U.S. Congress in session and the ministers of justice, clothed in magisterial robes in the courts of England, "but dignity and majesty have I seen but *once*, as it stood in chains, at midnight, in a dungeon in an obscure village of Missouri."[94]

Following the Saints' exile from Missouri in 1839, several former Church leaders remained. The Whitmers were among those who chose to stay in Missouri, independent of the Church. John Whitmer remained at Far West, and David Whitmer moved to Richmond to establish a successful livery stable and transportation business. Both brothers lived in Missouri another four decades. Father and Mother Whitmer died in Richmond in 1854 and 1856. Jacob Whitmer, a *Book of Mormon* witness and Missouri high councilor, became a farmer and shoemaker and was buried near his parents in 1856. Hiram Page, another early Church leader and relative to the Whitmers, died in 1852 a few miles away from David's home. Oliver Cowdery and his wife, Elizabeth, after returning to the LDS Church in 1848, also returned to Richmond, where Oliver died in 1850. David, who died in 1888, lived ten years longer than his brother John.

David lived in Richmond for fifty years. When he arrived in 1838, his sole capital was a wagon and team he used for general hauling. By his death in 1888, his private net worth may have been near ten thousand dollars.

David Whitmer's life in Missouri was pleasant. He was listed as a "livery keeper" in the 1860 census, and newspaper ads during the next twenty-five years indicate that this was his principal occupation. He served as a city councilman and filled the unexpired term of mayor in 1867–68.

DAVID WHITMER HOME SITE

The David Whitmer home site is located on the north side of Main Street between Thornton and Shaw streets.

David Whitmer Home, Richmond, Missouri
(David Whitmer gave numerous interviews here about early Mormonism)
LDS Historical Department—George E. Anderson, 1907

Historical Background

David Whitmer was born 7 January 1805 near Harrisburg, Dauphin County, Pennsylvania. He married Julia Ann Jolley on 9 January 1831 at Seneca County, New York. He was baptized in June 1829. He moved to Kirtland, Ohio, by June 1831 and to Jackson County, Missouri, by October 1832. He was one of the three witnesses of the *Book of Mormon* and was President of the Church in Missouri.

During David's lifetime, many members of the Church, reporters, and other interested parties interviewed him concerning his early activities in the Church.

David Whitmer's home was the site of many visits from Saints and nonbelievers who were interested in hearing about Mormonism for themselves. He was the most interviewed *Book of Mormon* witness. Those who interviewed Whitmer included Joseph F. Smith, Orson Pratt, George Q. Cannon, Joseph Smith III, and Zenos H. Gurley.

David called his family and friends together on the night before his death. He asked his physician to say if he thought David was in his right mind. The doctor responded "yes," and David Whitmer gave his last testimony:

> Now, you must all be faithful in Christ. I want to say to you all, that the Bible and the Record of the Nephites (Book of Mormon) are true, so you can say you have heard me bear my testimony on my death bed.[95]

RICHMOND CITY CEMETERY

The Richmond City Cemetery is located on Highway 10 just west of Richmond City Center.

City Cemetery, Richmond, Missouri
(David Whitmer and Austin King are buried here)
Ray County Historical Society—unknown, unknown

Historical Background

David Whitmer's grave is located in the Richmond City Cemetery along with Austin King's grave. King was an avid anti-Mormon. He was assigned as a judge over several Mormon cases and later became governor of Missouri.

David Whitmer died in 1888. The local papers published his death notice and commented favorably upon his life in Richmond. The *Democrat* reported:

> [N]o man ever lived here, who had among our people, more friends and fewer enemies. Honest, conscientious and upright in all his dealings, just in his treatment of all, he made lasting friends who loved him to the end.[96]

PIONEER CEMETERY

The Pioneer Cemetery is located on Highway 13 just north of the center of town.

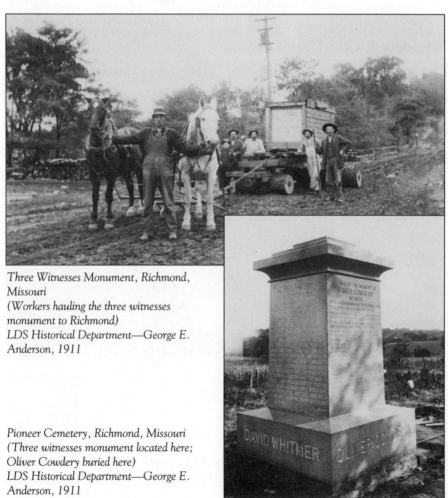

Three Witnesses Monument, Richmond, Missouri
(Workers hauling the three witnesses monument to Richmond)
LDS Historical Department—George E. Anderson, 1911

Pioneer Cemetery, Richmond, Missouri
(Three witnesses monument located here; Oliver Cowdery buried here)
LDS Historical Department—George E. Anderson, 1911

Historical Background

One of the three witnesses to the *Book of Mormon*, Oliver Cowdery, is buried in the Pioneer Cemetery. A monument to the *Book of Mormon*, the three witnesses, and Joseph Smith is located in this cemetery. Jacob Whitmer, one of the eight witnesses, is also buried here. One of the inscriptions on this monument states:

> The Book of Mormon, an account written by the hand of Mormon, upon plates taken from the plates of Nephi, translated and published by Joseph Smith, Junior Palmyra 1830.

Following Oliver Cowdery's return to the LDS Church in 1848, after a ten-year absence, he returned to Richmond, Missouri. He died on 3 March 1850 among friends, including David Whitmer, John Whitmer, Hiram Page, Phineas Young, and Jacob Whitmer. Young reported:

> His last moments were spent bearing testimony of the truth of the Gospel, revealed through Joseph Smith and the power of the Holy Priesthood which he had received through his administration.

He kissed his family goodbye and concluded, "Now I lay me down for the last time, I am going to my Savior." He died immediately, "with a smile on his face."[97]

ALEXANDER DONIPHAN MONUMENT

The Alexander Doniphan Monument is located in front of the Richmond County Courthouse in the town square.

Alexander Doniphan Monument, Richmond, Missouri
(Doniphan was an attorney and friend of the Saints in the 1830s)
RLDS Archives—unknown, unknown

Historical Background

Alexander Doniphan was born on 8 July 1808 in Mason County, Kentucky. He married Elizabeth Jane Thornton on 21 December 1837. Doniphan moved to Lexington, Missouri, in 1830 and removed to Liberty in 1833. He established a law practice in Clay County and served two consecutive terms in the state legislature between 1836–44. He was commissioned as a brigadier general in the state militia in 1838.

Doniphan represented the Mormons in 1833 and was outspoken against anti-Mormon activity in Missouri. In November 1838, he refused to carry out the order of General Lucus to execute Joseph Smith at Far West.

Liberty, Clay County, Missouri

Liberty, Missouri, is located approximately thirteen miles from the LDS Visitors Center and RLDS Auditorium/Temple.

In 1822, more than a dozen families were living in log cabins in Liberty. The first public sale of lots occurred in July of 1822, and the town was incorporated on 7 May 1829. Liberty is the oldest town in Clay County and is the county seat.

Following their expulsion from Jackson County, many Saints arrived in Clay County. Although the Saints were scattered in various communities in western Missouri, Church leaders in Ohio maintained close contact with them through postal communication and volunteers, who journeyed back and forth between the two states.

The Church established its new

Kansas Street, Liberty, Missouri (Mormons arrived in Liberty following their expulsion from Jackson County in 1833-34) Clay County Historical Society—unknown, c1865

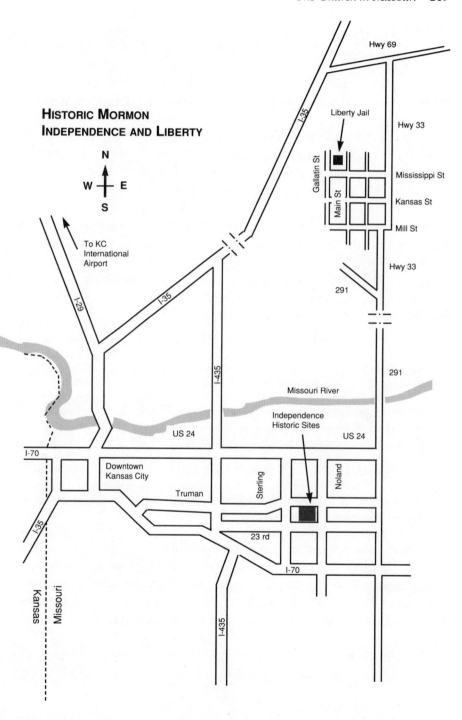

Hwy 69

I-35

Liberty Jail

Hwy 33

Gallatin St

Mississippi St

Main St

Kansas St

Mill St

HISTORIC MORMON
INDEPENDENCE AND LIBERTY

N
W — E
S

To KC
International
Airport

Hwy 33

291

I-29

I-35

I-435

291

Missouri River

Independence
Historic Sites

US 24

US 24

I-70

Downtown
Kansas City

Sterling

Noland

Truman

I-35

23 rd

I-70

Kansas

Missouri

I-435

Missouri headquarters in Liberty, Clay County, where most of the Saints had settled. This location also served as a base of operation for repeated legal attempts to recover the Saints' holdings in Jackson County. Twelve separate ecclesiastical branches were organized in Clay County by September 1834; and in July 1835, the Church organized the first high council in Clay County.

The residents of Clay County responded to the needs of the refugees in many ways. The residents' kindness did not go unnoticed in Jackson County, however. In an effort to stigmatize the people from Clay County who helped the Mormons, their Jackson County neighbors from across the river called them "Jack Mormons." The Saints welcomed the temporary relief from persecution and conflict. However, they soon realized they would not be restored to their lands across the Missouri River. The citizens of the county became uneasy; and by the middle of 1836, the situation was again critical. The most volatile non-Mormon residents noted the increase in Mormon population and brought forth old charges of collaboration with the Indians and the Saints' opposition to slavery.

Concerning the non-Mormons' apprehensions regarding the Mormon population within the county, one writer reported:

> They came to our county thus friendless and penniless, seeking (as they said) but a temporary asylum . . . They always declared . . . that, whenever a respectable portion of the citizens of this county should request it, they would promptly leave us in peace as they found us. That period had now arrived . . . Their rapid emigration, large purchases . . . they are eastern men, whose manners, habits, customs, and even dialect are essentially different from our own. They are non-slave holders and opposed to slavery. . . In addition to all this, they are charged, as they have hitherto been, with keeping up a constant communication with our Indian tribes on our frontier, with declaring, even from the pulpit, that the Indians are a part of God's chosen people, destined by heaven to inherit this land in common with themselves . . . The religious tenets of this people are so different from the present Churches of the age, that they always have and always will excite deep prejudices against them.[98]

In their grievances against their Mormon neighbors, the Clay County citizens admitted they had no constitutional right to expel the Saints from their midst. They suggested, however, that the removal of the Mormons was the only way to avert an armed crisis. "We, therefore, in the spirit of frank and friendly kindness," they wrote, "do advise them to seek a home where they may obtain large and separate bodies of land, and have a community of their own."[99]

The sparsely inhabited territory of Wisconsin was specifically recommended to Church leaders. Wisconsin as a possible alternative to Missouri brought forth various reactions, including one from Wisconsin itself. *The Dubuque Visitor*, a Wisconsin newspaper, responded to the citizens of Clay County with an editorial, "Do not, we pray you, make our territory the receptacle of *all* your nuisances." To Church leaders they wrote, "We pray you, be assured that your 'promised land' is not in Wisconsin; and although we are tolerably northern in latitude, we very much fear, should you follow the advice of your friends in Clay, you might find the climate too hot for you."[100]

A few days following the reception of the request to vacate, Church leaders in Missouri convened in a public meeting in Liberty to consider a course of action. The Saints responded to the citizens' request as follows:

> Resolved, first: For the sake of friendship, and to be in a covenant of peace with the citizens of Clay county and they to be in a covenant of peace with us, notwithstanding the necessary loss of property and expense we incur in moving, we comply with the requisitions of their resolutions in leaving Clay county.[101]

In early August 1836, the Saints began their exodus from Liberty, Clay County. The principal route of travel was over a ford of the Crooked River that led to Rockford Township. Eventually, Caldwell County, from the northern portion of Ray County, was created as a "Mormon county." When the Saints left Liberty in 1836, little did they know that their Church leaders in Ohio would return to the jail there for a bitter period of confinement.

The frontier community of Liberty built a small jail in 1833, about the time the Saints arrived from Jackson County. Joseph Smith, Sidney Rigdon, Lyman Wight, Alexander McRae, Caleb Baldwin, and Hyrum Smith were imprisoned in the Liberty Jail on 29 November 1838. The order committing them to the jail was issued on the same day they began their journey from Richmond, 29 November 1838. Austin A. King, the judge at the Richmond court, wrote:

> To the Keeper of the Jail of Clay County; Greetings: Whereas [the prisoners] have been brought before me, Austin A. King, Judge of the Fifth Judicial Circuit in the State of Missouri, and charged with the offense of treason against the State of Missouri, and the said defendants, on their examination before me, being held to answer further to said charge [in Daviess and Caldwell counties] and there being no jail in said counties: these [instructions] are therefore to command you that you receive the said [prisoners] into your custody in the jail of the said county of Clay, there to remain until they be delivered therefrom by due course of law.[102]

Liberty Jail, Liberty, Missouri
(Joseph Smith's 1839 epistle written here
became LDS D&C 121–123)
RLDS Archives—unknown, 1905

A crowd of people from Liberty and the surrounding area met Joseph Smith and his associates as they entered the jail. Their appearance disappointed several individuals in the crowd because the Church leaders resembled other men in appearance. After the men were unloaded from the wagon, "the door was opened, and, one by one, the tall and well

Liberty Jail, Stone Floor, Liberty, Missouri
(Sidney Rigdon was sick much of the time during his
imprisonment)
RLDS Archives—unknown, before 1910

proportioned forms of the prisoners entered. The Prophet Joseph was the last of the number who lingered behind," recalled Lyman O. Littlefield, a resident of Liberty. Joseph Smith "turned partly around, with a slow and dignified movement, and looked upon the multitude. Then turning away, and lifting his hat, he said, in a distinct voice, 'Good afternoon, gentlemen.' The next moment he had passed out of sight."[103] Joseph entered the only access to the jail, a single door that opened into the upper room.

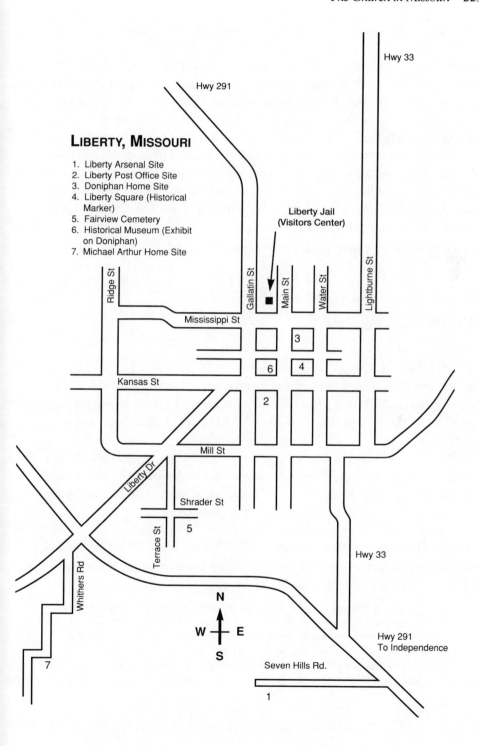

Hwy 33

Hwy 291

LIBERTY, MISSOURI

1. Liberty Arsenal Site
2. Liberty Post Office Site
3. Doniphan Home Site
4. Liberty Square (Historical Marker)
5. Fairview Cemetery
6. Historical Museum (Exhibit on Doniphan)
7. Michael Arthur Home Site

Liberty Jail
(Visitors Center)

Ridge St

Gallatin St

Main St

Water St

Lightburne St

Mississippi St

3

6   4

Kansas St

2

Mill St

Liberty Dr

Shrader St

Terrace St   5

Whithers Rd

Hwy 33

N

W ┼ E

S

Hwy 291
To Independence

7

Seven Hills Rd.

1

During the next several months, the six men were closely confined in a dark and cramped cell. The jail, a sturdy structure built in 1833 at a cost of six hundred dollars, consisted of two stories. It was about fourteen feet square, with only one small, heavily barred window measuring one foot by two feet. This window provided fresh air and natural light into their jail cell. The interior consisted of two rooms, an upper and a lower room. The lower room, or "dungeon," was lighted by two narrow window grates with heavy iron bars and was accessed by a trap door. The outside wall was made of rough-hewn limestone two feet thick, and an inside wall consisted of twelve-inch hewn oak logs. A twelve-inch space filled with loose rock separated the two walls. Combined, the walls made a formidable barrier four feet thick. For the Mormon prisoners, Liberty Jail was "hell surrounded with demons."[104]

LIBERTY JAIL (LDS VISITORS CENTER)

The Liberty Jail is located north of the Liberty town center and is situated on Mississippi Street between Gallatin and Main streets.

Historical Background

During Joseph Smith's incarceration in Liberty Jail, he dictated a letter to Church leaders in Quincy, Illinois. Sections 121, 122, and 123 of the LDS *Doctrine and Covenants* consist of extracts from this letter, which was written between 20 and 25 March 1839. The letter consists of two installments, both signed by the prisoners. The first, dated 20 March 1839, is approximately seventeen pages. The second installment is a continuation of the Church epistle consisting of another twelve pages, but it is not dated. The latter part is addressed to Emma Smith at Quincy, Illinois. A letter written by Joseph on 21 March gave instructions regarding the disposition of the letter; it was first to be read by the family and then delivered to Church leaders in Quincy.

We cannot adequately reconstruct Joseph Smith's experience in Liberty Jail between 1 December 1838 and 6 April 1839. This tragic experience lies hidden behind the phrases of those who languished there. Shortly before their anticipated departure, Joseph wrote to Emma:

> I sit down just as the sun is going down, as we peek through the grates of this lonesome prison, to write to you, that I may make known to you my situation. It is I believe . . . now about five months and six days since I have been under the grimace of a guard night and day, and within the walls, grates and screeching iron doors of a lonesome dirty prison. With emotions known only to God, do I write this letter. The contemplation of the mind under these circumstances

defies the pen, or tongue, or angels to describe or paint to the human being who never experienced what we experience. This night we expect, is the last night we shall try our weary joints and bones on our dirty straw couches in these walls, let our case hereafter be as it may . . . We cannot get into a worse hole than this. We shall not stay here but one night besides this, if that, thank God. We shall never cast a lingering wish after liberty in Clay County, Missouri. We have enough of it to last forever.[105]

Alexander Doniphan Home, Liberty, Missouri
(Alexander Doniphan brought new bride here in 1837)
Clay County Museum and Historical Society—unknown, unknown

ALEXANDER DONIPHAN HOME SITE

The Alexander Doniphan home site is located at 125 North Main and is situated on the east side of Main between Mississippi and Franklin streets.

Historical Background

Alexander Doniphan was a lawyer. One of his early legal clients in Clay County was the Mormons. The Saints had recently been run out of Jackson County and had asked Doniphan to represent them in several types of legal actions against those who had driven them from their homes. He continued to serve them as legal counsel and, as a member of the legislature, was instrumental in the creation of a "Mormon county," called Caldwell. Doniphan recalled, "I was a member of the legislature and drew the bill organizing Caldwell County for the Mormons exclusively, and the offices of the county were given to their people."[106]

With a temporary settlement completed between the Saints and their neighbors in Clay County, Doniphan turned his attention to other matters, including his marriage to Elizabeth Jane Thornton in 1837. He and his wife moved into a single-story brick home at 125 North Main where they lived until 1846.

While living in this home, Doniphan played another significant role in the history of the Saints in Missouri. His position as a leader of the Clay County Militia placed him at odds with his superiors in October 1838. When required to execute Church leaders at Far West, he refused.[107]

Several years later, Doniphan was visited at his home in Liberty by Orrin Porter Rockwell's mother. Her son had been arrested for attempted murder in the case of former Governor Boggs' attempted assassination. Doniphan took the case. Eventually, Rockwell was released when the Jackson County grand jury refused to indict him.

LIBERTY ARSENAL SITE

The Liberty Arsenal site is located approximately three miles south of Liberty and is situated on the south side of Seven Hills Road.

Liberty Arsenal, Liberty, Missouri
(Missouri Militia used this arsenal during the Mormon period)
Clay County Museum and Historical Society—unknown, unknown

Historical Background

The buildings (barracks, officers' quarters, magazine, storehouse, and utility buildings) were all constructed of brick. The original buildings and parade grounds covered ten acres on a hill overlooking the Missouri River Valley. In 1838, the Clay County Militia, known as the "Blues," drew supplies for an expedition to nearby Daviess and Caldwell counties under the direction of Alexander Doniphan. For the next several weeks and months, they tried to establish peace between the Mormons and the mobs. Eventually, they, along with several other units, witnessed the Saints' surrender at Far West, Missouri, just before the Saints' exodus from the state commenced.

LIBERTY SQUARE

Liberty Square is located in the center of town and is bounded by Main, Franklin, Water, and Kansas streets.

Historical Background

Located at Liberty Square is a State Historical Society marker that includes information about Liberty's founding and colorful history. The marker states, in part, "In Liberty is the site of the jail where Mormon Prophet Joseph Smith was held, 1838."

FAIRVIEW CEMETERY

The Fairview Cemetery is located southwest of the town center and is situated on the south side of Shrader Street.

Historical Background

Fairview Cemetery is the location of Alexander Doniphan's grave. Doniphan moved from Liberty, Missouri, in 1863 when he moved to St. Louis. Following the conclusion of the Civil War, he returned to western Missouri and settled in Richmond. For the next thirty years, Doniphan continued to practice law and to pursue other business ventures. He died on 8 August 1887 at his home in Richmond and was later buried at Fairview Cemetery. He has not only been honored by the Saints but also by many of his peers. U.S. Speaker of the House Champ Clark of Missouri stated in 1917, "If Doniphan had been a Massachusetts man . . . the world would hardly contain the books that would have been written about him."[108]

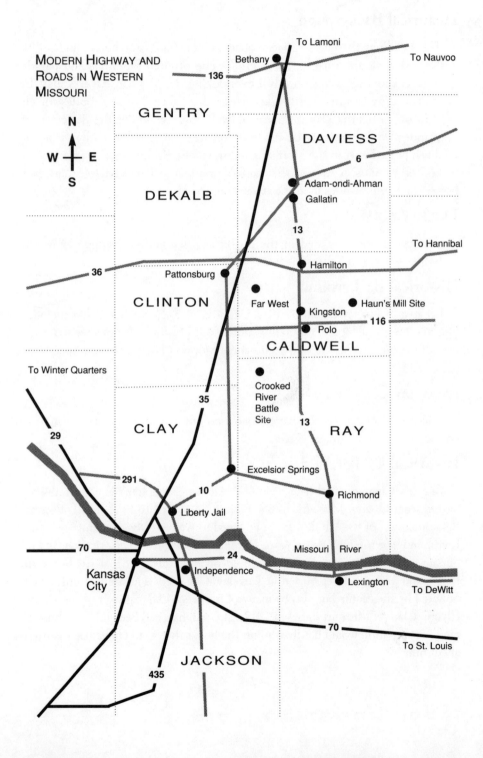

MODERN HIGHWAY AND
ROADS IN WESTERN
MISSOURI

N
W E
S

To Lamoni

To Nauvoo

Bethany

136

GENTRY

DAVIESS

6

DEKALB

Adam-ondi-Ahman

Gallatin

13

To Hannibal

36

Pattonsburg

Hamilton

CLINTON

Far West

Haun's Mill Site

Kingston

116

Polo

CALDWELL

To Winter Quarters

Crooked
River
Battle
Site

35

13

CLAY

RAY

29

Excelsior Springs

291

10

Richmond

Liberty Jail

70

Missouri   River

24

Kansas
City

Independence

Lexington

To DeWitt

70

To St. Louis

JACKSON

435

Liberty Post Office, Liberty, Missouri
(Post office in use during the Mormon period)
Clay County Museum and Historical Society—unknown, unknown

Kingston, Caldwell County, Missouri

Kingston is located approximately fifty-seven miles northeast of Independence.

The first white settler in Kingston was Jesse Mann, who came in March 1831. Within a few months, several other settlers arrived to begin residency. The first preachers visited Kingston as early as 1832. They lived in Richmond but preached in Kingston on circuit. Kingston was part of Ray County until 26 December 1836 when Caldwell County was

Main Street, Kingston, Missouri
(Large Mormon population here in 1838)
Kingston Historical Society—unknown, c1910

organized. The first school in Caldwell County was established in Kingston in 1838. The teacher was a Mormon, Mary Ann Duty.

STATE HISTORICAL MARKER

The state historical marker for Kingston is located in the courthouse yard at the southwest corner. The courthouse is situated in the center of town.

Historical Background

The marker states:

In fertile Shoal Creek Valley, Kingston was laid out in 1843 to replace Far West as the seat of Caldwell County. Organized in 1836, the county was to be for Latter Day Saints (Mormons) ejected from Jackson County in 1833 and asked to leave Clay County, 1836. Far West, here, was their county seat and Church headquarters. When the "Mormon War" began, Far West had 3,000 settlers. Hostilities between Latter Day Saints and their neighbors arose over political, social, and economic differences. First hostile acts were at the Latter Day Saints' settlement Adam-ondi-Ahman and DeWitt in Daviess and Carroll counties. Involved were Missouri Militiamen and Caldwell County Militia of Mormons. After massacre of 17 [now believed to be 18] Latter Day Saints at Haun's Mill, the Caldwell Militia surrendered at Far West, November 1, 1838.

Church leaders, Joseph Smith among them were accused of treason and ordered shot. They were jailed when Brig. Gen. Alexander W. Doniphan refused to enforce the order. Some were freed, others escaped, as charges were unsustained. About 12,000 Latter Day Saints removed to Illinois by June of 1839.

John Whitmer Gravestone, Kingston, Missouri
(John Whitmer, one of the eight witnesses, buried here in 1878)
LDS Historical Department—George E. Anderson, 1911

KINGSTON CEMETERY

The Kingston Cemetery is located just northeast of the Courthouse Square.

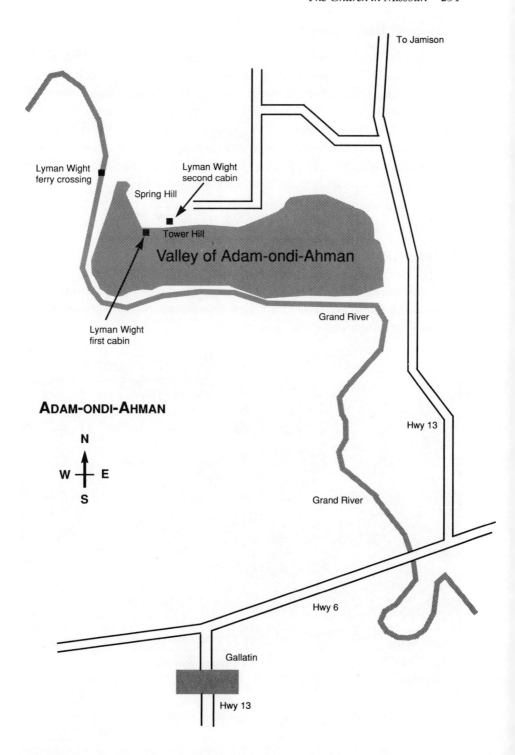

To Jamison

Lyman Wight
ferry crossing

Lyman Wight
second cabin

Spring Hill

Tower Hill

Valley of Adam-ondi-Ahman

Lyman Wight
first cabin

Grand River

ADAM-ONDI-AHMAN

N

W — E

S

Hwy 13

Grand River

Hwy 6

Gallatin

Hwy 13

Historical Background

John Whitmer's grave is located in the Kingston Cemetery. Whitmer, a Missouri Church leader and *Book of Mormon* witness, left the Church in 1838. He, along with most other dissenters, remained in Missouri during the 1838 Mormon War. He returned to Far West after the Saints' removal and remained in the area until his death in 1878.

He became a respected citizen in the area; and upon his death, a local newspaper printed a notice indicating that "Mr. Whitmer remained at Far West and has since been a highly respected and law abiding citizen."[109]

Adam-ondi-Ahman, Daviess County, Missouri

Adam-ondi-Ahman is located approximately eighty-five miles northeast of Independence. On 19 May 1838, Joseph Smith led a survey party to central Daviess County to found a new gathering place for the Saints. Within two years,

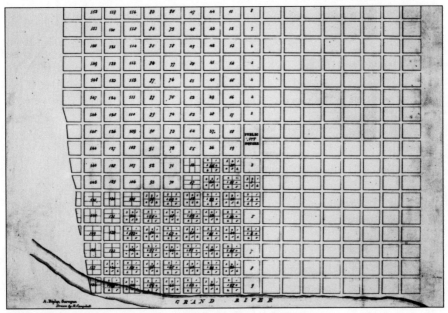

1838 Adam-ondi-Ahman Plat Map, Adam-ondi-Ahman, Missouri
(Proposed city at Diahman)
LDS Historical Department—R. Campbell, 1838

the settlement at Far West, approximately twenty-five miles to the southwest, had already doubled in size from its original mile-square plat. The new community was called Adam-ondi-Ahman. During this first visit, the Prophet received the following revelation:

> Adam-ondi-Ahman because, said he, it is the place where Adam shall visit his people or the Ancient of Days shall sit as spoken of by Daniel the Prophet.[110]

Joseph Smith directed the city to be laid out north and west of Tower Hill, because the remains of an ancient alter were found on its summit. The town square was then located at the top of the hill.

Lyman Wight, an early Mormon convert, had a home built at the foot of Spring Hill. He operated a ferry about a half mile upstream. Following Joseph Smith's visit, the community grew rapidly; and within weeks, several dozen log cabins were built.

During another visit on 28 June 1838, Joseph Smith organized a stake at Adam-ondi-Ahman. Joseph's uncle, John Smith, was sustained as stake president, with Reynolds Cahoon and Lyman Wight as counselors and Vinson Knight as acting bishop. The hymn "Adam-ondi-Ahman" was sung at the closing of the organizational meeting.

Other Saints arrived from the East; and in early October, part of Kirtland Camp, consisting of Saints coming from Kirtland, Ohio, settled in the community. Adam-ondi-Ahman was to have been two miles square in area with about six hundred inhabitants living within that locality.

Brigham Young dedicated a public square. The community had a functioning Church organization and a bishop's storehouse.

The Church experienced serious difficulties in Missouri, but the Saints also enjoyed happy days. During this period, Edward Stevenson recalled,

> I have often seen the Prophet [Joseph] indulge in a game of checkers. He was cheerful—often wrestling with Sidney Rigdon. One time he had his pants torn badly, but had a good laugh over it. In Missouri, when mob forces oppressed the Saints, we were encamped in Adam-ondi-Ahman, mostly around campfires without tents. One night the snow fell four or five inches. The Prophet, seeing our forlorn condition, called on us to form into two parties—Lyman Wight at the head of one line and he (Joseph) heading the other line—to have a sham battle. The weapons were snowballs. We set to with a will full of glee and fun.[111]

Another young man, Orange Wight, recalled,

> We often bathed in the limpid waters of the Grand River, although but a boy I was invited to bathe with [the Church leaders]. At one time we had a jolly time . . . There was Joseph the Prophet, my father Lyman Wight, Sidney Rigdon, and several others, our amusement consisted in part in seeing Brother Rigdon swim. He was so corpulent that he was forced to lay on his back to swim, he would swim in that way until his shoulders would strike the sand bar and then he could turn, but would flop back in deep water.[112]

Following disagreements between the Saints and the old settlers, severe persecution prompted the Mormons to leave northern Missouri. Albert Rockwood wrote:

> About this time [6 October 1838] the Sheriff of Caldwell County took forty stands of arms that were on the road to arm the mob. The Missourians gathered from all the upper counties to join the mob to the number of several hundreds, they continued to encamp in various places for several miles round Adam-ondi-Ahman for about two weeks, taking some prisoners, robbing and insulting in various ways many of the brethren, and driving many from their homes that were scattered about the county, but those at the city of Adam-ondi-Ahman were not molested only threatened. They were constantly under arms and on the watch. The brethren were from this place [Far West] by hundreds to their relief.[113]

By the end of 1838, the settlement was abandoned.

SPRING HILL

Spring Hill is located north of Grand River and northwest of Gallatin. The LDS Church has placed a marker at the crest relating the story of Spring Hill.

Historical Background

Joseph Smith, accompanied by other Church leaders, visited the Wight settlement at Spring Hill, where they laid out a city. The city was given the name "Adam-ondi-Ahman," in keeping with Joseph Smith's statement that it was so named by the Lord. The name was used as early as 1835.[114] W. W. Phelps wrote a hymn entitled "Adam-ondi-Ahman" and published it in the *Messenger and Advocate* in June 1835. The LDS D&C 78/RLDS D&C 77, published in the 1835 edition of *The Doctrine and Covenants*, spoke of establishing the "foundations of Adam-ondi-Ahman."

George W. Robinson, clerk for the First Presidency, described the visit on 19 May 1838:

In the after part of the day, Presidents Smith and Rigdon and myself, went to Wight's Ferry about a half mile from this place up the river, for the purpose of selecting and laying claim to City Plat near said ferry . . . which was called Spring Hill, a name appropriated by the brethren present, but afterwards named by the mouth of [the] Lord and was called Adam-Ondi-Ahman, because said he it is the place where Adam shall come to visit his people, or the Ancient of days shall sit as spoken by Daniel the Prophet.[115]

VALLEY OF ADAM-ONDI-AHMAN

The Valley of Adam-ondi-Ahman is located just north of the Grand River and is situated south of Spring Hill.

Aerial View, Adam-ondi-Ahman, Missouri
(Lyman Wight had a ferry on the Grand River in the background)
LDS Visual Resource Library—unknown, 1979

Historical Background

Unique to Mormon belief is Joseph Smith's teachings regarding the Valley of Adam-ondi-Ahman. The Saints believe that the first patriarch, Adam, called his righteous posterity together "into the valley of Adam-ondi-Ahman, and there bestowed upon them his last blessing."[116] Orson Pratt indicated that the name means "Valley of God, where Adam dwelt. It is in the original language spoken by Adam."[117]

Tower Hill, Adam-ondi-Ahman, Missouri
(Traditionally identified as site of an early sacred alter)
LDS Historical Department—George E. Anderson, 1907

TOWER HILL

Tower Hill is located east of Spring Hill.

Historical Background

During the visit of Church leaders to Wight's ferry in May 1838, George W. Robinson wrote,

> The next morning we struck our tents, and marched [across] Grand River at the mouth of Honey Creek at a place called Nelson's ferry. Grand River is a beautiful, deep and rapid stream . . . [W]e next kept up the river mostly in the timber for ten miles, until we came to Col. Lyman Wight who lives at the foot of Tower Hill, a name appropriated by Pres. Smith, in consequence of the remains of an old Nephitish Alter or Tower, where we camped for the sabbath.[118]

Lyman Wight Home (Second Cabin), Adam-ondi-Ahman, Missouri
(Lyman Wight was an initial and prominent settler here)
LDS Historical Department—unknown, before 1906

LYMAN WIGHT'S SECOND CABIN

Lyman Wight's second cabin was located about half way down Tower Hill, west of where the alter was located on the hill.

Lyman Wight Home (Second Cabin), Adam-ondi-Ahman, Missouri
(Saints evacuated their city January 1838 during the Mormon War)
LDS Historical Department—George E. Anderson, 1907

Historical Background

Lyman Wight's first cabin was located on the south side of Spring Hill. On the Grand River, Wight ran a ferry located northwest of this first cabin. He then built his second cabin on Tower Hill in 1838.

Lyman Wight's Stable, Adam-ondi-Ahman, Missouri
(Joseph Smith participated in a snowball fight near here)
BYU Harold B. Library—Edward Stevenson, 1895

Gallatin, Daviess County, Missouri

Gallatin, Missouri, is located approximately eighty-one miles northeast of Independence and is also about four miles south of Adam-ondi-Ahman.

Public Square, Gallatin, Missouri
(Site of "Election Day Battle" when the Mormons attempted to vote)
LDS Historical Department—George E. Anderson, 1907

Gallatin was named for Albert Gallatin, the secretary of the treasury who served under Presidents Jefferson and Madison. When Gallatin took office, the national debt was $10 million because the federal government had assumed the Revolutionary War debts of the states. When Gallatin left office, he had reduced the debt by half.

The Gallatin area was not permanently settled until the 1830s. The first business in Gallatin was established in 1835. On 29 December 1836, the County of Daviess was established; and Gallatin was incorporated in 1858.

Trouble openly broke out between the Saints and their neighbors on election day at Gallatin, Daviess County, on 6 August 1838. Colonel William P. Peniston, candidate for the state legislature, wanted to prevent the Mormons from casting their ballots. With his supporters, he harangued the crowd who gathered in town against the Mormons. Though outnumbered greatly, the Mormon men won the ensuing fight and proceeded to vote. No one was killed, but the exaggerated reports of the affair reached the governor's office in Jefferson City.

Governor Boggs issued his "extermination order" two months later. To General Clark, he wrote, "The Mormons must be treated as enemies and must be exterminated or driven from the state, if necessary for the public good. Their outrages are beyond all description."[119]

DAVIESS COUNTY HISTORICAL MARKER

The Daviess County historical marker is located just east of the courthouse in the Gallatin business square.

Historical Background

The Daviess County historical marker was erected by the State Historical Society of Missouri and the State Highway Commission in 1953.

The marker states:

> GALLATIN—This Grand River town, platted in 1837 as the seat of Daviess County, is named in honor of Albert Gallatin, Secretary of the Treasury, 1801–1813. Settlers were in the area as early as 1830 and in 1836 the county was formed. Adam-ondi-Ahman, 5 miles northwest was settled by the Mormons on direction of Prophet Joseph Smith, 1838. The name is said to mean "Adam's Consecrated Land," for here, according to Smith, Adam blessed all the patriarchs before his death. At this place, also known as "Adam's Grave," Smith announced the discovery of the altar, on a nearby hill, where, he said, these ancients worshipped. Hostilities broke out between the Mormons and the anti-Mormons and a sharp skirmish took place in Gallatin. In 1839, when the Mormons were expelled from Missouri, Adam-ondi-Ahman was abandoned. Established in Gallatin were the Daviess County Female Academy, chartered in 1849 and Daviess County Academy, and Masonic Hall, chartered in 1855. In 1893, Grand River College was moved here from Edinbury in Grundy County.

Crooked River, Ray County, Missouri

CROOKED RIVER BATTLE SITE

Crooked River is on private property and is unmarked. The battle site is located approximately thirty-five miles from Independence.

Historical Background

Following the first serious clash between the Mormons and non-Mormons in the northern counties at Gallatin, Daviess County, on 6 August 1838, relations

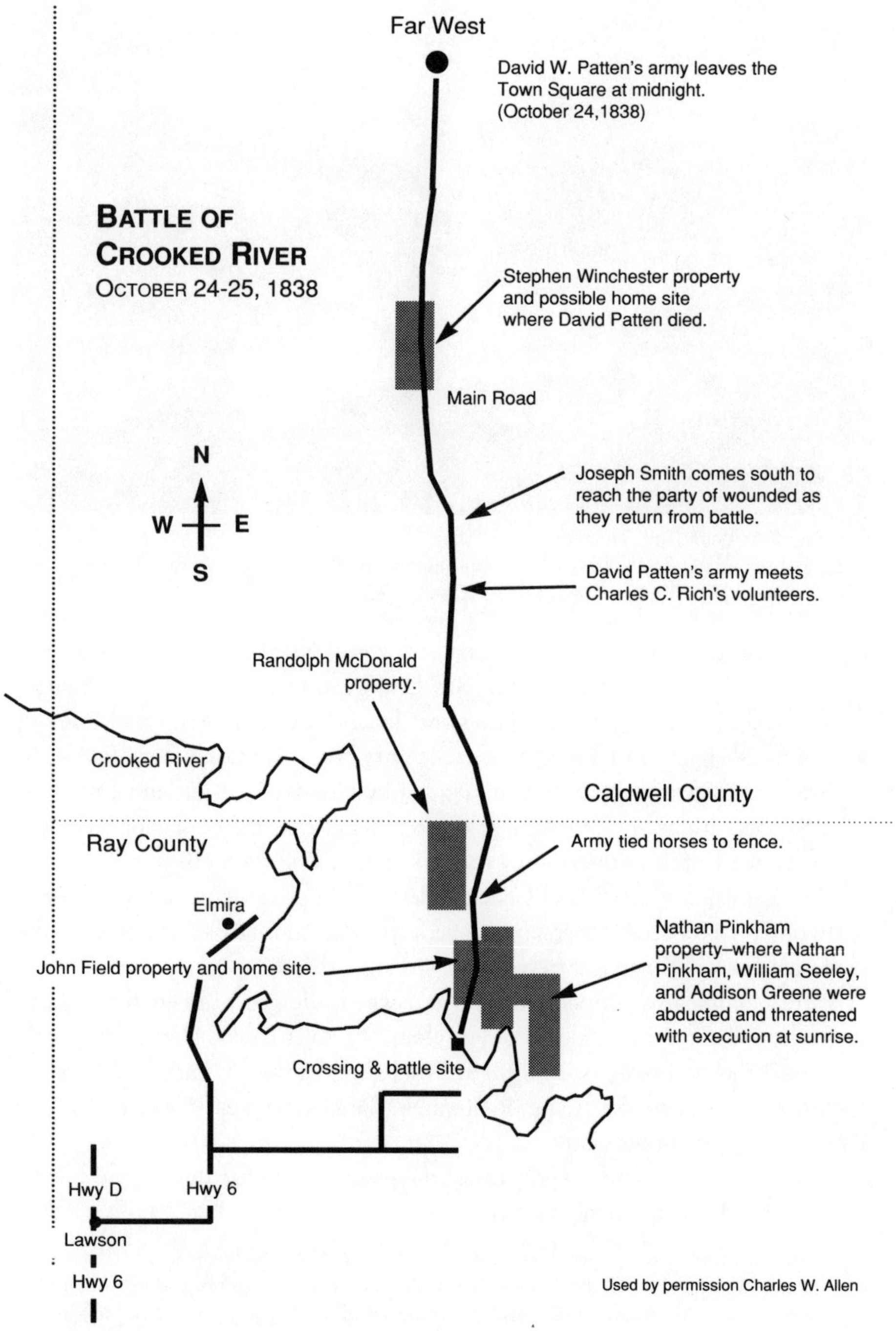

Far West

David W. Patten's army leaves the Town Square at midnight. (October 24,1838)

BATTLE OF CROOKED RIVER
OCTOBER 24-25, 1838

Stephen Winchester property and possible home site where David Patten died.

Main Road

N
W — E
S

Joseph Smith comes south to reach the party of wounded as they return from battle.

David Patten's army meets Charles C. Rich's volunteers.

Randolph McDonald property.

Crooked River

Caldwell County

Army tied horses to fence.

Ray County

Elmira

Nathan Pinkham property–where Nathan Pinkham, William Seeley, and Addison Greene were abducted and threatened with execution at sunrise.

John Field property and home site.

Crossing & battle site

Hwy D   Hwy 6

Lawson

Hwy 6

Used by permission Charles W. Allen

Crooked River Battle Site, Missouri
(Site of Mormon and Ray County militia confrontation in 1838)
LDS Historical Department—George E. Anderson, 1907

between the two groups went from bad to worse. Northern Missouri was in a state of civil war by 18 October. The Ray County militia, under Captain Samuel Bogart, mobilized six days later. The same day, his men captured two Mormons who were suspected of being spies. Seventy-five Mormons from Far West mobilized into two companies commanded by Charles C. Rich and David W. Patten, when drums beat at midnight calling them to the public square. They left Far West in an effort to rescue the prisoners held by Bogart's men.

Now known as the Battle of Crooked River, both groups engaged in a fight at dawn on 25 October. As dawn approached, the Mormons arrived at a ford on the banks of Crooked River, just twenty miles from Far West.

Patten's company, silhouetted by the dawn, made good targets for Bogart's men who were in a concealed position along the river banks. During the battle that freed the prisoners, two Mormons, including David W. Patten, were shot. Patten was taken to the home of Stephen Winchester near Far West, where Patten died several hours later.

James Hendricks and several other men were wounded during the battle. Drusilla Hendricks recalled this incident:

> The children soon came over and told me that their father said that Bro. Hendricks was shot. Then I went to the field to give vent to my feelings . . . I went back to the house and found the children all crying. I went to [the] loom

to try and weave to let on to them that I did not believe the report about their father. I could not weave at all, but had not sat there but a few moments when I saw Mr. T. Sniger, he did not belong to the Church, but was a good man, getting off his horse at the gate. I saw him wipe his eyes. I knew that he was crying. He came to the door and said, "Mr. Hendricks wishes you to come to him."

When she arrived at the location where her husband had been taken, she attempted to speak to him; but he was unable to speak or move "anymore than if he was dead." Drusilla wrote:

> My husband was shot in the neck where it cut off all feeling of his body. It is of no use for me to try and tell how I felt for that is impossible, but I could not have shed a tear if all had been dead before me. I went to work to try and get my husband warm, but could not. I rubbed and steamed him, but could get no circulation. He was dead from his neck down. One of the brethren told me how he fell . . . On hearing this it melted me to tears and I felt better.[120]

Exaggerated reports of this skirmish reached Jefferson City, the state capital. As a result of these rumors and false reports, Governor Boggs issued the executive order that the Saints must be "exterminated or driven from the state."

Haun's Mill, Caldwell County, Missouri

HAUN'S MILL SITE

Haun's Mill is difficult to find, and the roads are impassable in bad weather. The RLDS Church owns the site and has marked it. It is located approximately sixty-five miles from Independence.

Haun's Mill was the second settlement founded in what would become Caldwell County. In 1834, Jacob Haun came from Wisconsin and built a grist mill on Shoal Creek. Within a short time, other Mormons moved to the area and established a blacksmith shop and a sawmill and built several log cabins.

Haun's Mill Site, Missouri
(Near site where Haun's Mill massacre took place in 1838)
LDS Historical Department—George E. Anderson, 1907

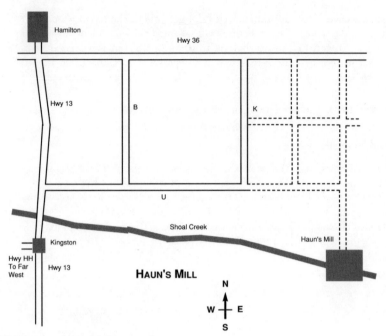

Historical Background

Abner Blackburn's impression of the land in the area of Haun's Mill rings with bright hope and optimism for the future:

> [We] started on our long journey to [Missouri]. Soon there were more prairies and fewer people, but the game was more plentiful. Deer, bear, turkey, wild hogs, and bees and snakes galore and no white man in sight for a whole day or more . . . This is prairie country with timber on the streams of water. This is the backwoods without a drought. [We] came to a beautiful place . . . The land was rich and wild game in abundance, wild strawberries and other kinds of wild fruit. Fish in the streams and bees in the forest with all kinds of nuts in the woods. This was truly a paradise on earth. We had a beautiful place for a home.[121]

Following the Battle of Crooked River, where two Mormons and one Missourian were killed, exaggerated reports of the skirmish spread across the state.

Three days later, on 30 October, a renegade Missouri militia unit arrived at Haun's Mill at Shoal Creek. Known as the Haun's Mill Massacre, what turned out to be the most savage action of the Mormon War occurred when Colonel Thomas Jennings' men killed eighteen people and wounded another fifteen.

Haun's Mill Site, Missouri
(Memorial mill stone at massacre site)
LDS Historical Department—George E. Anderson, 1907

During the afternoon, approximately two hundred forty men approached Haun's Mill. Joseph Young, Sr. described the incident:

> The banks of Shoal creek on either side teemed with children sporting and playing, while their mothers were engaged in domestic employments, and their fathers employed in guarding the mills and other property, while others were engaged in gathering in their crops for their winter consumption. The weather was very pleasant, the sun shone clear, all was tranquil, and no one expressed any apprehension of the awful crisis that was near us—even at our doors.[122]

The militia approached the area sometime around 4:00 P.M., which caused the women and children to flee for safety. Many of the men sought protection in the blacksmith shop near the mill. During a hail of bullets, Amanda Smith seized her two little girls. "Yet though we were women, with tender children, in flight for our lives, the demons poured volley after volley to kill us."[123]

Ten-year-old Sardius Smith, Amanda's son, was found hiding under the bellows and was quickly killed when a muzzle was placed against his head and fired. "Nits will make lice," the soldier said later, "and if he had lived he would have become a Mormon."[124] Another Smith child, seven-year-old Alma, saw his father and brother murdered and was himself shot. Those who survived hid themselves during the night in the woods nearby fearing another brutal attack by Missouri militia units roaming in the vicinity.

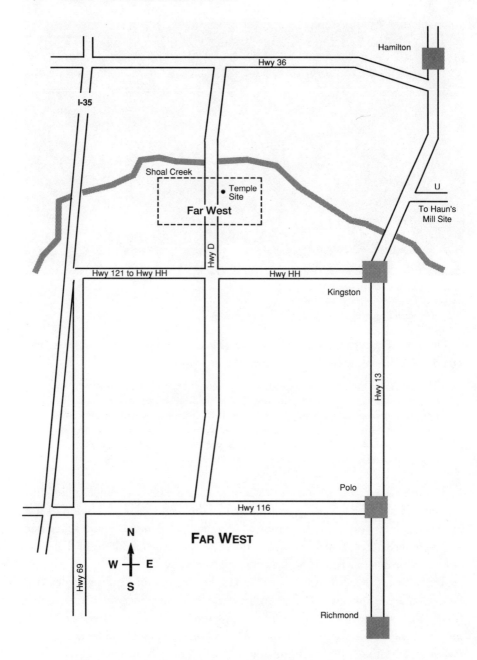

Far West, Caldwell County, Missouri

Far West is located approximately fifty-five miles northeast of Independence.

When the Saints left Jackson County, they were instructed by Church leaders in Ohio to remain in the area. Eventually, the majority crossed the Missouri River and found refuge in Clay County when they assured the communities that their asylum there was only temporary. Within two and a half years of their arrival, the old settlers of Clay became uneasy about the Mormon presence. On 29 June 1836, the county's leading citizens called upon the Saints to leave Clay County to avoid problems similar to those in Jackson County.

The Saints denied the complaints against them but made a "covenant of peace" to leave the county and accepted the offer of the local community leaders to raise funds by subscription in each township to help the Saints resettle in a more permanent location.

In August 1836, W. W. Phelps and John Whitmer, two counselors in the Missouri presidency, selected the 640-acre site for Far West. The site selected by Church leaders was in the sparsely settled northern area of Missouri. Settlement of this area at Shoal Creek began in October 1836. They petitioned for their own county, which they called Caldwell, with Far West as county seat.

By the fall of 1838, nearly two thousand farms were established. The Saints bought approximately 250,000 acres from the federal government at a cost of $318,000. In Far West, the Saints built nearly two hundred homes, several dry-goods stores, three family groceries, half a dozen blacksmith shops, and two hotels. They excavated for a temple and moved the local schoolhouse to the center of the town square to be used also as a church, town hall, and courthouse. The school section of land sold for $7.90 an acre, providing a school fund of about five thousand dollars. The town ordinances forbade saloons. A Church conference in October 1837 voted not to support any shops selling spirituous liquors, tea, coffee, or tobacco—an early observance of the Mormon dietary law known as the Word of Wisdom.

Albert Rockwell described the city in his journal:

> The public square in the center contains ten acres, the four main streets are each eight rods wide, the other [streets] are six rods wide. The squares contain four acres each, and are calculated for four buildings, (streets [are] marked First, Second, Third, Fourth, North Street also East, South, and West). The city is situated on a high rolling prairie, the timber is on Shoal and Goos creeks which are from two to four miles and nearly surrounds the city. The plan is the first square mile of the city. It is continued out on the same plan. The House of the

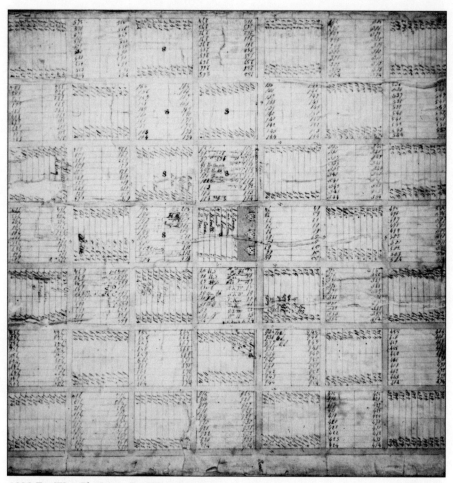

1838 Far West Plat Map, Far West, Missouri
(Far West plat conforms to "City of Zion" concept)
LDS Historical Department—unknown, c1838

Lord is to stand in the center of the public square. The corner stone was laid on the 4th of July last. Most of the lots in the first square mile are sold. City lots can be bought second handed but it is thought not advisable to purchase only of the Bishop. Plenty of lots are yet for sale in the second mile which brings the neighbors one half mile to the square.[125]

Far West was the largest Mormon community in Missouri before being abandoned in 1839. Albert P. Rockwood wrote from Far West during the difficult period following Joseph Smith's arrest on 3 November 1838 that "more than

6,000 men have been in Far West in one week, with orders from the Governor to exterminate the Mormons. The Brethren are hunted as wild beasts and shot down. Several have been shot in sight of the City." Later that month, he wrote again, "All the Mormons in Caldwell and Daviess Counties have been taken captive unless we would deny the faith." He concluded sorrowfully, "those that deny . . . have gone clear."[126]

General John B. Clark sought out Mary Rollins Lightner and her immediate family. He had been instructed to make sure that the Lightners were safely removed from danger. Governor Boggs protected her because of her service to the family as a seamstress. When Clark offered his protection to Mary, she asked if the other women and children at Far West would be allowed to leave the encircled city. When the answer was no, she announced resolutely, "Then, if that is the case, I refuse to go, for where they die, I will die, for I am a full blooded Mormon, and I am not ashamed to own it."[127]

After Far West was taken by Lucas' militia force on 31 October, no public meetings were held in the city until December. The High Council reconvened:

> [A]greeable to appointment the standing High Councilors met, when it was found that several were absent, some of them have had to flee for their lives, therefore it being necessary that those vacancies be filled the meeting was called for that purpose, and, also, to express each others feelings respecting the word of the lord. President Brigham Young presiding, the council was opened by prayer by Elder Heber C. Kimball.[128]

During the meeting, several brethren, including Simeon Carter, John Badger, Solomon Hancock, and Thomas Grover, bore testimony to the divinity of the restored gospel; and several said they "did not think Joseph was a fallen prophet."[129]

Because Thomas Marsh, President of the Twelve Apostles, had left the Church, David Patten, a senior member of the Twelve, had been killed at the Battle of Crooked River, and the First Presidency was incarcerated, Brigham Young assumed command and conducted the reorganization of the High Council and the evacuation of the Saints from Missouri. The High Council met in Far West for the last time on 16 January 1839, but this was not the last meeting of Church leaders in Missouri.

Shortly after Joseph Smith and Sidney Rigdon arrived at Far West in March 1838, they began organizing the Twelve Apostles for missionary work to England. The Church Presidency called several new apostles to fill the Quorum of the Twelve on 8 July 1838. This revelation told the Twelve to "take leave of my saints in the city of Far West, on the twenty-sixth day of April next [1839], on the building-spot of my house, saith the Lord."[130] Before the date, the Saints were driven from their homes and the city of Far West.

Wilford Woodruff, one of the newly called members of the Twelve, settled his family in Quincy, Illinois, in the spring of 1839. Soon after his arrival, he prepared himself "to accompany the Twelve to fulfill a certain revelation and commandment of the Lord,[131] which required us to take our leave of the Saints at Far West on the 26th day of April 1839 for the nations of the earth."[132]

This particular commandment was seemingly well known among the Saints and the anti-Mormons. The mobs in Missouri did not believe that Church leaders would attempt a return to Far West to fulfill the commandment but prepared for the possibility anyway.

Several members of the Twelve and those who were to be ordained traveled together. Brigham Young, Orson Pratt, and John Taylor accompanied Woodruff to Missouri from the safety of Illinois. The "roads were full of the Saints that were fleeing from Missouri to Illinois," Woodruff recorded. Sometimes traveling thirty miles a day, the party finally arrived near Far West on 23 April 1839. They hid themselves in a grove for two days waiting to enter Far West.

These Church leaders arrived in Far West just after midnight on 26 April 1839. Woodruff, along with about thirty other members, met under moonlight at the temple site to fulfill the revelation. Woodruff recorded:

> Elder Cutler, the master workman of the [temple] then recommenced laying the foundation of the LORD'S house agreeable to revelation by rolling up a large stone near the southeast corner. The following Twelve were present: Brigham Young, Heber C. Kimball, Orson Pratt, John E. Page and John Taylor, who proceeded to ordain (on the chief corner stone of the building) Wilford Woodruff and George A. Smith, who had been previously nominated by the First Presidency, accepted by the Twelve and acknowledged by the Church to the office of the Twelve to fill the place of those who had fallen.[133]

In the early morning hours following the solemn ceremony, Theodore Turley, one of the Saints who had gathered to witness the services, went to the home of dissident Isaac Russell to bid him farewell. Russell was amazed that Turley was in Far West with the Twelve and remained speechless when he learned that the commandment was obeyed, in spite of the dangerous situation for Church leaders.

During the difficult winter of 1838–1839, thousands of Saints left Missouri for safety. "The stakes of Zion," Elizabeth Haven wrote her cousin in February 1839, "will soon be bereft of all her children." The majority of Mormons emigrated to the Illinois shore of the Mississippi River near Quincy. The people of Illinois

Temple Site, Far West, Missouri
(Dedicated by Church leaders in 1838)
LDS Historical Department—George E.
Anderson, 1907

welcomed these refugees. There
Sarah Rich gave birth to her first
child. Elizabeth Haven found work as
a seamstress for "genteel people."
Drusilla Hendricks nursed her
wounded and ailing husband. For the
Saints, life went on—but with a note
of sadness. "By the river of Babylon
we can sit down," Elizabeth wrote.
"We weep when we remember Zion."[134]

Aerial View, Far West, Missouri
(Temple site, modern view)
LDS Visual Resources Library—unknown,
unknown

TEMPLE SITE

The temple site is located approximately one mile south of Shoal Creek and is
situated east of County Road "D," which runs between Highways 16 and 36.

Historical Background

The monument inscription at the temple site in Far West reads in part:

FAR WEST—A CONSECRATED AND HOLY LAND. From a Revelation to
Joseph Smith "Let the city Far West be a holy and consecrated land unto me

and it shall be called most holy for the ground upon which thou standest is holy."

"Therefore, I command you to build a house unto me for the gathering together of my Saints that they may worship me." Doctrine and Covenants 115:7

RLDS Far West Church/Visitors Center

The RLDS Far West Church/Visitors Center is located across the road from the Temple site.

Historical Background

An RLDS congregation was formed in Far West in 1873. Eventually, a white framed structure, which is still standing, was erected in 1905. Besides its use as a meeting house for the local RLDS members, it serves as a visitors center. Inside the visitors center, a display and a slide show are available.

Traditionally Identified as Joseph Smith Home, Far West, Missouri
(Joseph Smith lived here in 1838)
RLDS Archives—unknown, unknown

Joseph Smith Home Site

The location of the Joseph Smith home site is somewhat uncertain. Most scholars believe he lived near the temple. However, he owned land northeast of the temple site; and his farm was approximately five miles southwest of the temple site.

Historical Background

When Emma arrived at Far West from Ohio, she and Joseph stayed with George and Lucinda Harris for nearly two months before moving into their own home near the temple lot. On 2 June 1838, Emma gave birth to Alexander Hale Smith. Within a short time, bloody conflict arose in northern Missouri between the Saints and the state of Missouri.

Following his arrest by local militia units on 31 October 1838, Joseph was allowed to visit his family in their home at Far West before his move to Richmond, Missouri, to stand trial. Joseph's history states:

> Myself and the fellow prisoners were taken to the town, into the public square, and before our departure we, after much entreaty, were suffered to see our families, being attended all the while by a strong guard. I found my wife and children in tears, who feared we had been shot by those who had sworn to take our lives, and that they would see us no more. When I entered my house, they clung to my garments, their eyes streaming with tears, while mingled emotions of joy and sorrow were manifested in their countenances . . . I was then obliged to take my departure, who can realize the feelings which I experienced at that time, to be thus torn from my companion, and leave her surrounded with monsters in the shape of men, and my children, too, not knowing how their wants would be supplied . . . My partner wept, my children clung to me, until they were thrust from me by the swords of the guards. I felt overwhelmed while I witnessed the scene, and could only recommend them to the love of God whose kindness had followed me to the present time, and who alone could protect them and deliver me from the hands of my enemies, and restore me to my family.[135]

JOHN WHITMER HOME SITE

The John Whitmer home site is situated near the temple site. The exact location of the home site has not been established.

Historical Background

Following the Saints' exodus from Far West, former Church historian and *Book of Mormon* witness John Whitmer returned to an isolated farm around the abandoned city and temple lot. While there, he added his final comments to his Church history, which he had ended in March 1838. The entry in 1838, apparently the official end of his history, states:

John Whitmer Home, Far West, Missouri
(John Whitmer stayed in Far West following the Saints' departure in 1838)
LDS Historical Department—George E. Anderson, 1907

Therefore, I close this history of the Church of Latter Day Saints, hoping that I may be forgiven of my faults, and my sins be blotted out, and in the last day be saved in the kingdom of God, notwithstanding my private situation, which I hope will soon be bettered, and I find favor in the eyes of God, all men and his Saints, Farewell, March 1838.[136]

Water Routes in Missouri

Some of the first Mormons to arrive in Missouri came by water route. Members of the Colesville Branch had begun their journey in Colesville, New York. A short stay in Thompson, Ohio, was ended when Joseph Smith asked them to remove to the new Mormon Zion in Missouri. Their trip, about 1,250 miles from Broome County, New York, to Independence, Missouri, was a combination of land and water travel; but the vast majority was on the water. At St. Louis, Missouri, the Colesville Saints boarded a steamboat that took them on the Missouri River to Independence.

Long before Lewis and Clark made their way on "the muddy artery," the Missouri River was vital to the Indians, explorers, and trappers. After achieving statehood, Missouri soon was the center of all the Far West trade. Caravans of covered wagons and keelboats made their way west. The traders needed merchants to supply them and farmers to feed them. The expanding market attracted new settlements advancing along the Missouri Valley. Soon Lexington and Liberty were established in 1822 and Independence in 1827. By 1830, the entire eastern area of Missouri was filled; and these communities and other towns reached along the Big Muddy to the border on the west.

The steamboats on the Missouri River followed the *Yellowstone* on her first historic trip up the Missouri for the American Fur Company. Soon thereafter, other steamboats made trips from St. Louis to the various ports established on the river.

A common feeling during an earlier time was that "of all the variable things in creation, the most uncertain of all are the actions of a jury, the state of a woman's mind, and the condition of the Missouri River."[137] The couplet reflected the feelings of a people who knew the river well—a river that changed its course without the slightest notice and often left a river craft on a newly made sandbar. Settlers along the river could just as well expect a harvest of corn or catfish when the "Big Muddy" surged at the banks.

W. W. Phelps sent a description of the water routes traveled by the Saints to a newspaper in New York, the *Ontario Phoenix*. Phelp's description stated:

> The Ohio [River], opposite Indiana and Illinois, is a beautiful sheet of water, quite clear and studded with cotton wood, sycamore, locust, etc., and streaked with steamboats from one end to the other. The Mississippi [River] is a serpentine stream, right below St. Louis; guarded on the west, or Missouri shore, by huge bluffs, capt ever and anon with daring shot towers. It is said to be clear

above the Missouri. The Mississippi is the grand middle feeder of the Atlantic Ocean, and already steams and smokes with the commerce of nine states. The Missouri [River] is the capsheaf—it is always rily and bubbly, and received its "mountain rise" the last of June. It is said to possess mineral qualities, among which is magnesia. An uncommon heavy shower on the night of the 4th of July raised this stream in 24 hours, 8 feet![138]

When the Colesville Branch left St. Louis for Independence, Polly Knight was in a weakened condition. She had been sick for some time, but she refused to be left in Ohio by her family. Her "only or her greatest desire, was to set her feet upon the land of Zion, and to have her body interred in that land." Her husband was certain that she was going to die as they approached Independence and left the boat to obtain the necessary lumber to build her coffin. He later reported that the Lord gave her the desire of her heart, and she lived to stand upon that land.[139] Sister Knight died just two weeks following her arrival in Jackson County.

Following the dedication of the land as a place of gathering for the Saints and following the dedication of the temple site itself, Joseph Smith presided at a Church conference on 4 August 1831 in Kaw Township. The business completed, the Ohio Church leaders began their return journey home. This trip began on 9 August by canoe on the Missouri River.

Fort Osage, Sibley, Missouri
(Church leaders camped here in 1831)
Osage Historical Society—unknown, c1910

The Church leaders' first stop was Fort Osage, which stood on the south bank of the Missouri River fourteen miles northeast of Independence. Fort Osage was one of the first outposts built following the Louisiana Purchase. The fort was abandoned in 1827 but was used by Joseph Smith's party as a temporary camp. Two days later, the company experienced an accident when a canoe in which Joseph and Sidney Rigdon were riding ran into a tree lodged and bobbing in the river. The occupants almost drowned when the canoe was upset.

W. W. Phelps, among those returning to Ohio, said he saw a vision of "the destroyer in his most horrible power" riding upon the water. Some present reported hearing the noise of "the evil one." The experience left many of the group with strong impressions and fears about their travel on the Missouri.[140] The party landed and camped at McIlwaine's Bend, some one hundred miles from Independence. The location of McIlwaine's Bend is near present-day Miami, Saline County. On the following day, 12 August, Joseph received a revelation warning the Church leaders of the dangers of traveling on water.[141] Further, the revelation stated that Joseph, Sidney Rigdon, and Oliver Cowdery should leave the water route and travel by land to Cincinnati, Ohio. Reynolds Cahoon wrote that eleven men "then left the water [and] crossed with the Missouri at Chariton [a town that no longer exists]."[142]

At Chariton, Chariton County, Joseph met several brethren on their way to Zion, including his brother, Hyrum Smith, on 13 August 1831. Another revelation was received while the men met together.[143] Joseph and his company proceeded by land to Kirtland, while Hyrum Smith and his group continued their journey to Jackson County.

Lexington, Lafayette County, Missouri

Lexington is located approximately thirty miles east of Independence. Most of the early settlers of Lexington were from Lexington, Kentucky, which accounts for the name. The first permanent settler was Gilead Rupe in 1819. The river town became the county seat of Lillard (Lafayette) County in 1823 and was incorporated in 1845. Lexington, the county seat of Lafayette County, played a significant role in the Saints' history during the 1830s. Church leaders and members traveled to and from Lexington on political, economic, and Church business throughout the entire Mormon period.

Following their expulsion from Missouri in 1838, the Saints gathered in Illinois. For seven short years, they built the city of Nauvoo as the Church

View of Lexington, Missouri
(The steamboat Saluda exploded in 1852 at Lexington; among its passengers were many
Mormons on the way to Utah)
Missouri Historical Society—unknown, c1900

headquarters. During its turbulent history, Nauvoo grew from a small community to one of the largest cities in the state. Joseph and Hyrum Smith were killed in nearby Carthage, Illinois, by a mob during the difficult period of 1844. Many of the Saints prepared to depart the "City of Joseph" following an extended period of legal and extralegal prosecution and persecution. For many of these Saints and for those who followed them, Missouri was in their path to a refuge in the West.

One of the first groups to cross Missouri was the Mormon Battalion, which left Council Bluffs and traveled to Fort Leavenworth via the northwestern part of Missouri. Later, other Mormon emigrants passed through Missouri—in particular, St. Louis—on their way to Salt Lake City. The Mormon trails west have become well known and marked by official state and federal agencies. One lesser-known trail was the river route along the Missouri River.

The Missouri River was part of a nearly three-thousand-mile waterway that allowed the transportation of not only goods and products but also of people moving across the Midwest. During this period, hundreds of steamboats navigated along these waterways. During a period of almost eighty years, some three hundred steamboats were destroyed by fire or explosions, were crushed by ice, or were sunk by snags in the river. In 1852, the largest steamboat disaster in the United States took place on the Missouri River. The steamboat *Saluda* exploded near Lexington on 9 April 1852. Among the dead was a large group of Latter-day Saints en route to the Rocky Mountains.

In March 1852, the *Saluda* was loaded with Mormon emigrants, mostly from England and Wales, and a large hull of cargo from St. Louis. The destination of the steamboat was Council Bluffs, a Mormon staging ground for the land trek to Utah. The steamboat stopped at Lexington, some three hundred miles upriver, for supplies. The next several miles were among the most difficult to navigate. Just above the town wharf, the rocky edge and narrow channel forced the current into one of the swiftest, most deadly parts of the journey.

Francis T. Belt, the steamboat captain, attempted to bring his boat around the bend. Unable to do so, he tied up at the levee for the night. On the following two days, attempts were made to move upriver. For reasons unknown, possibly goaded by the complaints of some cold and frustrated passengers, the captain ordered the engineer to increase the steam pressure. No one can ascertain whether the boilers had already reached an unsafe level of pressure or whether the engineer was at fault for carelessly permitting the boilers to go dry and to get red hot. Nevertheless, when the pumps forced cold water into the boilers, the boilers exploded with a thunderous noise that could be heard for several miles.

Eye witnesses saw the boat and its passengers blown into the air, some people falling into the river and others landing on the wharf and nearby bluff. The steamboat was completely wrecked. The hull disintegrated. Timbers, splinters, pieces of boilers, engine parts, fragmented chimneys, bales, and freight were scattered everywhere. Hundreds of people, including the captain, were killed, while only about forty survived. Within ten minutes, the boat sank.

The town was stunned by the accident. One man on shore was killed when a piece of the boiler flue struck him; another man was killed by a broken timber. A large brick building nearby collapsed when hit by large pieces of iron from the boat.

A mass burial was performed the following day in the Lexington Cemetery for nearly eighty-five victims who were found. Many more were lost and washed away in the river never to be discovered. The town of Lexington demonstrated incredible compassion on those who suffered—both the survivors and the dead. A citizens' committee organized relief and raised funds to bury the dead, to care for the injured, and to find homes for the orphans.

Many survivors took immediate passage on another ship, the steamboat *Isbel*, which had arrived at Lexington the night before. The captain offered free passage to Council Bluffs, with provisions for the survivors. One man lost his wife and seven children in the accident; another individual lost her husband and three small children; but both traveled on alone without their families.

Panoramic View of DeWitt, Missouri
(A large group of Mormons arrived here in 1838)
DeWitt Historical Society—unknown, c1900

DeWitt, Carroll County, Missouri

DeWitt, Missouri, is located approximately forty-five miles east of Independence and is situated on a bluff approximately two miles from the Missouri River.

The first white settler in the area was Martin Palmer, who built a cabin near DeWitt in 1817. However, after a few months, he abandoned the cabin and returned to Chariton County. The first permanent resident was Jonathan Eppler from Alabama in 1826. Eli Gutherie actually laid out the town in approximately 1836 and called it Elderport. In 1837, Gutherie sold out to Henry Root; and the town's name was changed to DeWitt.

George M. Hinkle and John Murdock, high councilors in Far West, established the Mormon settlement in DeWitt, Carroll County, Missouri. The Missouri High Council sent Hinkle and Murdock to purchase land for the Saints.

The settlement is located near where the Missouri and Grand rivers meet. It was an ideal location as a port of entry for Mormon emigrants and for goods arriving from the East to support the settlements in northern Missouri. Hinkle and Murdock purchased a portion of the town plat from Henry Root on 23 June 1838 for five hundred dollars. The following month, several Mormon families began gathering to DeWitt; and by the fall, approximately seventy families were settled there.

When the Saints were driven from DeWitt, Zadoc Judd recalled:

> Our first days of travel brought us to a beautiful grove of timber; here we camped for the night. Here we buried old Sister Downey. She had travelled with us all the way from Canada. She was old . . . She was buried without much ceremony—without any coffin—wrapped in a quilt and put in the hole. It was a cold, frosty morning but the company was not long in getting started on the road.[144]

Zadoc's job as a ten-year-old boy included being a barefooted cowboy. He drove three cows from DeWitt on a frosty road. Soon, Zadoc found "his feet cold. The cows were anxious to eat but with whip and rocks I kept them on . . . [while] suffering with cold feet." While Zadoc was still moving along, a brother from Far West met him on horseback. He allowed Zadoc to ride while driving the cattle. Soon the company arrived safely in Far West.

Steamboat Landing, DeWitt, Missouri
(An important means of travel and commerce were the Missouri and Grand rivers)
DeWitt Historical Society—unknown, c1900

Although the Church leaders were somewhat apprehensive about water travel following the incidents at McIlwaine's Bend, the revelation written there stated that "the faithful among you shall not perish by the waters" and "it mattereth not unto me . . . whether they go by water or by land."[145] Water routes continued to be a major means of transportation of the Saints—members, missionaries, and Church leaders.

The banks of the Missouri River played a role in Church history after the Saints were expelled from Jackson County in 1833. After a series of attacks and confrontations, the Saints in the Independence area were forced to leave their homes in November and December 1833. The banks of the Missouri near the ferry were lined with refugees on both sides. Some of the Saints were able to bring a few of their household goods, but many were unable to do so. Parley P. Pratt recalled:

> Thursday, November 7 [1833] The shore began to be lined on both sides of the ferry with men, women and children; goods, wagons, boxes, provisions, etc., while the ferry was constantly employed; and when night again closed upon us the cottonwood bottom had much the appearance of a camp meeting. Hundreds of people were seen in every direction, some in tents and some in the open air around their fires, while the rain descended in torrents. Husbands were inquiring for their wives, wives for their husbands; parents for children, children for parents. Some had the good fortune to escape with their families, household goods, and some provisions; while others knew not the fate of their friends, and had lost all their goods. The scene was indescribable, and, I am sure, would have melted the hearts of any people on the earth, except our blind oppressors.[146]

DeWitt Historical Marker

The DeWitt historical marker is located in the town center on a bicentennial flagpole.

Historical Background

The marker states the following information about the Mormons:

> THE MORMONS In 1838, members of the Church of Jesus Christ of the Latter-day Saints (Mormons) living at Far West in Caldwell County, Missouri, were encouraged to settle at DeWitt by several landowners. Land was purchased near this location in June, and within a few months several hundred Mormons had created a village of tents and wagons. Land was cleared, crops were planted, and homes were built. However, the persistent misunderstandings which had followed the Mormons soon reached Carroll County. By October DeWitt was held in a virtual state of siege by non-Mormons from surrounding communities.

To avoid further violence on October 11, 1838, the Latter-day Saints loaded their possessions into seventy wagons and departed.

This marker was presented to the people of DeWitt, by The Church of Jesus Christ of Latter-day Saints, July 4, 1976.

First Capitol, Jefferson City, Missouri
(House of Representatives', senators', and governor's quarters from 1826-34)
Missouri Historical Society—unknown, unknown

Jefferson City, Cole County, Missouri

Jefferson City is located approximately one hundred twenty-five miles southwest of Independence.

Named after Thomas Jefferson, Jefferson City is Missouri's capital, established by the legislature on 31 December 1821. The 1820 constitution of Missouri stipulated that the capital of Missouri should be located on the bank of the Missouri within forty miles of the mouth of the Osage River. The reasoning was simple, as the major source of transportation was by river boat. However, because of several factors, including population growth in Jefferson City, the move of the capital from St. Charles to Jefferson City did not occur until October 1826. The capital was built on the bluffs above and along the south banks of the Missouri River.

The Lohman Building at the Jefferson Landing, on the banks of the Missouri, comprises a building from the Mormon period and is a rare example of Missouri River commercial architecture. Jefferson City's capital buildings were destroyed in 1837 and 1911.

During the Saints' sojourn in Missouri, Jefferson City played a significant role in their history. From the time of the first troubles in Jackson County until Joseph Smith's death in 1844, Jefferson City was continually involved in the Mormon question.

During the expulsion of the Saints from Jackson County, the Jefferson City newspaper, *Jeffersonian Republican*, noted the difficulties in Independence:

The people of Jackson . . . or rather factious portions of them, have taken very singular, and we think disreputable grounds, to redress their imaginary grievances . . . In Jackson . . . they killed, as we are informed, some of the *real* objects of their hatred: But it will, we should presume, require a more caustic remedy than *contempt*, to appease the offended majesty of the law in this case.[147]

Cole County Courthouse, Jefferson City, Missouri
(Temporary state capitol from 1837–40)
Cole County Historical Society—unknown, c1870

The paper announced that correspondence between the governor of the state and the judge of the circuit court was initiated and hoped that "justice will be administered." The newspapers, letters, and official government documents suggest that the state capital supported the Mormons' return to their lands. Eventually, this position weakened in the executive office; and the military support promised the Saints never materialized. The Saints were forced to accept their plight and to settle in adjoining counties.

When the Saints living in Clay County decided to establish settlements in northern Clay County, they hoped that the creation of a new county would be a positive move forward in solving many of the problems that existed between the Mormons and their neighbors. Church leaders transmitted a petition to Jefferson

City requesting the state legislature to form a new county for Mormon settlement.

Some non-Mormons hoped that in exchange for the privilege of having a "special county" created just for them, the Mormons would confine themselves to that specific area and refrain from settling elsewhere.

Many individuals were responsible for the creation of the Saints' new home, Caldwell County. Alexander Doniphan, a legal counselor to Church leaders, led the delegation to Jefferson City. The petition was presented before the Missouri House of Representatives on 29 November 1836. A committee returned to the House "A Bill to Organize the Counties of Caldwell and Daviess" on 19 December 1836. Eventually signed by Governor Boggs on 29 December, the new counties were legally organized.

From Jefferson City, Doniphan wrote Missouri Church leader W. W. Phelps:

> Dear Sir: I must apologize for my delay in giving you information in relation to your petition and the action on the same . . . I know the present limits of your country are contracted, and I regret it much, but you are aware of the prejudice and ignorance that are to be found and combatted everywhere in this country on this subject, as well with the Legislature as with the "Common Herd." In time, I hope you may add to its limits, when prejudices have subsided and reason and common sense have again assumed the helm. You shall hear from me and receive a copy of the Act laying off and organizing your county in a few days. My respects to Messrs. Partridge, Corrill, etc. What I have said here is secret to the world, not to your immediate friends.[148]

Although the size of the county was not as large as expected, the state legislature did act and did create a safe haven for the Saints, at least for a short period.

During the 1838 period, relations between the Saints and their neighbors in Caldwell and Daviess counties deteriorated to the point of civil war. The governor, Lilburn Boggs, a former Jackson County antagonist, supported militia activity against the Saints. Eventually, he issued the famous "extermination order" from his executive office in Jefferson City.

A committee appointed by the members of the Church living in Caldwell County prepared a memorial for the Missouri State Legislature on 10 December 1838. Signed by Edward Partridge, Heber C. Kimball, John Taylor, Theodore Turley, Brigham Young, Isaac Morley, George W. Harris, John Murdock, and John M. Burk, the long memorial stated in part:

> To the Honorable Legislature of the State of Missouri, in Senate and house of Representatives, convened.—We the undersigned petitioners, inhabitants of

Caldwell County Missouri, in consequence of the late calamity that has come upon us, taken in connection with former afflictions, feel it a duty we owe to ourselves and our country, to lay our case before your Honorable Body for consideration.[149]

David H. Redfield, who carried the Saints' petitions to the capital in mid-December, said the city was buzzing with excitement regarding the Mormon War and filled with rumors that the Mormons were keeping the Danite system to spill more blood before they left Missouri.

The state legislature met in session to debate the governor's actions. Representative David Atchison of Clay County denounced the "extermination order." His speech was reported in the *Missouri Republican:*

This order he looked upon as unconstitutional, and he wished to have an expression of the Legislature upon it. If the Governor of the state, or any other power, had the authority to issue such orders, he wished to know it, for, if so, he would not live in any state where such authority was given.[150]

Second State Capitol, Jefferson City, Missouri
(State legislature met here from 1840–1912)
Missouri Historical Society—Thomas Easterly, 1850

The Saints' representative from Caldwell County asked the legislature to rule on the order's constitutionality, for he wanted to know whether Missouri officials could legally force the Mormons to deed over their property and leave the state. The *Missouri Republican* noted that James Chiles, the Jackson County representative, said:

We got rid of a great evil when we drove them from Jackson County, and we have had peace there ever since; and the state will always be in difficulty so long as they suffer them to live in the state; and the quicker they get that petition from before this body, the better.[151]

The state legislature continued to investigate the Mormon War and in December appropriated two thousand dollars for relief to Mormons and non-Mormons who had been rendered homeless, an amount that was too little, too late. Some members of the legislature called for an investigation into the matter. State Senator William M. Campbell said, "To leave the whole matter to the Governor looked . . . like submitting the lamb to the keeping of the wolf."[152]

Not only were the governor's actions called into question but also the state militia's participation in the affair was challenged. Earlier, the *Missouri Republican* lampooned the state militia by reprinting an out-of-state article that included the following view of affairs:

It is said, that a company of twenty Missourians espied a big Mormon near the north east corner of Caldwell County on Tuesday last. They retreated for the time being, but intended, as soon as they are reinforced by thirty or forty of their companions, to [hazard] an attack upon him.[153]

Once the Saints left the state and Joseph Smith escaped imprisonment to the safety of Illinois, many hoped that the end of the Mormon trouble had arrived. However, it was not an end but was just a lull in the anti-Mormon activities. Within a short period, the state of Missouri attempted to extradite Joseph from his home in Illinois to stand trial for alleged crimes against the people and state of Missouri.

Joseph Smith was arrested, but eventually he was set free by Judge Stephen Douglas. A second attempt to extradite Joseph Smith immediately followed the attempted assassination of the former Missouri state governor, Lilburn Boggs. The current governor, Thomas Reynolds, petitioned Illinois Governor Thomas Carlin to arrest Joseph. Carlin ordered Joseph's arrest, and Joseph was taken into custody on 8 August 1842. Again, Smith was set free by a local municipal court, to the chagrin of Carlin and Reynolds.

Following a series of events, Joseph went to the Illinois state capital in Springfield to meet with the new governor, Thomas Ford, and with Stephen A. Douglas and Justin Butterfield. A trial formally convened on 4 January 1843, and again Joseph was vindicated.

Missouri officials in Jefferson City refused to accept defeat and issued another indictment against Joseph in the spring of 1843. Now, for unknown reasons, Ford collaborated with Missouri Governor Reynolds in issuing a new warrant for Joseph's arrest.

In June 1843, Jackson County Sheriff Joseph H. Reynolds captured Joseph Smith in Dixon, Illinois. On their way to Quincy, Joseph escaped and returned to Nauvoo. In Nauvoo, the city court released him. The Missouri governor asked Governor Ford to retake Joseph by military force, but Ford refused. Later, Ford argued that the courts of Illinois had ruled in Joseph's favor and therefore Ford was unable to arrest Joseph again. Soon thereafter, Missouri Governor Reynolds committed suicide. These events, along with several failed attempts to bring Joseph to Missouri for trial, ended Missouri's attempts to extradite him.

St. Louis, St. Louis County, Missouri

Jean Jacques Blaise d'Abbadie, commander of the province of Louisiana, granted to Gilbert Antoine Maxent and Pierre Laclede exclusive trading privileges with Indian tribes along the Missouri River west of the Mississippi in 1763. Laclede left New Orleans two months later to select an outpost for the newly acquired trading dominion. He chose a site on the side of a high hill on the west bank of the Mississippi, about twenty miles below the river's confluence with the Missouri. The crest of the hill offered commanding views of the Mississippi Valley; but more importantly, the site was relatively safe from flooding. A fellow traveler, Auguste Chouteau, returned to the site a few months later with thirty woodsmen to clear the bluff for the outpost and to lay out the village in February 1764, the official founding date of St. Louis.

Panoramic View of St. Louis, St. Louis, Missouri
(Important and busy river town that Church leaders visited)
Missouri Historical Society, R. Benecke, 1867

The village of St. Louis was named for Louis IX, the patron saint of Louis XV, reigning monarch of France in 1764. French families living on the east bank of the Mississippi constituted many of the earliest settlers. These families simply ferried across the river when news arrived that France had ceded to England its lands east of the Mississippi in the treaty at the end of the Seven Years War. These early inhabitants did not know, however, that Louis XV had already given France's vast Louisiana holdings to Spain. St. Louis did not come under direct Spanish administrative control, though, until 1770 and always remained a French colonial village in culture and language until after the United States purchased the area as part of the Louisiana Purchase in 1803.

St. Louis was engulfed by an invasion of westward-bound American pioneers and entrepreneurs following the Louisiana Purchase by the United States. St. Louis was well positioned to become a hub of commerce, exploration, and military operations. During the same year of the purchase, Lewis and Clark's famous expedition set out from the East and established their winter quarters near St. Louis. The crew of fifty-one young frontiersmen spent the cold months in St. Louis learning frontier techniques in preparation for their journey west.

The Lewis and Clark expedition left its staging ground in the spring of 1804 and headed up the Missouri, traveling in an iron-reinforced keelboat and two pirogues. They spent the summer traveling up the Big Muddy, stopping frequently to make scientific observations and to talk with Indians. Upon their return, interest in the western country was aroused by tales of mountains teeming with beaver, of friendly Indians, and of an all-water route along the Missouri River to the rich hunting grounds. Eager traders flocked into St. Louis through

Boat Landing, St. Louis, Missouri
(Numerous Saints and missionaries traveled through St. Louis)
Missouri Historical Society—Thomas Easterly, c1868

the winter of 1806-1807, ready to start west in a procession of canoes, keel boats, and pirogues laden with a load of trading merchandise as soon as ice broke in the Missouri.

The steamboat *Zebulon Pike* docked at St. Louis in 1817, bringing a new era of commerce to the town. French was still the prevailing language in St. Louis until the time that the first Mormon missionaries arrived in the city in 1831; but in the ensuing decades, English speakers flooded in. The population of the city mushroomed from about 5,900 in 1830 to 16,700 in 1840 and then to 78,000 in 1850.

When the first Mormon missionaries arrived in St. Louis, they found a sixty-seven-year-old settlement and a nine-year-old city. St. Louis became one of the most important non-Mormon cities in LDS Church history during the first half of the nineteenth century.[154]

The Saints often used the famous Boonslick Trail between St. Louis and Jackson County, Missouri. The Indians and early traders traced it before it eventually became the first ford to the Far West, a main highway out of which grew the more famous Santa Fe, California, and Oregon trails. Daniel Boone and his son extended the early trail to some salt springs, an animal licking place in Saline County, by 1805. The Daughters of the American Revolution marked this route between St. Louis and Franklin; the first marker is located behind the old courthouse on Fifth Street in St. Louis. Another maker, the first LDS meeting house in St. Louis, is located on the northwest corner of Fourth Street and Washington Avenue. A Mormon Pioneer Trail Foundation plaque is located on the Missouri Athletic Club Building.

The missionaries to the Lamanites (native American Indians), Oliver Cowdery, Parley P. Pratt, Frederick G. Williams, Ziba Peterson, and Peter Whitmer, Jr., were the first Mormons to use the famous route in early 1831. Pratt mentioned this trip in his autobiography published several years later:

> We halted for a few days in Illinois, about twenty miles from St. Louis . . . [A]lthough in the midst of strangers, we were kindly entertained, found many friends, and preached to large congregations in several neighborhoods. In the beginning of 1831 we renewed our journey; and, passing through St. Louis and St. Charles we traveled on foot for three hundred miles.[155]

Following their arrival in Independence, the missionaries sent Pratt back to Church leaders in Kirtland, Ohio, to report the missionaries' activities. Pratt noted, "In nine days I arrived at St. Louis . . . I spent a few days with a friend in the country, at the same place we had tarried on the way out: and took a steamer in St. Louis bound for Cincinnati."[156]

Later, in June, Joseph Smith and a party of Church leaders from Kirtland traveled on the famous trail on foot for the entire 240 miles from St. Louis to Independence, Missouri. The New York Colesville Branch of the Church stayed in St. Louis from 13–18 June waiting for a steamboat to take them up the Missouri River to Independence, where they met Joseph Smith's party to dedicate the land of Missouri for the gathering of the Saints.

Missionary activities continued in and around St. Louis during most of the period before the 1838 Mormon War in Missouri. The St. Louis newspapers began to take notice of the Saints in 1833 when the *Free Press* published an article entitled "Intolerance" just before the Saints' expulsion from Jackson County:

> A society of *Mormonites*, a religious sect, were settled in Jackson county, in this state, where they had established a printing press, and published a paper entitled the "Star." The citizens of Jackson county having had a meeting on the subject of these "obnoxious" people, were determined to drive them from the county and raze their printing office to the ground. Their resolutions were prevented from being carried into execution by a subsequent agreement in which the Mormonites stipulated for their removal of their society and the discontinuance of the publication of the "Star."
>
> We profess to know but little of the character of this religious sect; nor do we pretend to vouch for the soundness of their doctrines; but we protest against the justness of this course of intolerance towards these people, however absurd and fanatical their modes of worship may have been. We have no right to interfere with the religious creeds of our neighbors; and if their conduct towards us is regulated by the laws of the land, we can have no just cause of complaint . . . but to proceed against them as a religious body, not discriminating between the innocent and the guilty, must be considered *persecution* in the most odious sense of the word, and a disregard for the provisions of our Constitution.[157]

During the Mormon War period, the Saints are mentioned almost seven hundred times in St. Louis newspapers. During the initial stages of the conflict, the *St. Louis Daily Evening Gazette* reported the troubles in the western part of the state between the Saints and their neighbors; and on 20 December, the *Missouri Argus* expressed its support of the Saints who were suffering from the effects of the state's handling of the affair. Almost universally, the leading St. Louis newspapers condemned Governor Boggs' "extermination order" and his handling of the events of 1838. Although such support did little to prevent the Saints' expulsion from their lands in Caldwell and Daviess counties, the support may be one reason why no Mormons in St. Louis were expelled.

St. Louis acted as a refuge for the Saints when they fled persecution in western Missouri in the 1830s and again when they sought protection from Illinois mobs in the mid-1840s. St. Louis' size and cosmopolitan nature may be one of the reasons the Saints fared so well in the city. At different times, citizens of St. Louis held meetings to raise funds to assist the destitute exiles. Although many Mormons attempted to leave the state as a result of the "extermination order," a few others eventually made their home in St. Louis. Thomas Wrigley remembered:

> We for some time felt afraid of the exterminating orders of Governor Boggs, which were still in force, but our numbers began to increase in that city and we took courage and a few met in a private house and organized a branch . . . but it was sometimes hard work having to contend with the prejudice of the people of the world and every apostate that left Nauvoo came here and did their best to bring persecution on us.[158]

The *People's Organ,* a St. Louis newspaper, reported that the Saints met on Morgan [now Delmar] Street in a school house. Brigham Young and other Church leaders visited St. Louis a week later for a Church conference. Young reported, "We arrived in St. Louis; I preached in the evening; the Branch numbered about 700 members."[159]

The leaders left the following day for Cincinnati. "We left St. Louis on board Louis Phillpie," Young wrote, "[with] Captain J. J. Woman [and] with about two hundred passengers; many of them were from the Osprey. I was called upon to deliver a lecture on the principles of the church, which allayed some prejudice which had been manifested against the Elders on board."[160] Shortly thereafter, Joseph Smith was murdered in Illinois and in character. The St. Louis newspapers condemned the act as "Murder of the most deliberate cold-blood, atrocious and cowardly description."[161]

The St. Louis Branch of the Church continued to grow following Joseph's assassination in 1844. Although the time was turbulent for the Saints in St. Louis, the increased number of emigrants who flooded into the city caused local Church leaders to rent a concert hall on Market Street (between Second and Third streets, west side) for sabbath services. Eventually, Branch President Felt divided the branches into several other units, which consisted of about four thousand members by September 1849.

Church leaders moved their Sunday meetings from the concert hall to the "Old Methodist Church on Fourth Street." This was a spacious building with a gallery and a basement consisting of three rooms, suitable for councils and storage. The St. Louis Stake was created on 4 November 1854. The Church had moved from a small presence to a significant organization during the first twenty-five years of contact with the city, known as the "Gateway to the West."

St. Louis not only was a place of refuge for the Saints during this period but also became an important way station for Mormon emigrants. The first wave of convert emigrants from Europe passed through the city beginning in April 1841; and until 1855, St. Louis remained an important port for thousands of European converts on their way to Nauvoo, Illinois, and later to Utah. Emigrants who came up the Mississippi from New Orleans were forced to change boats at St. Louis for their continued trip to Nauvoo.

Many Mississippi river boats transported missionaries, Church leaders, and Mormon emigrants on the major rivers in the area to Church gathering points, missionary locations, Church conferences, and pioneer staging grounds. These steamboats, including the *Alex Scott* and *Grand Turk*, all docked at St. Louis.

The *Alex Scott*, a popular riverboat, transported several Mormon emigrant companies from New Orleans to St. Louis. The boat, according to John Greenhow, "made rapid progress till we passed the mouth of the Ohio, when we soon after run aground and remained there three days; on our deliverance we got to within ninety miles of St. Louis, where we had to remain three weeks for want of water."[162] On another occasion, when the boat transported Saints to St. Louis, a female member of the Church, while drawing a bucket of water, fell overboard during the trip and drowned.

From St. Louis, many steamboats headed west on the Missouri River to Mormon pioneer staging grounds. The *Clara* left St. Louis on 12 March 1855 for Atchison, Kansas. Encountering low water, the vessel was compelled to land at Leavenworth. There she remained for several weeks, during which time twenty Saints died from cholera. On the way to Atchison, nine more deaths occurred.

Several emigrants' layovers in St. Louis lasted longer than the necessary days to change steamboats. These emigrants stayed in the city to work and to recoup their finances. The Church newspaper, *St. Louis Luminary*, reported:

> St. Louis is a fine, large, and flourishing city, and has furnished employment to many hundreds and thousands of our brethren . . . there are few public buildings of any consideration in this city that our brethren have not taken an active and prominent part in erecting or ornamenting. There are few factories, foundries, or mercantile establishments, but have taken, or are taking an active part in establishing or sustaining.[163]

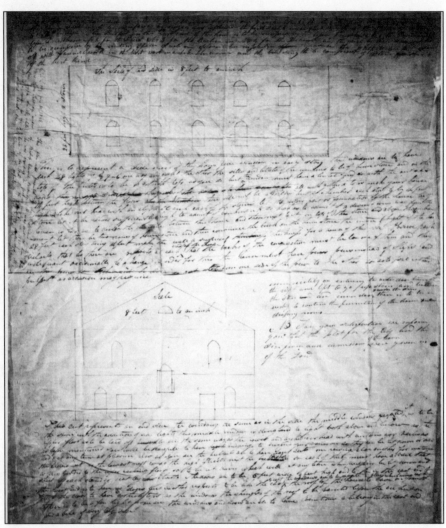

Independence Temple, Independence, Missouri
(Sketch of proposed temple to be built at Zion.)
LDS Historical Department– Oliver Cowdery, 1833

5

EPILOGUE

The Saints have a rich heritage from the early Ohio and Missouri period (1831–39). A "window" to how this season is understood by those who accept Joseph Smith as their Church founder is exemplified in the "three churches on Walnut Street."[1] When you visit Walnut Street in Independence, Missouri, you encounter three separate and distinct religious organizations that have been drawn to this small area of land because of their connection with the early Saints. The Church of Jesus Christ of Latter-day Saints (LDS) Visitors Center is located on one side of the street. The Reorganized Church of Jesus Christ of Latter Day Saints (RLDS) Auditorium and Temple complex are only hundreds of feet away, and just across the street from the RLDS buildings is the headquarters of the Church of Christ (Temple Lot).

Although all three churches have a common beginning and share some beliefs and practices with each other, their interpretations of the events that transpired during the Ohio and Missouri period, particularly of the Kirtland experience, have created a doctrinal and organizational division among them. Once the three churches openly and heatedly debated each other; now all three exist side by side in friendship and cooperation. The LDS and RLDS churches, in particular, have been involved in many cooperative exchanges and projects while remaining faithful to their individual beliefs and practices.

In general, the three churches on Walnut may be understood by the period of Church history they tend to emphasize. The Church of Christ (Temple Lot) retains the New York church's name, the Church of Christ. The doctrinal and organizational developments of the Ohio, Missouri, and Illinois period have been basically rejected by this church; therefore, it emphasizes the New York period (the revelations, scripture, and organizational structure).

The RLDS Church, on the other hand, has incorporated the phrase "Church of Jesus Christ of Latter Day Saints," an Ohio and Missouri designation for the Church, as part of its name. The name reflects the theological perspective of the RLDS movement, as its members accept the organizational development of the Church in Ohio and Missouri.[2] The only temple built by the Saints during this period, the Kirtland Temple, remains in the possession of the RLDS Church and stands as a symbolic representation of the RLDS Church and its Ohio beliefs.

The LDS Church, on the other hand, owns the temple site in Nauvoo, the second temple built by the Saints. The temple doctrine and theological significance of the Nauvoo Temple stand in marked contrast to the Kirtland Temple. In Kirtland, the temple endowment was an endowment of "power"; while in Nauvoo, the temple endowment was a richly symbolic series of ordinances. The LDS Church not only accepts the religious messages and organizational structures developed in Ohio and Missouri but more importantly accepts Joseph Smith's teachings and revelations from the Nauvoo period (1839–44).

In a very general sense, the Church of Christ (Temple Lot) is the New York organization; the RLDS Church is the Ohio organization; and the LDS Church is the Nauvoo organization.

For the LDS and RLDS churches,the doctrinal and organizational development of the early Church was both significant and profound in Ohio. The offices and administrative functions of the Church, such as the office of high priest, a Church First Presidency (the leading Church administrative body), patriarchs and patriarchal blessings, and the Kirtland Stake (administrative geographical boundary), set the two churches apart from the Church of Christ (Temple Lot). In addition to these prominent features, Joseph organized and called the Aaronic and Melchizedek Priesthood quorums, the First Quorum of Seventy, and the Quorum of Twelve Apostles, all of which had significant impacts upon the modern churches' governing structures.

In addition to Church government, Ohio represents a rich spiritual heritage. The first modern Church scriptures (1835 *Doctrine and Covenants*), the first Church hymnal (1835), and a second edition of the *Book of Mormon* (1837) were printed in Kirtland, Ohio. In addition, Joseph Smith's translation of the *Bible* was basically accomplished during this period. Some eighty-four revelations were recorded by Joseph during this time; by far the vast majority of Joseph's printed revelations come from the Ohio and Missouri era. Missionary work commenced in Canada and the British Isles, where thousands of people were converted and eventually gathered to America. For Joseph and many of the Saints, the gifts of the spirit and the religious experiences of Kirtland set this period of Church history apart from any other time. The Saints' accomplishments in Kirtland will remain an important part of their "sacred past."

Kirtland also represents a difficult period of Church history, sometimes called the "first great apostasy" in the restored Church. The "Parrish Party," a group of about thirty former members and leaders led by Warren Parrish, may be considered the first real "splinter group." The dissent and open rebellion against Joseph Smith's leadership in Kirtland continued in western Missouri during 1837 and 1838 as well.

A number of Saints left the Church, and as many as one-third of the leaders (many of the witnesses to the *Book of Mormon* and early supporters of Joseph included) chose to disassociate themselves from the Church to which they had given so much faithful service, both in time and money. Although many simply "disappeared from the scene," others vigorously fought against their former friends and Church leaders. This dissension was the cause of much frustration and sorrow for the Saints who remained committed to the Church and to Joseph Smith's leadership.

Between 1844 and 1880, the ownership of the Kirtland Temple was in question, as any individual or group that held possession of the building did not have an acceptable title. In 1879, the RLDS Church decided to obtain legal title to the Temple. On 23 February 1880, Judge Sherman rendered the court decision that gave actual title to the RLDS Church. Since then, the RLDS Church has maintained and used the building for public activities and special church services. Today, the RLDS Church conducts complimentary tours of this beautiful edifice.

The LDS presence in Kirtland for the first time since the 1840s began when Wilford C. Wood purchased the Newel K. Whitney store in the 1950s. The first LDS proselyting missionaries arrived in Kirtland in 1978 and moved into the store. Following consultation with local RLDS Church representatives, LDS Church officials expanded their proselyting activities to include the town of Kirtland itself. The Newel K. Whitney store was eventually restored and dedicated in 1984. Today, the LDS Church conducts tours of the restored Newel K. Whitney store in Kirtland and of the John Johnson farm in Hiram, Ohio.

The LDS and RLDS churches have committed significant resources to preserve the Church's Ohio past. The John Johnson farm in Hiram, Ohio, and the Newel K. Whitney store and the temple in Kirtland stand as visual reminders of these early industrious "pioneers" who came to Ohio because they wanted to feel the power of God in a house built to his name and to participate in a religiously motivated effort to experience a change of heart so they would be the "people of God." The Church left Ohio and removed to Missouri, where Church settlements had previously been established.

To many of those who honor Joseph Smith as the founder of their faith, the state of Missouri is not only a place of tragic history but also a land with a glorious future. Since Joseph's death in 1844, many members of the restoration movement have talked and have written about a return to the Mormon Zion in Missouri. Following Joseph's death, the members of the Church felt "like sheep without a shepherd, their beloved Prophet having been taken away."[3] The majority of Nauvoo Saints followed Brigham Young to the Rocky Mountains, just as the Saints seven years earlier had followed Brigham Young from Missouri. Other groups remained behind—some tired of moving and others unhappy about the Church's leadership in Nauvoo. Within a short time, several groups claimed succession rights to the Church presidency. Although they differed in beliefs and practices, nearly all groups still held in common a belief that the Saints must gather again in Missouri before the Second Coming of Christ. A few restoration churches began to relocate in Missouri following the end of the American Civil War.[4]

The Church of Christ, a small restoration group, moved from Woodford County, Illinois, to Jackson County during the winter of 1866–67. They are credited with being the first group to return to Independence following the expulsion from Jackson County in 1833. The small church came into possession of a portion of the original temple lot in 1869. Although this ownership was challenged in the courts in the 1890s, legal possession was upheld; and the temple site remains in its custody today. This church is commonly called the Church of Christ (Temple Lot), or Hedrickite Church.

Albert and Maria Noble are reported to be the first RLDS members to return to Independence. They arrived in 1867 and settled near the Missouri River. Henry Etzenhouser's family moved to the area soon thereafter, and E. C. Brand of Lee's Summit organized a branch meeting in the Independence Courthouse on 25 May 1873. Eventually, the RLDS Independence District was organized in 1878.

The RLDS Church purchased land for a church building in 1879 and dedicated the land on 6 July 1884. In 1888, they built a beautiful stone building, known as the Stone Church, just outside of the original temple-lot boundary. The RLDS Independence Stake was organized in April 1901. Joseph Smith III, the RLDS Church president, remained in Lamoni, Iowa, where the RLDS Church headquarters were located and where Graceland College, owned and operated by the RLDS Church, is located. In 1906, President Smith moved to Independence, Missouri, where he spent the last years of his life.

Officially, the RLDS Church moved its headquarters to Independence in 1918. The RLDS Auditorium was constructed between 1926–62, and the new RLDS Temple was begun in 1990. Both are situated on 25 acres of the original temple lot.

The LDS Church, with its headquarters in Salt Lake City, Utah, purchased twenty-five acres of the original temple lot in Independence on 14 April 1904. An LDS chapel was built on this property in 1914, and a mission home was constructed in 1917. In 1978, a new stake center replaced the chapel a little farther down the street. In 1971, the LDS Church built a visitors center on property that was part of the original 63 acres purchased by Edward Partridge in 1831.

Since the time the LDS Church purchased the first Missouri historical property in Independence, the Church has bought Liberty Jail and several hundred acres at Far West and Adam-ondi-Ahman.

Several other restoration churches are also located in the Independence area, including the Church of Jesus Christ, situated at 807 South Cottage. Often called Cutlerites, members of the Church of Jesus Christ moved with the Saints to Winter Quarters, located on the west bank of the Missouri River in Indian Territory, following their exodus from Nauvoo. Alpheus Cutler's group did not proceed west with Brigham Young and eventually settled in Manti, Iowa. Following Cutler's death, the group migrated to Clitherall, Minnesota. In 1928–29, most of the young members moved to Independence, Missouri, where they established their church.[5] Other restoration congregations, including the Independent Restoration Branch movement, have established meeting houses in western Missouri during the past few years. Although these organizations look forward to the future, the past remains ever present, particularly the difficult days of turmoil and destruction.

Although persecution of minority groups, including Catholics and abolitionists, was not uncommon in ante-bellum America, when both the number of people and the length of time involved are considered, the Mormons stand as a unique object of social and religious intolerance in nineteenth-century American history.[6]

Another group, native American Indians, deserve special mention because of a unique historical incident. Just as the Saints were being driven from Missouri during the winter of 1838–39, General Winfield Scott began the twelve-hundred-mile forced march of the Cherokee Indians from their lands in Georgia, North Carolina, and Tennessee to the Indian Territory in the West. Now known as the "Trail of Tears," the march resulted in the deaths of as many as four thousand people as a result of exposure. They crossed the Mississippi River beginning in January 1839 near present-day Cape Girardiau in southern Missouri—at the very moment when the Saints were being forced to cross the same river in the north.

Much of the suffering from the Missouri persecution occurred when the Saints left the state during the winter of 1838–39. Several factors may have caused the Church's leadership to make the decision to leave rather than wait until spring when the deadline had been set.

First, many Saints had the means to leave; for them, no reason existed to remain. Others were forced to flee because the Missouri militia was hunting them down.

Second, others believed that incarcerated Church leaders, including Joseph Smith, would be released as soon as all Mormons had left the state. Therefore, in an effort to expedite the leaders' release, the Saints chose to leave.

Third, many Saints felt that the time required to move such a large group by the deadline necessitated beginning the move early. Although a break in the weather at Far West occurred, regretfully, the Saints encountered harsher weather near the Illinois border.

Finally, the food supply at Far West was insufficient to support the Saints. Many Saints needed a safe refuge to recover their health—away from continued harassment by mobs and militia units.

The winter relocation caused many who enjoyed good health to fall ill, and the condition of those in bad health worsened. Much of the sickness and many of the premature deaths in Nauvoo, Illinois, in 1839–40 resulted from the exposure the Saints suffered during their expulsion from their homes and lands in Missouri.

The Saints' experiences in Missouri, especially the difficult period in 1838, hold a unique position in Mormon history. Names such as Lilburn Boggs, George Hinkle, and Alexander Doniphan and events such as the Gallatin Election Battle, the Battle of Crooked River, the "extermination order," and Haun's Mill Massacre still spark strong emotions in the institutional memory of the Saints. The events of 1838 seem to typify the manner in which the dominant culture treated the Mormons throughout the entire nineteenth century and early twentieth century. The Missouri experience continues to cast a long shadow on the Church's history, even to the present period. The feeling of the Saints in Nauvoo, as well as the feeling of present-day Saints, is expressed in the following passage in their newspaper, the *Times and Seasons:*

> We can never forget the injuries done in Missouri. They are ever present in our minds. We feel it impossible to efface them from our memories.[7]

Although the injustices suffered in Missouri are not forgotten, time has healed many of the old wounds among the Saints, their non-Mormon neighbors, and the dissenters. The "extermination order" was enforced only for a short time after it was issued. On 25 June 1976, Missouri State Governor Christopher S. Bond rescinded the order in honor of the Bicentennial Celebration of the nation. (See Appendix One.) Since the troubled days of the 1830s, many descendants of former persecutors and dissenters have become members of the restoration churches. Many of George Hinkle's descendants are active in the RLDS Church, and even Governor Lilburn Boggs has posterity who are Latter-day Saints today.

THE EXTERMINATION ORDER AND ITS RESCINDING

Governor Boggs issued orders to General Clark, conferring upon him the most plenary authority for putting down the so-called Mormon insurrection following the receipt of several appeals from mob leaders and citizens in northern Missouri and pressured by advisors to act immediately. This document, now known as the "extermination order," was issued on 27 October 1838.

Headquarters of the Militia
City of Jefferson, October 27, 1838
Gen. John B. Clark.

Sir:—Since the order of this morning to you, directing you to cause four hundred mounted men to be raised within your division, I have received by Amos Rees, Esq. of Ray county and Wiley C. Williams, Esq., one of my aids, information of the most appalling character, which entirely changes the face of things, and places the Mormons in the attitude of an open and avowed defiance of the laws, and of having made war upon the people of this State. Your orders are, therefore, to hasten your operations with all possible speed. The Mormons must be treated as enemies, and must be exterminated or driven from the State if necessary, for the public peace—their outrages are beyond all description. If you can increase your force, you are authorized to do so, to any extent you may consider necessary. I have just issued orders to Maj. Gen. Willock of Marion county, to raise five hundred men, and to march them to the northern part of Daviess, and there unite with General Doniphan, of Clay, who has been ordered with five hundred men to proceed to the same point for the purpose of intercepting the retreat of the Mormons to the north. They have been directed to communicate with you by express, you can also communicate with them if you find it necessary. Instead, therefore, of proceeding as at first directed to reinstate the citizens in their homes, you will proceed immediately to Richmond and then operate against the Mormons. Brig. Gen. Parks of Ray, has been ordered to have four hundred of his Brigade in readiness to join you at Richmond. The whole force will be placed under your command.

I am very respectfully,
Your Ob't Serv't,

L. W. BOGGS, Commander-in-Chief.

In late 1975, RLDS Far West, Missouri Stake President Lyman F. Edwards wrote Governor Christopher Bond inviting him to participate in the RLDS annual stake conference kicking off the 1976 summer reunion. President Edwards suggested that some kind of gesture during the American Bicentennial might be appropriate in the heart of "Mormon War Country." RLDS Church leaders also worked through the chair of the Republican Committee in the area. The Governor's Office responded positively to the invitation, but no promises were made as to his availability.

In February 1976, Lyman and his wife Nancy attended the Lincoln Day Dinner at the Mila Club in St. Joseph, Missouri, where Governor Bond was in attendance. President Edwards was assisted by the local Episcopal priest, who was interested in helping arrange Bond's attendance at the RLDS conference. Nancy was most winsome and persuasive; and Governor Bond responded that he was really quite intrigued by the project and that he would continue to follow up with his staff.

The Missouri State Patrol contacted RLDS Church leaders regarding security arrangements at the stake conference in case Governor Bond could appear but cautioned that his reelection campaign might take priority.

Just one month before the conference, the Governor's Office asked for additional details and for information about who should be invited, in case the gesture materialized. The RLDS First Presidency's Office was contacted, along with LDS Church leaders in Salt Lake City.

Governor Bond arrived at the conference and addressed the gathering. He then presented an official Governor's Executive Order that technically rescinded the "extermination order" and that presented apologies to the Saints and other people of Missouri for the unfortunate developments of that earlier day. Lyman Edwards recalled:

> The order was tasteful and even passionate in its seriousness, even as we were aware that the current setting was somewhat focused on a patriotic celebration.

After reading it, the Governor presented the Executive Order to President W. Wallace Smith [RLDS Church] to receive it on behalf of the Saints of the Restoration Movement. Governor Bond stayed for the conference and mingled with the Saints after the meeting before departing with our appreciation.[1]

Governor Bond's order reads as follows:

WHEREAS, on October 27, 1838, the Governor of the State of Missouri, Lilburn W. Boggs, signed an order calling for the extermination or expulsion of Mormons from the State of Missouri; and

WHEREAS, Governor Boggs' order clearly contravened the rights to life, liberty, property and religious freedom as guaranteed by the Constitution of the United States, as well as the Constitution of the State of Missouri; and

WHEREAS, in this bicentennial year as we reflect on our nation's heritage, the exercise of religious freedom is without question one of the basic tenets of our free democratic republic;

Now, THEREFORE, I, CHRISTOPHER S. BOND, Governor of the State of Missouri, by virtue of the authority vested in me by the Constitution and the laws of the State of Missouri, do hereby order as follows:

Expressing on behalf of all Missourians our deep regret for the injustice and undue suffering which was caused by the 1838 order, I hereby rescind Executive Order Number 44 dated October 27, 1838, issued by Governor W. Boggs.

In witness I have hereunto set my hand and caused to be affixed the great seal of the State of Missouri, in the city of Jefferson, on this 25 day of June, 1976. (Signed) Christopher S. Bond, Governor.

Appendix Two

PHOTOGRAPHIC SOURCES

Amherst Historical Society, Amherst, Ohio. Local history and photograph collection of Amherst, Ohio.

Ashtabula Historical Society, Ashtabula, Ohio. Local history and photograph collection of Ashtabula, Ohio.

Boone County Historical Society, Columbia, Missouri. Local history and photograph collection of Boone County. The society has also published one book and one album.

Brigham Young University, Harold B. Lee Library Archives and Special Collections, Provo, Utah. Collection includes large holdings of Mormon history material and photographs.

The Church of Jesus Christ of Latter-day Saints, Historical Department, Salt Lake City, Utah. Large holdings include George Edward Anderson Collection, photo album presented to Joseph F. Smith by George E. Anderson, Junius F. Wells Collection, Daniel Shupe Collection, Robert Spencer Collection, Harry Allsworth Collection, and Joseph F. Smith Memorial Dedication Trip Collection.

The Church of Jesus Christ of Latter-day Saints, Visual Resources Library, Salt Lake City, Utah. Collection includes recent color photographs and slides of LDS Church history sites.

Cincinnati Public Library, Cincinnati, Ohio. Local history and photographs of Cincinnati, Ohio.

Clay County Museum and Historical Society, Richmond, Missouri. Local history and photographs of Clay County.

Cole County Historical Society, Jefferson City, Missouri. Local history and photographs of Cole County.

DeWitt Historical Society, DeWitt, Missouri. Local history and photographs of DeWitt, Missouri.

Geauga County Historical Society, Burton, Ohio. Local history and photographs of Geauga County.

Jackson County Historical Society, Independence, Missouri. Local history and photographs of Jackson County. The society maintains an extensive bookstore.

Kansas State Historical Society, Kansas City, Kansas. Large holdings include local histories and photographs for the state of Kansas.

Lake County Historical Society, Mentor, Ohio. Collection of local history and large collection of photographs of Lake County.

Missouri Historical Society, St. Louis, Missouri. Large holdings include local histories and photographs including the Thomas Easterly collection for the state of Missouri.

Oberlin College, Oberlin, Ohio. Collection includes history and photographs of Oberlin College.

Ray County Historical Society, Richmond, Missouri. Collection of local history and photographs of Ray County.

The Reorganized Church of Jesus Christ of Latter Day Saints Library-Archives, Independence, Missouri. Large holdings include early Mormon history and photographs.

Shaker Historical Society, Cleveland, Ohio. History and photograph collection of the North Union (Shaker Heights) Shaker community.

United States Department of Agriculture, National Archives and Records Service, Cartographic and Architectural Branch, Washington, D.C. Collection contains aerial photographs of any location in the United States.

Utah State Historical Society, Salt Lake City, Utah. Collection includes Utah state history and photographs of LDS Church historical sites.

Village of Mantua, Mantua, Ohio. Collection of history and photographs of Mantua, Ohio.

John Waldsmith Collection, Sycamore, Ohio. One of the largest stereograph collections on Ohio history.

Western Reserve Academy, Hudson, Ohio. Collection of history and photographs pertaining to the Western Reserve College.

Western Reserve Historical Society, Cleveland, Ohio. Holdings include history and photographs of villages, townships, and counties in the Western Reserve.

Willoughby Historical Society, Willoughby, Ohio. Local history and photograph collection of Willoughby, Ohio.

ENDNOTES

PREFACE

1. William Cupp Darrah, Stereo Views: A *History of Stereographs in America and Their Collection* (Gettysburg: Times and News Publishing Co.,1964), 167.

2. "Journal of George Edward Anderson," 24 April 1907, LDS Church Historical Department Archives Division, Salt Lake City, Utah, hereafter cited as LDSCA. All material at the LDSCA used by permission.

3. Anderson, 25 April 1907.

PERSONAL VOICES

1. Charles Mackay, *The Mormons: or Latter-day Saints* (London: Office of National Illustrated Library, 1852), iv.

2. Quoted in Larry C. Porter, "A Study of the Origins of the Church of Jesus Christ in the States of New York and Pennsylvania, 1816–1831," Ph.D. dissertation, Brigham Young University, 1971, 19.

3. *Journal of Discourses* (Liverpool and London: F. D. Richards and S. W. Richards, 1856) 3:51.

4. "Martha Cox Notebook," LDSCA.

5. *The Juvenile Instructor*, 1 October 1882.

6. *The Saint's Herald*, 1 June 1881.

7. Joseph Smith, Jr., trans. *The Book of Mormon* (Palmyra: E. G. Grandin, 1830); Herald Heritage Reprint (Independence: Herald Publishing House, 1970).

8. The LDS Church, headquartered in Salt Lake City, Utah, uses "Latter-day Saints," while the RLDS Church, headquartered in Independence, Missouri, retained the early separated form, "Latter Day Saints," as part of its title.

9. Dean C. Jessee, "Joseph Knight's Recollection of Early Mormon History," *BYU Studies* 17 (Autumn 1976): 37.

10. "Sarah Leavitt Autobiography," LDSCA.

11. *The Doctrine and Covenants of The Church of Jesus Christ of Latter-day Saints* (Salt Lake City: The Church of Jesus Christ of Latter-day Saints, 1981), Section 37, hereafter cited as LDS D&C; *The Book of Doctrine and Covenants* (Independence: Herald Publishing House, 1970), Section 37, hereafter cited as RLDS D&C.

12. "Emily Young Autobiography," Harold B. Lee Library Archives, Brigham Young University, Provo, Utah, hereafter cited as BYUHBLL.

13. "Caroline Crosby Memoirs," LDSCA.

14. "Mary A. Noble Journal," BYUHBLL.

15. *The Latter-day Saints' Millennial Star*, 11 July 1863, hereafter cited as *Millennial Star*.

16. Quoted in William Mulder and A. Russell Mortensen, *Among the Mormons* (New York: Alfred A. Knopf, 1969, 118.

17. "Jonathan Crosby Autobiography," LDSCA.

18. *Woman's Exponent*, 1 August 1880.

19. "Reminiscences of Drusilla Hendricks," LDSCA.

20. "George Burkett Diary," LDSCA.

21. "1883 School of the Prophets," LDSCA.

22. "Luke Johnson Statement," LDSCA.

23. "Caroline Crosby Memoirs," LDSCA.

24. *The Juvenile Instructor*, 1 March 1892.

25. "Mosiah L. Hancock Autobiography," BYUHBLL.

26. "Benjamin F. Johnson Journal," LDSCA.

27. "Hyrum Smith Diary," LDSCA.

28. "Hepzibah Richards Correspondence," LDSCA.

29. "John Smith Journal," LDSCA.

30. "Sarah Rich Autobiography," LDSCA.

31. Dean C. Jessee and David J. Whittaker, eds., "The Last Months of Mormonism in Missouri: The Albert Perry Rockwood Journal," *Brigham Young University Studies*, hereafter cited as *BYU Studies*, 28 (Winter 1988): 22.

32. *The Saints Herald*, 15 July 1879.

33. "Emma Smith to Joseph Smith, 9 March 1839," LDSCA.

34. Quoted in Kenneth W. Godfrey, Audrey M. Godfrey, and Jill Mulvay Derr, *Personal Voices: The Untold History of the Latter-day Saints 1830–1900* (Salt Lake City: Deseret Book

Company, 1982), 114.

35. "Nancy Tracy Autobiography," Utah Historical Society, Salt Lake City, Utah.

36. *Doctrine and Covenants of the Church of Jesus Christ of Latter Day Saints* (Nauvoo: Printed by John Taylor, 1844).

37. *Woman's Exponent*, 15 February 1879.

38. *The Juvenile Instructor*, 15 August 1892.

39. Ibid., 15 May 1893.

40. "Joseph Fielding Diary," LDSCA.

41. "Curtis Bolton Journal," LDSCA.

42. Joseph H. Buckingham, *Illinois As Lincoln Knew It: A Boston Reporter's Record of a Trip in 1847* (Springfield: Abraham Lincoln Association, 1938), 109.

THE CHURCH IN OHIO

1. *History of Geauga and Lake Counties, Ohio* (Evansville: Unigraphic, Inc., 1973), 246. Two exhaustive studies dealing with the Saints during the Ohio period are Milton V. Backman, Jr., *The Heavens Resound* (Salt Lake City: Deseret Book Company, 1983) and Karl Ricks Anderson, *Joseph Smith's Kirtland* (Salt Lake City: Deseret Book Company, 1989).

2. Quoted in Christopher Gore Crary, "Frontier Living Conditions in Kirtland," in *Ohio's Western Reserve: A Regional Reader*, Edited by Harry F. Lupold and Gladys Haddad (Kent: Kent State University Press, 1988), 74.

3. Parley P. Pratt, *Autobiography of Parley P. Pratt* (Salt Lake City: Deseret Book Company, 1973), 48.

4. Mary Lightner, "Mary Elizabeth Rollins Lightner," *The Utah Genealogical and Historical Magazine*, 17 (July 1926): 194.

5. Parley P. Pratt, *Mormonism Unveiled: Zion's Watchman Unmasked* (New York: O. Pratt and E. Fordham, 1838), 40–41.

6. *Painesville Telegraph*, 16 November 1830.

7. *The Latter Day Saints' Messenger and Advocate*, October 1836, hereafter cited as *Messenger and Advocate*.

8. "Milo Andrus Autobiography," BYUHBLL.

9. Ibid.

10. "Caroline Crosby Memoirs," LDSCA.

11. "Wilford Woodruff Journal," LDSCA; also found in Scott G. Kenney, *Wilford Woodruff's Journals: 1883–1898 Typescript*, 9 vols. (Midvale: Signature Books, 1987) 1:8; see also Dean C. Jessee, "The Kirtland Diary of Wilford Woodruff," *BYU Studies* 12 (Summer 1972): 368.

12. *Journal of Discourses* 4:34–35.

13. LDS D&C 105/RLDS D&C 102. See Roger D. Launius, *Zion's Camp: Expedition to Missouri, 1834* (Independence: Herald Publishing House, 1984).

14. Hereafter, *The Evening and the Morning Star* is cited as the *Star;* for a study of early Mormon publication efforts, see Wayne Ham, comp., *Publish Glad Tidings: Readings in Early Latter Day Saint Sources* (Independence: Herald Publishing House, 1970).

15. The *Latter Day Saints' Messenger and Advocate* was published from October 1834 to September 1837 at Kirtland, Ohio, hereafter cited as *Messenger and Advocate.*

16. The *Elders' Journal* was published at Kirtland, Ohio, from October to November 1837; thereafter, it continued to be published under the title *Elders' Journal of the Church of Jesus Christ of Latter Day Saints* from July to August 1838 at Far West, Missouri. Hereafter, all references will be *Elders' Journal.*

17. *Messenger and Advocate,* July 1835.

18. Ibid.

19. Ibid., March 1835.

20. Ibid., February 1835.

21. Joseph Smith, *History of The Church of Jesus Christ of Latter-day Saints,* edited by B. H. Roberts, 7 vols., 4th ed. (Salt Lake City: The Church of Jesus Christ of Latter-day Saints, 1964) 2:443, hereafter cited as *History of the Church.*

22. *Messenger and Advocate,* June 1836.

23. Quoted in Leonard J. Arrington, "Oliver Cowdery's Kirtland, Ohio, 'Sketch Book,'" *BYU Studies* 12 (Summer 1972): 417–18.

24. Kenney, *Wilford Woodruff Journals* 1:140–41; see also Jessee, "Kirtland Diary," 395–96.

25. *Messenger and Advocate,* March 1835.

26. "Joseph Smith Diaries," LDSCA; also found in Dean Jessee, *The Personal Writings of Joseph Smith* (Salt Lake City: Deseret Book Company, 1984), 20–21; see also Scott H. Faulring, *An American Record: The Diaries and Journals of Joseph Smith* (Salt Lake City: Signature Books, 1989), 14.

27. Ebenezer Robinson, "Items of Personal History of the Editor," *The Return,* August 1889, hereafter cited as *The Return.*

28. *History of the Church* 2:519–20.

29. *Messenger and Advocate,* July 1835.

30. Richard P. Howard, ed., *The Memoirs of President Joseph Smith (1832–1914)* (Independence: Herald Publishing House, 1979), 2.

31. Jessee, *Personal Writings,* 60–61; see also Faulring, *Prophet's Record,* 36.

32. *History of the Church* 2:502–03.

33. *Messenger and Advocate,* November, 1836.

34. LDS D&C 88/RLDS D&C 85.

35. *Messenger and Advocate*, February 1835.

36. *Journal of Discourses* 7:158.

37. *Des Moines Daily News*, 16 October 1882.

38. *Doctrine and Covenants of the Church of the Latter Day Saints: Carefully Selected from the Revelations of God* (Kirtland: Frederick G. Williams, 1835); Herald Heritage Reprint (Independence: Herald Publishing House, 1971).

39. "William E. McClellan Letter," 4 August 1832, Reorganized Church of Jesus Christ of Latter Day Saints, Library-Archives, Independence, Missouri.

40. LDS D&C 66/RLDS D&C 66.

41. Jessee, *Personal Writings*, 146; see also Faulring, *Prophet's Record*, 118–19.

42. Jessee, *Personal Writings*, 146–47; see also Faulring, *Prophet's Record*, 119.

43. Kenney, *Wilford Woodruff Journal*, 1:106–07; see also Jessee, "Kirtland Diary," 368.

44. "Sarah Leavitt Autobiography," LDSCA.

45. *Messenger and Advocate*, December 1835.

46. *History of the Church* 2:348.

47. *Times and Seasons*, 1 March 1842; eventually, this material was republished by the LDS Church as part of its *Pearl of Great Price* (Liverpool: Franklin D. Richards, 1851) under the title "Book of Abraham."

48. Elden Jay Watson, *Manuscript History of Brigham Young 1801–1844* (Salt Lake City: Smith Secretarial Services, 1968), 16.

49. *Messenger and Advocate*, September 1836.

50. "Joseph Fielding Journal," LDSCA.

51. "Journal of Heber C. Kimball," LDSCA.

52. *Messenger and Advocate*, January 1837.

53. *History of the Church* 1:145–46.

54. Lucy Mack Smith, *History of Joseph Smith by His Mother*, edited by Preston Nibley (Salt Lake City: Bookcraft, 1954), 224.

55. Howard, *The Memoirs of President Joseph Smith III*, 1–2.

56. Quoted in Edward W. Tullidge, *The Women of Mormondom* (New York: Tullidge and Crandell, 1877), 41–43.

57. *Deseret News*, 19 May 1858; see also *History of the Church*, 1:215.

58. Kenney, *Wilford Woodruff Journals*, 1:137; see also Jessee, "Kirtland Diary," 393.

59. Kenney, *Wilford Woodruff Journals*, 1:137; see also Jessee, "Kirtland Diary," 394.

60. *Messenger and Advocate*, August 1835.

61. Kenney, *Wilford Woodruff Journals*, 1:106–11; see also Jessee, "Kirtland Diary," 371–73.

62. Kenney, *Wilford Woodruff Journals*, 1:146; see also Jessee, "Kirtland Diary," 397.

63. *History of the Church* 2:301, 316, 344, 347.

64. LDS D&C 41/RLDS D&C 41.

65. Wilford Woodruff quote in *Conference Report* (April 1898): 57.

66. "Oliver Cowdery Letter Book," Huntington Library, San Marino, California.

67. *History of the Church* 2:469.

68. *The Return*, May 1889.

69. Baptism for the dead allowed living descendants to be vicariously baptized for deceased relatives or friends, a proxy baptism; see 1 Corinthians 15:29.

70. Lyndon W. Cook and Milton V. Backman, Jr. eds. *The Kirtland Elders' Quorum Record: 1836–1841* (Provo: Grandin Book Company, 1985), 59.

71. Jessee, *Personal Writings*, 102; see also Faulring, *Prophet's Record*, 75.

72. Jessee, *Personal Writings*, 106; see also Faulring, *Prophet's Record*, 78.

73. Jessee, *Personal Writings*, 66; see also Faulring, *Prophet's Record*, 42–43.

74. Jessee, *Personal Writings*, 92–94; see also Faulring, *Prophet's Record*, 68.

75. Jessee, *Personal Writings*, 105; see also Faulring, *Prophet's Record*, 78.

76. *Journal of Discourses* 1:215.

77. Ibid., 3:121.

78. *Messenger and Advocate*, December 1835.

79. Ibid., January 1837.

80. Pratt, *Mormonism Unveiled*, 41.

81. Susan Easton Black, "Kirtland Cemetery List," BYUHBLL.

82. *Woman's Exponent*, 1 June 1888.

83. Jessee, *Personal Writings*, 143–44; see also Faulring, *Prophet's Record*, 116–17.

84. LDS D&C 109/see *The History of the Reorganized Church of Jesus Christ of Latter Day Saints* (Independence: Herald Publishing House, 1983) 2:38–44, 6 vols., hereafter cited as *RLDS History*.

85. LDS D&C 109:22, 34, 78-80/*RLDS History* 2:40–41, 44.

86. "Ira Ames Autobiography," Utah State Historical Society, Salt Lake City, Utah.

87. Nicholas G. Morgan, comp., *Eliza R. Snow: An Immortal: Selected Writings of Eliza R. Snow* (Salt Lake City: Nicholas G. Morgan, Sr. Foundation, 1957), 62.

88. *Messenger and Advocate*, March 1836.

89. Jessee, *Personal Writings*, 186; Faulring, see also *Prophet's Record*, 157–58 and LDS D&C 110:1–4/*RLDS History* 2:46–47.

90. *Painesville Telegraph*, 31 May 1838; the *Painesville Telegraph* became the *Painesville Republican* on 24 November 1836, and the name was changed back to *Painesville Telegraph* sometime in 1837.

91. Roger D. Launius, *An Illustrated History of the Kirtland Temple* (Independence: Herald Publishing House, 1986), 15–16.

92. *Messenger and Advocate*, 3 July 1837.

93. Kenney, *Wilford Woodruff Journals*, 1:120; see also Jessee, "Kirtland Diary," 381.

94. "Kirtland Revelation Book," LDSCA.

95. Jessee, *Personal Writings*, 163; see also Faulring, *Prophet's Record*, 136.

96. Jessee, *Personal Writings*, 92; see also Faulring, *Personal Record*, 67.

97. *Journal of Discourses* 10:165.

98. *History of the Church* 2:161.

99. LDS D&C 20/RLDS D&C 17.

100. "Kirtland Revelation Book," LDSCA.

101. This material was eventually published by the RLDS Church in 1867 as *The Holy Scriptures, Translated and Corrected by the Spirit of Revelation by Joseph Smith, Jr., the Seer* (Plano: The Reorganized Church of Jesus Christ of Latter Day Saints, 1867); see also *The Holy Scriptures, Inspired Version*, Joseph Smith, Jr., trans. (Independence: Herald Publishing House, 1974).

102. LDS D&C 65/RLDS D&C 65.

103. LDS D&C 76/RLDS D&C 76.

104. *The Juvenile Instructor*, 15 May 1892.

105. "Eliza R. Snow Life Sketch," LDSCA.

106. Eliza R. Snow Smith, *Biography and Family Record of Lorenzo Snow* (Salt Lake City: Deseret News Company, Printers, 1884), 36.

107. *Messenger and Advocate*, October 1834.

108. Elden J. Watson, ed. *Orson Pratt Journals* (Salt Lake City: Elden J. Watson, 1975) 60.

109. LDS D&C 37/RLDS D&C 37.

110. LDS D&C 54:8/RLDS D&C 54:2b.

111. *Elders' Journal*, October 1837.

112. Watson, *Manuscript History of Brigham Young*, 22–23.

113. Ibid., 58–59.

114. Quoted in Richard L. Anderson, "Jackson County in Early Mormon Description," *Missouri Historical Review*, 65 (April 1971): 268–69.

115. See Frank Wilcox, *The Ohio Canals* (Kent: The Kent State University Press, 1969).

116. *History of the Church* 1:118.

117. Ibid., 5:217–18.

118. LDS D&C 61:30–31/RLDS D&C 11:5 c–d.

119. *History of the Church* 4:167.

120. See *History of the Church* 5:202.

121. *History of the Church* 6:521.

122. Quoted in Arrington's "Kirtland Sketch Book," *BYU Studies* 12 (Summer 1972): 414.

123. *The Return*, July 1889.

124. *Cleveland Herald*, 25 November 1830.

125. F. Mark McKiernan and Roger D. Launius, eds., *An Early Latter Day Saint History: The Book of John Whitmer* (Independence: Herald Publishing House, 1980), 51.

126. Jessee, *The Personal Writings*, 36.

127. Quoted in Lawrence R. Flake, "A Shaker view of a Mormon mission," *BYU Studies*, 20 (Fall 1979): 95.

128. LDS D&C 49/RLDS D&C 49.

129. McKiernan and Launius, *An Early Latter Day Saint History*, 59–60.

130. Ibid., 61.

131. Flake, "A Shaker View," 97.

132. McKiernan and Launius, *An Early Latter Day Saint History*, 98.

133. Bari Oyler Stith, *Lake County, Ohio* (Northridge: Windsor Publications, Inc., 1983), 21–26.

134. Quoted in Richard L. Anderson, "The Impact of the First Preaching in Ohio," *BYU Studies* 11 (Spring 1971): 489.

135. E. D. Howe, *Autobiography and Recollections of a Pioneer* (Painesville: By the Author, 1878), 45.

136. Ibid., 38.

137. Watson, *The Orson Pratt Journals*, 75.

138. Lucy Mack Smith, *History of Joseph Smith*, 207.

139. Jessee, *Personal Writings*, 96; see also Faulring, *Prophet's Record*, 70.

140. *Millennial Star*, 19 November 1864.

141. Josiah Jones, "History," *Evangelist* 9 (1841): 133.

142. *Times and Seasons*, 1 September 1843.

143. Pratt, *Autobiography*, 107.

144. Jessee, *Personal Writings*, 95–96; see also Faulring, *Prophet's Record*, 69.

145. Jessee, *Personal Writings*, 16; see also Faulring, *Prophet's Record*, 10.

146. Jessee, *Personal Writings*, 31, 647; see also Faulring, *Prophet's Record*, 25–26.

147. *Chardon Spectator and Geauga Gazette*, 12 July 1834.

148. Jessee, *Personal Writings*, 65; see also Faulring, *Prophet's Record*, 40–41.

149. LDS D&C 49/RLDS D&C 49.

150. Newel Knight, *Scraps of Biography—Tenth Book of the Faith Promoting Series* (Salt Lake City: Juvenile Instructor Office, 1883), 69.

151. "Joseph Knight's Incidents of History from 1827 to 1844," LDSCA.

152. LDS D&C 54/RLDS D&C 54.

153. *Painesville Telegraph*, 28 June 1831.

154. Jessee, *Personal Writings*, 63; Faulring, *Prophet's Record*, 38.

155. Jessee, *Personal Writings*, 70–71; *Faulring*, Prophet's Record, 46.

156. History of the Church *1:219*.

157. *See Donald Q. Cannon and Lyndon W. Cook, eds.* Far West Record: Minutes of The Church of Jesus Christ of Latter-day Saints, 1830–1844 *(Salt Lake City: Deseret Book Company, 1983), 19–26.*

158. *LDS D&C 66/RLDS D&C 66.*

159. *Cannon and Cook*, Far West Record, *21.*

160. *See D. Kelly Ogden, "The Kirtland Hebrew School (1835–36),"* Regional Studies in Latter-day Saint History, Ohio (Provo: Department of Church History and Doctrine, Brigham Young University, 1990), 63–87.

161. History of the Church *2:356*

162. Ibid., 2:396.

163. Messenger and Advocate, *January 1835*.

164. *The* Star, *August 1834*.

165. History of the Church *2:64*.

166. Pratt, *Autobiography*, *117*.

167. Ibid., 127.

168. Ibid., 128.

169. Quoted in Ronald E. Romig and Donald Moore, "New Portage: City of Refuge, City of Safety in the Ohio," *Restoration Studies 2 (1983): 85*.

170. *History of the Church 3:1*.

171. Pratt, *Autobiography*, *28*.

172. Ibid.

173. Ibid., 48.

174. Ibid., 49.

175. Ibid., 49–50.

176. Ibid., 49–51.

177. LDS D&C 75/RLDS D&C 75.

178. "Revelation Relative to the Bishop's Search for an Agent," 8 March 1833, BYUHBLL.

179. "Wesley Perkins Letter," 11 February 1832, BYUHBLL.

PHOTOGRAPHIC ESSAY

1. See "Kirtland Temple (Mormon), Kirtland, Lake County, Ohio," *Architectural Forum* 64 (March 1936): 178–83.

2. Ibid., 178–79.

3. Elwin C. Robinson and Priscilla Graham, "Builders of the Kirtland Temple," unpublished manuscript in possession of the authors, 1.

4. Lauritz G. Petersen, "The Kirtland Temple," BYU Studies 12(summer 1972): 400–09. Current initials reflect RLDS usage.

5. The information contained in these captions was prepared by Paul Anderson, Senior Exhibit Designer, Museum of Church History and Art, The Church of Jesus Christ of Latter-day Saints, Salt Lake City, Utah.

THE CHURCH IN MISSOURI

1. LDS D&C 52:42–43/RLDS D&C 52:9e–f.

2. LDS D&C 57/RLDS D&C 57.

3. [LDS D&C 58/RLDS D&C 58.

4. LDS D&C 59/RLDS D&C 59.

5. LDS D&C 60/RLDS D&C 60.

6. LDS D&C 61/RLDS D&C 61.

7. LDS D&C 62/RLDS D&C 62.

8. LDS D&C 63/RLDS D&C 63.

9. Mulder and Mortensen, *Among the Mormons*, 71–72.

10. Ibid., 72.

11. LDS D&C 1/RLDS D&C 1.

12. LDS D&C 133/RLDS D&C 108.

13. LDS D&C 69/RLDS D&C 69.

14. Cannon and Cook, *Far West Record*, 44.

15. LDS D&C 82/RLDS D&C 81.

16. LDS D&C 83/RLDS D&C 82.

17. *A Book of Commandments, for the Government of the Church of Christ Organized According to Law, on the 6 April 1830* (Zion: W. W. Phelps and Co., 1833); Herald Heritage Reprint (Independence: Herald Publishing House, 1972).

18. LDS D&C 85.

19. Cannon and Cook, *The Far West Record*, 52.

20. *The Star*, April 1833.

21. Mulder and Mortensen, *Among the Mormons*, 72–74.

22. Emily M. Austin, *Mormonism or Life Among Mormons* (Madison: M. J. Cantwell, 1882), 72–73.

23. LDS D&C 103/RLDS D&C 106.

24. See LDS D&C 105:30–32/RLDS D&C 102:8 c–d, 9.

25. See LDS D&C 107:72–73.

26. Quoted in *History of the Church* 1:445.

27. *History of the Church* 2:104.

28. LDS D&C 105/RLDS D&C 102.

29. Cannon and Cook, *Far West Record*, 69.

30. Ibid., 100.

31. "Reminiscences of Drusilla Hendricks," LDSCA.

32. LDS D&C 115:4/*RLDS History*, 2:153–54. The LDS Church uses the modern form *Latter-day*, and the RLDS Church retains the original form.

33. LDS D&C 116/*RLDS History*, 2:166.

34. Faulring, 210.

35. LDS D&C 118:6/*RLDS History* 2:166.

36. "Levi Hancock Journal," LDSCA.

37. Ibid.

38. Jessee and Whittaker, "Rockwood Journal," 21.

39. "James Aldrich to Daniel Aldrich," 30 September 1838, LDSCA.

40. Jessee and Whittaker, "Rockwood Journal," 18.

41. Ibid., 15

42. Although most Danite activities were nonmilitary and certainly legal, the extremist faction led by Avard generated hostile and bitter feelings before the Mormon War.

43. *History of the Church* 3:190.

44. For the complete text of the letter that includes LDS D&C 121–123, see Jessee, *Personal Writings*, 388–407; see also *RLDS Church History* 2:324–26.

45. Ibid.

46. Cannon and Cook, *Far West Record*, 211–20.

47. "Reminiscences of Drusilla Hendricks," LDSCA.

48. "Sarah D. Rich Autobiography," LDSCA.

49. LDS D&C 121–123/*RLDS Church History* 2:324–36.

50. See Parley P. Pratt, *History of the Late Persecution Inflicted by the State of Missouri upon the Mormons* (Detroit: Dawson & Bates, Printers, 1839), 29.

51. "Morris Phelps, Account of Missouri Imprisonment," LDSCA.

52. Pratt, *Autobiography*, 252.

53. Ibid., 277–78.

54. "Autobiography of Milo Andrus," BYUHBLL.

55. Quoted in T. Edgar Lyon, "Independence, Missouri 1827–1833," *BYU Studies* 13 (Autumn 1972): 16.

56. LDS D&C 52/RLDS D&C 52. The most exhaustive study of the Saints' experiences in Jackson County is found in Warren A. Jennings, "Zion is Fled: The Expulsion of the Mormons from Jackson County, Missouri," Ph.D. dissertation, University of Florida, 1962.

57. *Times and Seasons*, 15 February 1844.

58. See *Messenger and Advocate*, September 1835.

59. LDS D&C 57:3/RLDS D&C 57:1d.

60. LDS D&C 58/RLDS D&C 58

61. *Journal of Discourses* 18:160–61.

62. Jessee, "Joseph Knight's Recollections," 39.

63. Quoted in Ronald E. Romig and John H. Siebert, "Historic Views of the Temple Lot," *John Whitmer Historical Association Journal* 7 (1987): 22.

64. Cannon and Cook, *Far West Record*, 50–51.

65. Quoted in Mulder and Mortensen, *Among the Mormons*, 76.

66. John Corrill, *A Brief History of The Church of Christ of Latter Day Saints* (St. Louis: Printed for the author, 1839), 19.

67. Wilford Woodruff, *Leaves from My Journal*, (Salt Lake City: Juvenile Instructor Office, 1881), 12.

68. Quoted in Ronald E. Romig and John H. Siebert, "First Impressions: The Independence, Missouri, Printing Operation, 1832–33," *John Whitmer Historical Association Journal* 10 (1990): 54.

69. Cannon and Cook, *Far West Record*, 49–50.

70. Mary Lightner, "Mary Elizabeth Rollins Lightner," 196.

71. Quoted in Romig and Siebert, "Historic Views of the Temple Lot," 26.

72. For a full description, see *History of the Church* 1:357–62.

73. *History of the Church* 1:358–59.

74. Ibid., 1:196.

75. LDS D&C 97:3–5/RLDS D&C 94:2a–c.

76. LDS D&C 28/RLDS D&C 27.

77. LDS D&C 30, 32/RLDS D&C 29, 31.

78. LDS D&C 28:9/RLDS D&C 27:3c–d.

79. Pratt, *Autobiography*, 39.

80. Eleanor Atkinson, "The Winter of Deep Snow," *Transactions of the Illinois State Historical Society for the Year 1909*, 49.

81. Pratt, *Autobiography*, 52.

82. Ibid.

83. Ibid.

84. Ibid., 56.

85. Ibid., 57.

86. Ibid., 44.

87. Quoted in *History of the Church*, 2:450.

88. See Michael S. Riggs, "The Economic Impact of Fort Leavenworth on Northwestern Missouri 1827–1838. Yet Another Reason for the Mormon War?" *Restoration Studies* 4 (1988): 124–33.

89. *Elders' Journal*, July 1834.

90. Riggs, "The Economic Impact of Fort Leavenworth," 124–33.

91. Jessee, *Personal Writings*, 367.

92. Ibid.

93. Pratt, *Autobiography*, 211.

94. Ibid.

95. Preston Nibley, *Witnesses of the Book of Mormon* (Salt Lake City: Stevens and Wallis, 1946), 102.

96. *Richmond Democrat*, 26 January 1888.

97. *Millennial Star*, 9 December 1878.

98. The most exhaustive study of the Saints' Clay County experiences is found in Max H. Parkin, "A History of the Latter-day Saints in Clay County, Missouri from 1833 to 1837," Ph.D. dissertation, Brigham Young University, 1976; this citation is on p. 258.

99. Gentry, "A History of the Latter-day Saints," 29.

100. Ibid., 44.

101. *History of the Church* 2:453.

102. *Journal of History* 9 (April 1916): 178.

103. Quoted in Andrew Jenson, ed. *Historical Record* (October 1888): 667–68.

104. Jessee, *Personal Writings*, 390.

105. Ibid., 376.

106. *Kansas City Journal*, 12 June 1881.

107. See Roger D. Launius, "Alexander W. Doniphan: Missouri's Forgotten Leader." In *Missouri Folk Heroes of the 19th Century*, F. Mark McKiernan and Roger D. Launius, eds. (Independence: Herald Publishing House, 1990).

108. Quoted in Launius, "Alexander Doniphan," 81.

109. Quoted in McKiernan and Launius, *An Early Latter Day Saint History*, 21.

110. See LDS D&C 116/RLDS History 2:153–54. The most exhaustive studies of the Mormon experiences in northern Missouri are found in Leland H. Gentry, "A History of the Latter-day Saints in Northern Missouri from 1836–1839," Ph.D dissertation, Brigham Young University, 1965, and Stephen C. Lesueur, "'High Treason and Murder': The Examination of Mormon Prisoners at Richmond, Missouri, in November 1838," *BYU Studies* 26 (Spring 1986): 3–30.

111. "Autobiography of Edward Stevenson," LDSCA.

112. "Orange Wight Autobiography," BYUHBLL.

113. Jessee and Whittaker, "Rockwood Journal," 18.

114. See LDS D&C 107/RLDS D&C 104.

115. "The Scriptory Book of Joseph Smith," LDSCA.

116. LDS D&C 107:53/RLDS D&C 104:28a.

117. *Journal of Discourses* 18:343.

118. "The Scriptory Book of Joseph Smith," LDSCA.

119. Quoted in William A. Linn, *The Story of the Mormons from the Date of Their Origin to the Year 1901* (New York: Macmillan Co., 1923), 205.

120. "Reminiscences of Drusilla Hendricks," LDSCA.

121. "Abner Blackburn Diary," LDSCA.

122. *History of the Church* 3:184.

123. Andrew Jenson, *The Historical Record* (5 July 1886): 84.

124. Andrew Jenson, *The Historical Record* (December 1888): 673.

125. Jessee and Whittaker, "Rockwood Journal," 21.

126. Ibid.

127. Mary Lightner, "Mary Elizabeth Rollins Lightner," 199.

128. Cannon and Cook, *Far West Record*, 221.

129. Ibid.

130. LDS D&C 118:5/*RLDS History*2:166.

131. Ibid.

132. Kenney, *Wilford Woodruff*1:324–25.

133. Ibid., 1:327.

134. Quoted in Godfrey, *Women's Voices*, 83.

135. *History of the Church* 3:193.

136. McKiernan and Launius, *An Early Latter Day Saint History*, 160.

137. Quoted in Pearl Wilcox, *Jackson County Pioneers* (Independence: By Author, 1975), 35.

138. Quoted in Anderson, "Jackson County in Early Mormon Descriptions," 273.

139. Newel Knight, *Scraps of Biography* (Salt Lake City: Juvenile Instructor Office, 1883), 70.

140. See *History of the Church* 1:203.

141. LDS D&C 61/RLDS D&C 61.

142. "Reynolds Cahoon Journal," LDSCA.

143. Now known as LDS D&C 62/RLDS D&C 62.

144. "Zadoc Judd Autobiography," BYUHBLL.

145. LDS D&C 61:6,22/RLDS D&C 61:1e;3f.

146. Pratt, *Autobiography*, 102.

147. *Jeffersonian Republican*, 30 November 1833.

148. Quoted in Gentry, "History of Latter-day Saints in Northwestern Missouri," 63–64.

149. Cannon and Cook, *Far West Record*, 211–21.

150. *Missouri Republican*, 27 December 1838.

151. Carrie Johnston and William Harvey Sheridan McGlumphy, *History of Clinton and Caldwell Counties* (Topeka: Historical Publishing Co., 1923), 250.

152. *Missouri Republican*, 9 January 1839.

153. Ibid., 19 November 1838.

154. See Stanley B. Kimball, "The Saints and St. Louis, 1831–1857: An Oasis of Tolerance and Security," *BYU Studies* 13 (Summer 1973): 489–519.

155. Pratt, *Autobiography*, 52

156. Ibid.

157. *Free Press*, 15 August 1833.

158. Quoted in Kimball, "The Saints and St. Louis," 499.

159. Watson, *Manuscript History*, 167.

160. Ibid.

161. *St. Louis Evening Gazette*, 1 July 1844.

162. *Times and Seasons*, 1 November 1843.

163. *St. Louis Luminary*, 3 February 1855.

EPILOGUE

1. See Janet Brigham, "Three Churches on Walnut Street," *Ensign* 9 (June 1979): 52; for an overview of the various organizations that have roots to the restoration, see Steven L. Shields, *Divergent Paths of the Restoration: A History of the Latter Day Saint Movement*, 4th ed., revised and enlarged (Los Angeles: Restoration Research, 1990).

2. See Roger Launius, *Father Figure: Joseph Smith III and the Creation of the Reorganized Church* (Independence: Herald Publishing House, 1990), 39–58.

3. *History of the Church* 7:229.

4. See Wayne A. Ham, "Center-Place Saints," *Restoration Studies* 3 (1983): 123–32.

5. See Rupert J. Fletcher and Daisy Whiting Fletcher, *Alpheus Cutler and the Church of Jesus Christ* (Independence: The Church of Jesus Christ, 1974).

6. See David Brion Davis, "Some Themes of Counter Perversion: An Analysis of Anti-Masonic, Anti-Catholic and Anti-Mormon Literature," *Mississippi Valley Historical Review*, 47 (September 1960): 205–44.

7. *Times and Seasons*, 15 January 1844.

APPENDIX ONE

1. Personal correspondence, 14 March 1991.

SELECTED BIBLIOGRAPHY OF PUBLISHED MATERIALS

General American History

Brown, Richard M. *Strain of Violence; Historical Studies of American Violence and Vigilantism.* New York: Oxford University Press, 1975.

Griffin, C. S. *The Ferment of Reform, 1830–1860.* New York: Thomas Y. Crowell Co., 1967.

Pressen, Edward. *Jacksonian America: Society, Personality, and Politics.* Rev. ed. Homewood: The Dorsey Press, 1978.

Reiner, Robert. "Militia and Public Order in Nineteenth-Century America," *Journal of American Studies* 11 (April 1977): 81–101.

Riegel, Robert E. *Young America 1830–1840.* Norman: University of Oklahoma Press, 1949.

Ohio and Missouri

Anderson, Hattie M. "The Evolution of a Frontier Society in Missouri, 1815–1828." *Missouri Historical Review* 32 (April 1938): 298–326; 32 (July 1938): 458–83; 33 (October 1838): 23–44.

————. "Missouri, 1804–1828: Peopling a Frontier State." *Missouri Historical Review* 31 (January 1937): 150–80.

Billington, Ray Allen. *Westward Expansion: A History of the American Frontier.* Holt, Rinehart and Winston, 1906.

Boyd, W. W. "Secondary Education in Ohio Previous to the Year 1840." *Ohio Archaeological and Historical Publications* 25 (1916): 118–34.

Chittenden, Hiram Martin. *History of Early Steamboat Navigation on the Missouri River.* Minneapolis,: Ross & Haines, Inc., 1962.

Conlin, Mary Lou. *The North Union Story.* Shaker Heights: The Shaker Historical Society Museum, 1974.

Crary, Christopher Gore. "Frontier Living Conditions in Kirtland." In *Ohio's Western Reserve: A Regional Reader*, 71–75. Edited by Harry F. Lupold and Gladys Haddad. Kent: The Kent

State University Press, 1988.

Feldberg, Michael. *The Turbulent Era: Riot and Disorder in Jacksonian America*. New York: Oxford University Press, 1980.

Hayden, Amos Sutton. *Early History of the Disciples in the Western Reserve, Ohio*. Cincinnati: Chase & Hall, 1876. New York: Arono Press, 1972.

The History of Caldwell and Livingston Counties, Missouri. St. Louis: National Historic Company, 1886.

Hopkins, Charles Edwin. *Ohio the Beautiful and Historic*. Boston: L. C. Page & Co., 1931.

Illustrated Historical Atlas of Carroll County, Missouri. N.p.: Brink, McDonough, and Co., 1876.

Mattes, Merrill J. "The Jumping Off Places on the Overland Trail." In *The Frontier Reexamined*, 27–39. Edited by John Francis McDermoot. Urbana: University of Illinois Press, 1967.

McReynolds, Edwin C. *Missouri: A History of the Crossroads State*. Norman: University of Oklahoma Press, 1962.

Nagel, Paul C. *Missouri: A Bicentennial History*. New York: W. W. Norton & Company, 1977.

Smith, Thomas H. *An Ohio Reader: 1750 to the Civil War*. Grand Rapids: William B. Eerdmans, 1975.

Religion in America

Ahlstrom, Sidney E. *A Religious History of the American People*. New Haven: Yale University Press, 1972.

Allen, James B. "Why Did People Act That Way? Some Observations on Religious Intolerance and Persecution in the American Past." *Ensign* 8 (December 1978): 21–24.

Andrews, Edward. *The People Called Shakers: A Search for the Perfect Society*. New York: Oxford University Press, 1953.

Backman, Milton V. Jr. *American Religions and the Rise of Mormonism*. Salt Lake City: Deseret Book Company, 1970.

_____. *Christian Churches of America: Origins and Beliefs*. Rev. ed. New York: Charles Scribner's Sons, 1983.

Barlow, Philip L. *Mormons and the Bible: The Place of Latter-day Saints in American Religion*. New York: Oxford University Press, 1991.

Brown, Ira V. "Watchers for the Second Coming: The Millennarian Tradition in America." *Mississippi Valley Historical Review* 39 (1952): 441–458.

Foster, Lawrence. *Religion and Sexuality: Three American Communal Experiments of the Nineteenth Century*. New York: Oxford University Press, 1981.

Gaustad, Edwin. *A Documentary History of Religion in America to the Civil War*. Grand Rapids: Eerdmans Publishing Company, 1982.

Johnson, Charles A. *The Frontier Camp Meeting, Religion's Harvest Time*. Dallas: Southern

Methodist University Press, 1955.

MacLean, J. P. *Shakers of Ohio*. Philadelphia: Porcupine Press, 1975.

Sweet, William Warren. *Religion in the Development of the American Culture*. New York: Charles Scribner's Sons, 1952.

Weigel, Gustave S. J. *Churches in North America: An Introduction*. Baltimore: Helicon Press, 1961.

LDS/RLDS Churches

Allen, James B., and Glen M. Leonard. *The Story of the Latter-day Saints*. Salt Lake City: Deseret Book, 1976.

Arrington, Leonard J., and Davis Bitton. *The Mormon Experience: A History of the Latter-day Saints*. New York: Alfred A. Knopf, 1979.

Barlow, Philip L. *Mormons and the Bible: The Place of the Latter-day Saints in American Religion*. New York: Oxford, 1991.

Barrett, Ivan J. *Joseph Smith and the Restoration: A History of the LDS Church to 1846*. Provo: Brigham Young University Press, 1972.

Blair, Alma R. "Reorganized Church of Jesus Christ of Latter Day Saints: Moderate Mormonism." In *The Restoration Movement: Essays in Mormon History*, 207–30. Edited by F. Mark McKiernan, Alma R. Blair, and Paul Edwards. Lawrence: Coronado Press, 1973.

Bushman, Richard L. "The Book of Mormon in Early Mormon History." In *New Views of Mormon History: Essays in Honor of Leonard J. Arrington*, 3–18. Edited by Davis Bitton and Maureen Ursenbach Beecher. Salt Lake City: University of Utah Press, 1987.

Church History in the Fullness of Times: The History of The Church of Jesus Christ of Latter-day Saints. Salt Lake City: The Church of Jesus Christ of Latter-day Saints, 1989.

Hill, Marvin S. *The Quest for Refuge: The Mormon Flight from American Pluralism*. Salt Lake City: Signature Books, 1989.

Launius, Roger D. "Whither Reorganization Historiography?" *John Whitmer Historical Association Journal* 10 (1990): 24–38.

Linn, William A. *The Story of the Mormons*. New York: Macmillan, 1902.

Mackay, Charles. *The Mormons: or the Latter-day Saints*. London: Office of the National Illustrated Library, 1852.

Roberts, B. H. *A Comprehensive History of The Church of Jesus Christ of Latter-day Saints, Century 1*. 6 vols. Salt Lake City: The Church of Jesus Christ of Latter-day Saints, 1930.

_____. *The Missouri Persecutions*. Salt Lake City: Bookcraft, 1965.

Robertson, R. J. "The Mormon Experience in Missouri, 1830–1839." *Missouri Historical Review* 68 (April 1974): 280–98.

Shields, Steven L. *The Latter Day Saint Churches: An Annotated Bibliography*. New York: Garland Publishing, 1986.

_____. *Divergent Paths of the Restoration, A History of the Latter Day Saint Movement.* Los Angeles: Restoration Research, 1990.

Smith, Emma, comp. *A Collection of Sacred Hymns for the Church of the Latter Day Saints.* Kirtland: F. G. Williams and Co., 1835; Heritage Reprint. Independence: Herald Publishing House, 1983.

Smith, Gregory. "The House of the Lord." *Saints Herald* 123 (February 1986): 5–6.

Smith, Joseph. *History of The Church of Jesus Christ of Latter-day Saints.* 7 vols. Edited by B. H. Roberts. Salt Lake City: The Church of Jesus Christ of Latter-day Saints, 1932–51.

Smith, Joseph III, and Heman C. Smith, eds. *History of the Reorganized Church of Jesus Christ of Latter Day Saints.* 6 vols. Independence: Herald Publishing House, 1973.

LDS/RLDS in Ohio and in Missouri

Anderson, Karl Ricks. *Joseph Smith's Kirtland: Eyewitness Accounts.* Salt Lake City: Deseret Book, 1989.

Anderson, Lavina Fielding. "Kirtland's Resolute Saints." *Ensign* 9 (January 1979): 49–55.

_____. "Like Gold Seven Times Purified: Early Saints in Missouri." *Ensign* 9 (April 1979): 51–55.

Anderson, Richard L. "The Impact of the First Preaching in Ohio." *BYU Studies* 11 (Summer 1971): 474–96.

_____."New Data for Revising the Missouri 'Documentary History.'" *BYU Studies* 14 (Summer 1974): 488–501.

Anderson, William C., and Eloise Anderson. *Guide to Mormon History Travels.* Provo: by the authors, 1991.

Backman, Milton V. Jr. "Flight from Kirtland." In *Regional Studies in Latter-day Saint History, Ohio,* 139–54. Edited by Milton V. Backman, Jr. Provo: Department of Church History and Doctrine, Brigham Young University, 1990.

_____. *The Heavens Resound: A History of the Latter-day Saints in Ohio 1830–38.* Salt Lake City: Deseret Book, 1983.

_____. "Kirtland: The Crucial Years." *Ensign* 8 (January 1979): 24–28.

Berbert, Geri. "Disaster on the Missouri." *Ensign* 11 (September 1981): 28–30.

Bitton, Davis. "The Waning of Mormon Kirtland." *BYU Studies* 12 (Summer 1972): 455–64.

Brack, Nancy J. "A Mormon Interlude in Kirtland." *Lake County Historical Quarterly* 31 (March 1989): 1–8.

Britton, Rollin J. "Early Days on Grand River and the Mormon War." *Missouri Historical Review* 13 (January 1919): 112–34; (April 1919): 287–310; (July 1919): 388–98; 14 (October 1919): 89–110; (January 1920): 233–45.

Bushman, Richard L. "Mormon Persecutions in Missouri, 1833." *BYU Studies* 3 (Autumn 1960): 11–20.

Corrill, John. *A Brief History of The Church of Jesus Christ of Latter Day Saints*. St. Louis: For the Author, 1839.

Crary, Christopher Gore. "Frontier Living Conditions in Kirtland." In *Ohio's Western Reserve: A Regional Reader*. Harry F. Lupold and Gladys Haddad. Kent: Kent State University Press, 1988.

Crawley, Peter, and Richard L. Anderson. "The Political and Social Realities of Zion's Camp" *BYU Studies* 14 (Summer 1974): 406–20.

Dyer, Alvin R. *The Refiner's Fire: Historical Highlights of Missouri*. Salt Lake City: Deseret Book Company, 1972.

Jenson, Andrew. *Church Chronology: A Record of Important Events*. Salt Lake City: Deseret News, 1914.

_____. *Encyclopedic History of The Church of Jesus Christ of Latter-day Saints*. Salt Lake City: Deseret News Publishing Company, 1941.

_____. *Historical Record*. 8 vols. Salt Lake City: Andrew Jenson, 1881–1889.

_____. *Latter-day Saint Biographical Encyclopedia*. 4 vols. Salt Lake City: Andrew Jenson History Company, 1901.

Kimball, Stanley B. *Discovering Mormon Trails New York to California 1831–1868*. Salt Lake City: Deseret Book Company, 1979.

_____. "Sources on the History of the Mormons in Ohio: 1830–1838." *BYU Studies* 11 (Summer 1971): 524–40.

Lesueur, Stephen C. *The 1838 Mormon War in Missouri*. Columbia: University of Missouri Press, 1987.

Lyon, T. Edgar. "Independence, Missouri, and the Mormons, 1827–1833." *BYU Studies* 13 (Autumn 1972): 10–19.

McGrane, Reginald Charles. *The Panic of 1837*. Chicago: University of Chicago Press, 1927.

Parkin, Max H. "Missouri's Impact on the Church." *Ensign* 9 (April 1979): 57–63.

Wilcox, Pearl. *The Latter Day Saints on the Missouri Frontier*. Independence: Peal G. Wilcox, 1972.

Wood, Gordon S. "Evangelical America and Early Mormonism." *New York History* 61 (October 1980): 359–86.

Biographical Studies

Anderson, Mary Audentia Smith. *Ancestry and Posterity of Joseph Smith and Emma Hale*. Independence: Herald Publishing House, 1929.

Anderson, Richard L. *Investigating the Book of Mormon Witnesses*. Salt Lake City: Deseret Book, 1981.

_____. "What Were Joseph Smith's Sisters Like?" *Ensign* 9 (March 1979): 42–45.

_____. "The Whitmers." *Ensign* 9 (August 1979): 35–40.

Arrington, Leonard J. *Brigham Young: American Moses*. New York: Alfred A. Knopf, 1985.

_____. *Charles C. Rich—Mormon General and Western Frontiersman*. Provo: Brigham Young University Press, 1974.

_____, and Joann Jolley. "The Faithful Young Family: The Parents, Brothers and Sisters of Brigham." *Ensign* 10 (August 1989): 52–57.

_____, and Susan Arrington Madsen. "Lucy Mack Smith." In *Mothers of the Prophets*, 3–26. Salt Lake City: Deseret Book, 1987.

_____. *Sunbonnet Sisters: True Stories of Mormon Women and Frontier Life*. Salt Lake City: Bookcraft, 1984.

Avery, Valeen T., and Linda K. Newell. *Mormon Enigma: Emma Hale Smith*. Garden City: Doubleday and Company, Inc., 1984.

Barron, Howard H. *Orson Hyde: Missionary, Apostle, Colonizer*. Bountiful: Horizon, 1977.

Beecher, Maureen Ursenbach. "Leonora, Eliza, and Lorenzo: An Affectionate Portrait of the Snow Family." *Ensign* 10 (June 1980): 64–69.

Black, Susan Easton, comp. *Membership of The Church of Jesus Christ of Latter-day Saints: 1830–48*. Fifty volumes. Provo: BYU Religious Studies Center, 1989.

Brodie, Fawn M. *No Man Knows My History: The Life of Joseph Smith*. New York: Alfred A. Knopf, Inc. 1971.

Corbett, Pearson H. *Hyrum Smith, Patriarch*. Salt Lake City: Deseret Book, 1963.

Easton, Susan, and Keith Perkins, comps. *A Profile of Latter-day Saints of Kirtland, Ohio, and Members of Zion's Camp: 1830–1839*. Provo: Religious Studies Center, Brigham Young University, 1983.

Gunn, Stanley R. *Oliver Cowdery, Second Elder and Scribe*. Salt Lake City: Bookcraft, 1962.

Hartley, William G. "The Knight Family: Ever Faithful to the Prophet." *Ensign* 19 (January 1989): 43–49.

_____. *"They Are My Friends," A History of Joseph Knight Family, 1825–1850*. Provo: Grandin Book Company, 1986.

Hill, Donna. *Joseph Smith: The First Mormon*. Garden City: Doubleday & Company, Inc., 1977.

Jensen, Richard L. "The John Taylor Family." *Ensign* 10 (February 1980): 50–56.

Jesse, Dean C. "Joseph Knight's Recollection of Early Mormon History." *BYU Studies* 17 (Autumn 1976): 27–39.

_____. "'Steadfastness and Patient Endurance': The Legacy of Edward Partridge." *Ensign* 9 (June 1979): 40–47.

Launius, Roger D. "Alexander W. Doniphan: Missouri's Forgotten Leader." In *Missouri Folk Heroes of the Nineteenth Century*. F. Mark McKiernan and Roger D. Launius, eds. Independence: Herald Publishing House, 1989: 63–82.

Launius, Roger D. *Father Figure: Joseph Smith III and the Creation of the Reorganized Church*.

Independence: Herald Publishing House, 1990.

Legg, Phillip R. *Oliver Cowdery: The Elusive Second Elder of the Restoration.* Independence: Herald Publishing House, 1989.

Madsen, Truman G. *Joseph Smith the Prophet.* Salt Lake City: Bookcraft, 1989.

McKiernan, F. Mark. "The Conversion of Sidney Rigdon to Mormonism." *Dialogue* 5 (Summer 1970): 71–78.

_____. *The Voice of One Crying in the Wilderness: Sidney Rigdon, Religious Reformer 1793–1876.* Lawrence: Coronado Press, 1971.

Newell, Linda King, and Valeen Tippetts Avery. *Mormon Enigma: Emma Hale Smith.* Garden City: Doubleday & Company, Inc., 1984.

Nibley, Preston. *Witnesses of the Book of Mormon.* Salt Lake City: Deseret Book Co., 1953.

Perkins, Keith. "A House Divided: The John Johnson Family." *Ensign* 9 (February 1970): 54-59.

Porter, Larry C. "Alvin Smith: Reminder of the Fairness of God." *Ensign* 8 (September 1978): 65–67.

Pratt, Parley P. *Autobiography of Parley P. Pratt.* Salt Lake City: Deseret Book Company, 1973.

Pratt, R. Steven. "The 5 Sons of Jared and Charity Pratt." *Ensign* 9 (October 1979): 52–57.

Quinn, Michael. "The Newel K. Whitney Family." *Ensign* 8 (December 1978): 42–45.

Rollmann, Hans. "The Early Baptist Career of Sidney Rigdon in Warren, Ohio." *BYU Studies* 21 (Winter 1981): 37–50.

Rounds, W. J. "Colonel George M. Hinkle (Was He a Hero or a Villain?)" *Restoration Trail Forum* 9 (August 1983): 3–4.

Smith, Lucy Mack. *Biographical Sketches of Joseph Smith, the Prophet, and His Progenitors for Many Generations.* Independence: Herald Publishing House, 1969, reprint.

_____. *History of Joseph Smith.* Edited by Preston Nibley. Salt Lake City: Bookcraft, 1954.

Snow, Eliza R., comp. *Biography and Family Record of Lorenzo Snow.* Salt Lake City: Deseret News, 1884.

Snow LeRoi C. "How Lorenzo Snow Found God." *Improvement Era* 40 (February 1937): 82–84, 105.

_____. "Who Was Professor Joshua Seixas?" *Improvement Era* 39 (February 1936): 67–71.

Van Orden, Bruce A. "W. W. Phelps: His Ohio Contributions, 1835–36." In *Regional Studies in Latter-day Saint Church History, Ohio,* 45–62. Edited by Milton V. Backman Jr. Provo: Department of Church History and Doctrine, Brigham Young University, 1990.

Wilcox, Pearl. *Jackson County Pioneers.* Independence: Pearl Wilcox, 1975.

Woodford, Robert J. "Jesse Gause, Counselor to the Prophet." *BYU Studies.* 15 (Spring 1975): 362–64.

Contemporary Accounts and Recollections

Anderson Richard L. "The Reliability of the Early History of Lucy and Joseph Smith." *Dialogue* 4 (Summer 1969): 13–28.

Andrus, Hyrum L., and Helen Mae Andrus, comps. *They Knew the Prophet*. Salt Lake City: Bookcraft, Inc., 1974.

_____, and Richard E. Bennett, eds. *Mormon Manuscripts to 1846: A Guide to the Holdings of the Harold B. Lee Library*. Provo: Harold B. Lee Library, Brigham Young University, 1977.

Arrington, Leonard J. "James Gordon Bennett's 1831 Report on 'The Mormonites.'" *BYU Studies* 10 (Spring 1970): 353–64.

_____. "Oliver Cowdery's Kirtland, Ohio, 'Sketch Book.'" *BYU Studies* 12 (Summer 1972): 410–26.

Backman, Milton V. Jr. "Truman Coe's 1836 Description of Mormonism." *BYU Studies* 17 (Spring 1977): 347–55.

_____. "Witnesses of the Glories of Heaven." *Ensign* 11 (March 1981): 58–61.

Bitton, Davis. *Guide to Mormon Diaries and Autobiographies*. Provo: Brigham Young University Press, 1977.

Cannon, Donald Q., and Lyndon W. Cook, eds. *Far West Record*. Salt Lake City: Deseret Book, Co., 1983.

_____, and David J. Whittaker, eds. *Supporting Saints: Life Stories of Nineteenth-Century Mormons*. Provo: BYU Religious Studies Center, 1985.

Cook, Lyndon, and Milton V. Backman, Jr., eds. *Kirtland Elders' Quorum Record: 1836–41*. Provo: Grandin Book Company, 1985.

Crawley, Peter. "Two Rare Missouri Documents." BYU Studies 14 (Summer 1974): 502–27.

Elders' Journal of The Church of Latter Day Saints. October–November 1837, Kirtland, Ohio; *Elders' Journal of the Church of Jesus Christ of Latter Day Saints*. July–August 1838, Far West, Missouri.

The Evening and the Morning Star. June 1832–July 1833, Independence, Missouri; December 1833–September 1834, Kirtland, Ohio.

"The Far West Dissenters and the Gamblers at Vicksburg: An Examination of the Documentary Evidence and Historical Context of Sidney Rigdon's Salt Sermon." *Restoration* 3 (January 1986): 21–27.

Faulring, Scott H., ed. *An American Prophet's Record: The Diaries and Journals of Joseph Smith*. Salt Lake City: Signature Books, 1987.

Flake, Chad J. "The Newell K. Whitney Collection." *BYU Studies* 11 (Summer 1971): 322–28.

Godfrey, Kenneth W., Audrey M. Godfrey, and Jill Mulvay Derr. *Women's Voices: An Untold History of the Latter-day Saints, 1830–1890*. Salt Lake City: Deseret Book Company, 1982.

Ham, Wayne, ed. *Publish Glad Tidings: Readings in Early Latter-day Saint Sources.* Independence: Herald Publishing House, 1970.

Hinkle, George. "Letter to W. W. Phelps, August 14, 1844." *Journal of History* 13 (October 1920): 448–53.

Howard, Richard P., ed. *The Memoirs of President Joseph Smith (1832–1914).* Independence: Herald Publishing House, 1979.

Jennings, Warren A. "'What Crime Have I been Guilty of?': Edward Partridge's Letter to an Estranged Sister." *BYU Studies* 18 (Summer 1978): 520–28.

Jesse, Dean C. "Joseph Smith, Jr.—In His Own Words, Part 1." *Ensign* 14 (December,1984): 22–31.

_____. "Joseph Smith, Jr.—In His Own Words, Part 2." *Ensign* 15 (January 1985): 18–24.

_____. "Joseph Smith, Jr.—In His Own Words, Part 3." *Ensign* 15 (February 1985): 6–13.

_____. "The Kirtland Diary of Wilford Woodruff." *BYU Studies* 12 (Summer 1972): 365–99.

_____, ed. *The Papers of Joseph Smith: Autobiographical and Historical Writings.* Vol. 1. Salt Lake City: Deseret Book Company 1989.

_____, ed. *The Personal Writings of Joseph Smith.* Salt Lake City: Deseret Book Company, 1983.

_____, and William G. Hartley. "Joseph Smith's Missionary Journal" *New Era* 4 (February 1974): 34–36.

_____, and David J. Whittaker. "The Last Months of Mormonism in Missouri: The Albert Perry Rockwood Journal." *BYU Studies* 28 (Winter 1988): 5–41.

Johnson, Clark V. "The Missouri Persecution: The Petition of Isaac Leany." *BYU Studies* 23 (Winter 1983): 94–104.

_____."The Missouri Redress Petitions: A Reappraisal of Mormon Persecutions in Missouri." *BYU Studies* 26 (Spring 1986): 31–44.

Journal of Discourses. 26 vols. Liverpool and London: F. D. Richards and S. W. Richards, 1856.

Keller, Karl, ed. "I Never Knew a Time When I Did Not Know Joseph Smith: A Son's Record of the Life and Testimony of Sidney Rigdon" *Dialogue* 1 (Winter 1966): 15–42.

Kenney, Scott G., ed. *Wilford Woodruff's Journals: 1833–1898 Typescript.* 9 vols. Midvale: Signature Books, 1983.

Kimball, Stanley B. "Missouri Mormon Manuscripts: Sources in Selected Societies." *BYU Studies* 14 (Summer 1974): 458–87.

Knight, Newel. *Scraps of Biography—Tenth Book of the Faith Promoting Series.* Salt Lake City: Juvenile Instructor Office, 1883.

Latter Day Saints' Messenger and Advocate. October 1834–September 1837, Kirtland.

The Latter-day Saints' Millennial Star. Manchester and Liverpool.

McKiernan, F. Mark, and Roger D. Launius, ed. *An Early Latter Day Saint History: The Book of*

John Whitmer, Kept by Commandment. Independence: Herald House, 1980.

Mulder, William, and A. Russell Mortensen, eds. *Among the Mormons: Historic Accounts by Contemporary Observers.* New York: Alfred A. Knopf, 1969.

Reid, J. M. *Sketches and Anecdotes of the Old Settlers, and New Comers, The Mormon Bandits and Danite Band.* Keokuk: R. B. Ogden, Publisher, 1876.

The Saints' Herald. January 1860–present, Plano and Lamoni. Reorganized Church of Jesus Christ of Latter Day Saints.

Times and Seasons. 1839–1846, Nauvoo, Illinois.

Watson, Elden Jay, ed. *Manuscript History of Brigham Young, 1801–1844.* Salt Lake City: Smith Secretarial Services, 1968.

_____, Elden Jay, comp. *The Orson Pratt Journals.* Salt Lake City: Elden Jay Watson, 1975.

Doctrinal Development

Allen, James B. "Line upon Line." *Ensign* 9 (July 1979): 32–39.

Anderson Richard L. "Joseph Smith and the Millinarian Time Table." *BYU Studies* 3 (Spring–Summer 1961): 55–66.

Alexander, Thomas G. "The Word of Wisdom: From Principle to Requirement." *Dialogue* 14 (Autumn 1981): 78–88.

Bachman, Daniel W. "New Light on an Old Hypothesi: The Ohio Origins of the Revelation on Eternal Marriage" *Journal of Mormon History* 5 (1978): 19–32.

A Book of Commandments, for the Government of the Church of Christ, Organized According to Law, on 6th of April, 1830. Zion: W. W. Phelps & Co., 1833; Herald Heritage Reprint. Independence: Herald House, 1972.

Book of Mormon. Joseph Smith, Jr., trans. Palmyra: E. B. Grandin, 1830; Heritage Reprint. Independence: Herald Publishing House, 1980.

Burton, Alma P. *Toward The New Jerusalem.* Salt Lake City: Deseret Book, 1985.

Bush, Lester E. Jr. "The Word of Wisdom in Early Nineteenth-Century Perspective." *Dialogue* 14 (Autumn 1981): 46–65.

Cannon, Donald Q., Larry E. Dahl, and John W. Welch. "The Restoration of Major Doctrines Through Joseph Smith: Priesthood, the Word of God, and the Temple." *Ensign* 19 (February 1989): 7–13.

_____. "The Restoration of Major Doctrines Through Joseph Smith: The Godhead, Mankind, and The Creation." *Ensign* 19 (January 1989): 27–33.

Clark, James R., ed. *Messages of the First Presidency of The Church of Jesus Christ of Latter-day Saints 1833–1964.* 6 vols. Salt Lake City: Bookcraft, 1964–1965.

A Collection of Sacred Hymns, for the Church of the Latter Day Saints. Kirtland: F. G. Williams & Co., 1835. Herald Heritage Reprint, 1973.

Cook, Lyndon. *Joseph Smith and the Law of Consecration.* Provo: Grandin Book Company,

1985.

_____. *The Revelations of the Prophet Joseph Smith*. Salt Lake City: Deseret Book Company, 1985.

Dahl, Larry E., and Charles D. Tate, Jr., eds. *The Lectures on Faith: In Historical Perspective*. Provo: Religious Studies Center, 1990.

Doctrine and Covenants of the Church of Latter Day Saints: Carefully Selected from the Revelations of God. Kirtland: Frederick G. Williams, 1835; Herald Heritage Reprint. Independence: Herald House, 1971.

The Doctrine and Covenants of The Church of Jesus Christ of Latter-day Saints. Salt Lake City: The Church of Jesus Christ of Latter-day Saints, 1981.

The Book of Doctrine and Covenants. Independence: Herald Publishing House, 1970.

Esplin, Ronald K. "The 1840–41 Mission to England and the Development of the Quorum of the Twelve." In *The Mormons in Early Victorian Britain*, 70–91. Edited by Richard L. Jensen and Malcom R. Thorp. Salt Lake City: University of Utah Press, 1989.

Garrett, H. Dean. "The Coming Forth of the Doctrine and Covenants." In *Regional Studies of Latter-day Saint Church History, Ohio*, 89–104. Edited by Milton V. Backman, Jr. Provo: Department of Church History and Doctrine, Brigham Young University, 1990.

Gentry, Leland H. "What of the Lectures on Faith?" *BYU Studies* 19 (Fall 1978): 5–19.

Harrell, Charles R. "The Development of the Doctrine of Preexistence, 1830–1844." *BYU Studies* 28 (Spring 1988): 75–96.

The Holy Scriptures, Inspired Version. Joseph Smith, trans. Independence: Herald Publishing House, 1974.

Howard, Richard P. *Restoration Scriptures: A Study of Their Textual Development*. Independence: Herald Publishing House, 1969.

Jesse, Dean C. "Joseph Smith and the Beginning of Mormon Record Keeping." In *The Prophet Joseph Smith: Essays on the Life and Mission of Joseph Smith*, 138–60. Edited by Larry C. Porter and Susan Easton Black. Salt Lake City: Deseret Book Company, 1988.

Journal of Discourses. 26 vols. Liverpool and London: F. D. Richards and S. W. Richards, 1856; reprinted 1967.

Kirkham, Francis W. *A New Witness for Christ in America: The Book of Mormon*. 2 vols. Salt Lake City: Utah Printing Company, 1967.

Launius, Roger D. "A Survey of Priesthood Ordination: 1830–1844." *Restoration Trail Forum* 9 (May 1983): 3–4, 6.

Madsen, Truman G., ed. *Concordance of Doctrinal Statements of Joseph Smith*. Salt Lake City: I.E.F. Publishing, 1985.

Matthews, Robert J. "How We Got the Book of Moses." *Ensign* 16 (January 1986): 43–49.

_____. *"A Plainer Translation": Joseph Smith's Translation of the Bible; a History and Commentary*. Provo: Brigham Young University Press, 1975.

_____. "The 'New Translation' of the Bible, 1830–1833: Doctrinal Development During the Kirtland Era." *BYU Studies* 11 (Summer 1971): 400–22.

Millet, Robert L., and Kent P. Jackson, eds. *Studies in Scripture: Volume One, the Doctrine and Covenants*. Sandy: Randall Book Co., 1984.

Murdoch, Norman H. "Joseph Smith, the Book of Mormon, and Mormonism: A Review Essay." *New York History* 67 (1986): 224–30.

The Pearl of Great Price. Liverpool: Franklin D. Richards, 1851; Salt Lake City: The Church of Jesus Christ of Latter-day Saints, 1989.

Pratt, John P. "The Restoration of Priesthood Keys on Easter 1836, Part 1." *Ensign* 15 (June 1985): 59–68.

_____. "The Restoration of Priesthood Keys on Easter 1836, Part 2: Symbolism of Passover and of Elijah's Return." *Ensign* 15 (July 1985): 55–64.

Quinn, Michael. "The Evolution of the Presiding Quorums of the LDS Church," *Journal of Mormon History* 1 (1974): 21–38.

Smith, Joseph Fielding, comp. *Teachings of the Prophet Joseph Smith*. Salt Lake City: Deseret Book Company, 1961.

Todd, Jay. *Saga of the Book of Abraham*. Salt Lake City: Deseret Book Co., 1969.

Underwood, Grant. "Book of Mormon Usage in Early LDS Theology." *Dialogue* 17 (Autumn 1984): 35–74.

_____. "Millenarianism and the Early Mormon Mind." *Journal of Mormon History*. 9 (1982): 41–51.

Van Wagoner, Richard S., Steven C. Walker, and Allen D. Roberts. "The 'Lectures on Faith': A Case Study in Decanonization." *Dialogue* 20 (Fall 1987): 71–77.

Woodford, Robert J. "The Doctrine and Covenants: A Historical Overview." In *Studies in Scripture Volume One: Doctrine and Covenants*, 3–22. Edited by Robert L. Millet and Kent P. Jackson. Salt Lake City: Randall Book, 1984.

_____. "How the Revelations in the Doctrine & Covenants were Received and Compiled." *Ensign* 15 (January 1985): 26–33.

Young, Joseph. *History of the Organization of the Seventies*. Salt Lake City: Deseret News, 1878.

Individual Sites

Anderson, Paul L. "Heroic Nostalgia: Enshrining the Mormon Past." *Sunstone* 5 (July–August 1980): 47–55.

Anderson, William C., and Eloise Anderson. *Guide to Mormon History Travel*. Provo: Published by the Authors, 1991.

Backman, Milton V. Jr. "Establish a House of Prayer, a House of God: The Kirtland Temple." In *The Prophet Joseph: Essays on the Life and Mission of Joseph Smith*, 208–25. Edited by Larry C. Porter and Susan Easton Black. Salt Lake City: Deseret Book, 1988.

Backman, Milton V. Jr. "The Quest for a Restoration: The Birth of Mormonism in Ohio." *BYU Studies* 12 (Summer 1972): 346–64.

Barrett, Ivan J. "A Map of Northwestern Missouri in the Late 1830s." *BYU Studies* 26 (Spring 1986): 2.

Black, Susan Easton. "Joseph's Experience in Hiram, Ohio: A Time of Contrasts." In *Regional Studies in Latter-day Saint Church History Ohio*, 27–44. Edited by Milton V. Backman, Jr. Provo: Department of Church History and Doctrine, Brigham Young University, 1990.

Blair, Alma R. "The Haun's Mill Massacre." *BYU Studies* 13 (Autumn 1972): 62–76.

Brack, Nancy J. "A Mormon Temple in the American Rural Tradition." *Lake County Historical Quarterly* 31 (September 1989): 17–26.

Brigham, Janet. "Church History Sites—Separating Fiction and Fact." *Ensign* 9 (March 1979): 74–75.

Cowan, Richard O. "The House of the Lord in Kirtland: A 'Preliminary' Temple." In *Regional Studies of Latter-day Saint Church History, Ohio*, 105–22. Edited by Milton V. Backman, Jr. Provo: Department of Church History and Doctrine, Brigham Young University, 1990.

Durham, Reed C. "The Election Day Battle at Gallatin." *BYU Studies* 13 (Autumn 1972): 36–61.

Fant, Kathleen Griffin. *Orange Township . . . Orange Community*. Salem, Ohio: The Orange Community Historical Society, 1982.

Gentry, Leland H. "The Land Questions at Adam-ondi-Ahman." *BYU Studies* 26 (Spring 1986): 45–56.

Hayden, Dolores. *Seven American Utopias: The Architecture of Communitarian Socialism, 1790–1975*. Cambridge: MIT Press, 1976.

Hill, Marvin S. "Cultural Crisis in the Mormon Kingdom: A Reconsideration of the Causes of Kirtland Dissent." *Church History* 49 (September 1980): 286–97.

Hitchcock, Mrs. Peter S. "Joseph Smith and the Kirtland Temple." *Historical Society Quarterly* 7 (November 1965): 1–4.

Jackson, Don H. *The Heritage of Liberty*. Liberty: City of Liberty, 1976.

Jackson, Richard H. "The Mormon Village: Genesis and Antecedents of the City of Zion Plan." *BYU Studies* 17 (Winter 1977): 223–40.

Jennings, Warren A. "The Expulsion of the Mormons from Jackson County, Missouri." *Missouri Historical Review* 64 (October 1969): 41–63.

Jesse, Dean C. "'Walls, Grates, and Screeching Iron Doors': The Prison Experience of Mormon Leaders in Missouri, 1838–1839." In *New Views of Mormon History: Essays in Honor of Leonard J. Arrington*, 19–42. Edited by Davis Bitton and Maureen Ursenbach Beecher. Salt Lake City: University of Utah Press, 1987.

Kidney, Walter C. *Historic Building in Ohio*. Pittsburgh: Ober Park Associates, 1972.

Kimball, Stanley B. "The Saints and St. Louis, 1831–1857: An Oasis of Tolerance and Security." *BYU Studies* 13 (Summer 1973): 489–519.

_____. "Two More Mormon Trails." *Ensign* 9 (August 1979): 48–50.

Launius, Roger D. *An Illustrated History of the Kirtland Temple*. Independence: Herald House,

1986.

_____. *The Kirtland Temple: A Historical Narrative*. Independence: Herald House, 1986.

Layton, Robert J. "Kirtland: A Perspective in Time and Place." *BYU Studies* 11 (Summer 1971): 423–38.

"Maser Detail Series: Historic American Buildings: Kirtland Temple." *Architectural Forum* 64 (March 1936): 177–83.

Parkin, Max H. "Kirtland: A Stronghold for the Kingdom," In *The Restoration Movement: Essays in Mormon History*, 63–98. Edited by Mark McKiernan, Alma R. Blair, and Paul Edwards Lawrence. Coronado Press, 1973.

_____. "The Courthouse Mentioned in the Revelation on Zion." *BYU Studies* 14 (Summer 1974): 451–57.

Peatross, C. Ford. *Historic America: Buildings, Structures, and Sites*. Washington D.C.: Library of Congress, 1983.

Petersen, Lauritz G. "The Kirtland Temple." *BYU Studies* 12 (Summer 1972): 400–09.

Pioneer and General History of Geauga County. Geauga County: The Historical Society of Geauga County, 1880.

Prusha, Anne B. *A History of Kirtland, Ohio*. Mentor: Lakeland Community College Press, 1982.

Romig, Ronald E., and Donald Moore. "New Portage: City of Refuge, City of Safety in the Ohio." *Restoration Studies* 2 (1983): 80–88.

_____. and John H. Siebert. "First Impressions: The Independence, Missouri, Printing Operation, 1832–33." *John Whitmer Historical Association Journal* 10 (1990): 51–66.

_____, and John H. Siebert. "Historic Views of the Temple Lot." *John Whitmer Historical Association Journal* 7 (1987): 21–27.

Saari, Alma. "The Fairport Harbor Story." *Historical Quarterly, Lake County, Ohio* 8 (May 1966): 1–5.

Thompson, John E. "A Chronology of Danite Meetings in Adam-ondi-Ahman, Missouri, July to September 1838." *Restoration* 4 (January 1985): 11–14.

_____. "The Initial Survey Committee Selected to Appoint Lands for Gathering in Daviess County, Missouri (1837–1838)." In *Restoration Studies* 3 (1986): 305–13.

Photography

Anderson, James J., and Jeannette Grosvenor. *Geauga County, Ohio: A Pictorial History*. Norfolk, Virginia: The Donning Company, 1989.

Holzapfel, Richard Neitzel, and T. Jeffery Cottle. *Old Mormon Nauvoo and Southeastern Iowa: Historic Photographs and Guide*. Santa Ana: Fieldbrook Productions, Inc., 1991.

Holzapfel, Richard Neitzel, and T. Jeffery Cottle. *Old Mormon Palmyra and New England: Historic Photographs and Guide*. Santa Ana: Fieldbrook Productions, Inc., 1991.

Tobler, Douglas S., and Nelson B. Wadsworth. *The History of the Mormons in Photographs and Text: 1832 to the Present*. New York: St. Martin Press, 1989.

"The Way it Looks Today: A Camera Tour of Church History Sites in New England, New York, Pennsylvania, and Ohio." *Ensign* 8 (September 1978): 33–49.

"The Way it Looks Today: A Camera Tour of Church History Sites in Kirtland Neighborhood." *Ensign* 9 (January 1979): 31–48.

Winckler, Suzanne. *The Smithsonian Guide to Historic America: The Great Lakes States*. New York: Stewart, Tabori and Chang, 1989.

_____. *The Smithsonian Guide to Historic America: The Plains States*. New York: Stewart, Tabori and Chang, 1990.

Specialized Studies

Anderson, Richard Lloyd. "Atchison's Letters and the Causes of Mormon Expulsion from Missouri." *BYU Studies* 26 (Summer 1986): 3–47.

Andrew, Laurel Blank. *The Early Temples of the Mormons: The Architecture of the Millennial Kingdom of God in the American West*. Albany: New York State University, 1978.

Arrington, Leonard J. "Early Mormon Communitarianism: The Law of Consecration and Stewardship." *Western Humanities Review* 7 (Autumn 1953): 341–69.

_____."An Economic Interpretation of 'The Word of Wisdom.'" *BYU Studies* 1 (Winter 1959): 37–49.

_____, Feramoz Y. Fox, and Dean L. May. *Building the City of God*. Salt Lake City: Deseret Book, 1976.

Bishop, M. Guy. "Preparing to 'Take the Kingdom': Childbearing Directives in Early Mormonism." *Journal of the Early Republic* 7 (Fall 1987): 275–90.

Bitton, Davis. "Early Mormon Lifestyles: or The Saints as Human Beings." In *Restoration Movement: Essays in Mormon History*, 273–305. Edited by F. Mark McKiernan, Alma R. Blair, and Paul Edwards. Lawrence: Coronado Press, 1973.

_____. "Kirtland as a Center of Missionary Activity, 1830–1838." *BYU Studies* 11 (Summer 1971): 497–516.

Bushman, Richard L. "Family Security in the Transition from Farm to City, 1750–1850." In *The Underside of American History*, vol. 1, 315–32. Edited by Thomas R. Frazier. New York: Harcourt Brace Jovanovich, Publishers, 1987.

Campbell, Alexander. *Delusions*. Boston: Benjamin H. Greene, 1832.

Cook, Lyndon. "The Apostle Peter and the Kirtland Temple." *BYU Studies* 15 (Summer 1975): 550–52.

Crawley, Peter. "A Bibliography of The Church of Jesus Christ of Latter-day Saints in New York, Ohio, and Missouri." *BYU Studies* 12 (Summer 1972): 465–537.

Dahl, Curtis. "Mound Builders, Mormons, and William Cullen Bryant." *New England Quarterly* 34 (March 1961): 178–90.

Davis, David Brion. "Some Themes of Counter Perversion: An Analysis of Anti-Masonic, Anti-Catholic, and Anti-Mormon Literature." *Mississippi Valley Historical Review* 47 (September 1960): 205–24.

DePillis, Mario S. "The Quest for Religious Authority and the Rise of Mormonism." *Dialogue* 1 (Spring 1966): 68–88.

Doxey, Graham W. "Missouri Myths." *Ensign* 9 (April 1979): 64–65.

Fales, Susan L., and Chad J. Flake, comps. *Mormons and Mormonism in U.S. Government Documents: A Bibliography*. Salt Lake City: University of Utah Press, 1989.

Flake, Chad J., ed. *A Mormon Bibliography: 1830–1930*. Salt Lake City: University of Utah Press, 1978.

_____, and Larry W. Draper, comps. *A Mormon Bibliography 1830–1930: Ten Year Supplement*. Salt Lake City: University of Utah Press, 1989.

Flake, Lawrence R. "A Shaker View of a Mormon Mission." *BYU Studies* 20 (Fall 1979): 94–98.

Gayler, George R. "Attempts by the State of Missouri to Extradite Joseph Smith, 1841–1843." *Missouri Historical Review* 58 (October 1963): 21–36.

Gentry, Leland H. "The Danite Band of 1838." *BYU Studies* 14 (Summer 1974): 421–50.

Godfrey, Kenneth W. "The Zelph Story." *BYU Studies* 29 (Spring 1989): 31–56.

Ham, Wayne. "Center-Place Saints." *Restoration Studies* 3 (1986): 123–32.

Hartley, William G. "Mormon Sundays." *Ensign* 8 (January 1978): 19–25.

Hicks, Michael. *Mormonism and Music: A History*. Urbana: University of Illinois Press, 1989.

_____. "Poetic Borrowing in Early Mormonism." *Dialogue* 18 (Spring 1985): 132–44.

Hill, Marvin S., C. Keith Rooker, and Larry T. Wimmer. *The Kirtland Economy Revisited*. Provo: Brigham Young University Press, 1977.

Huff, Kent W. "The United Order of Joseph Smith's Times." *Dialogue* 19 (Summer 1986): 146–49.

Irving, Gordon. "The Mormons and the Bible in the 1830s." *BYU Studies* 13 (Summer 1973): 473–-88.

Jennings, Warren A. "The Army of Israel Marches into Missouri." *Missouri Historical Review* 62 (Winter 1968): 107-35.

_____. "Factors in the Destruction of the Mormon Press in Missouri, 1833." *Utah Historical Quarterly* 35 (Winter 1967): 5676.

Jessee, Dean C. "The Reliability of Joseph Smith's History." *Journal of Mormon History* 3 (1976): 34-39.

Kemp, Thomas Jay. *The Office of the Patriarch to the Church in The Church of Jesus Christ of Latter-day Saints*. Stanford, Thomas J. Kemp, 1972.

Kimball, Stanley B. "The First Road West From New York to Kirtland, 1831." *Ensign* 9 (January 1979): 29-30.

Launius, Roger D. *Zion's Camp: Expedition to Missouri, 1834.* Independence: Herald House, 1984.

Lesueur, Stephen C. "'High Treason and Murder': The Examination of Mormon Prisoners at Richmond, Missouri, in November 1838." *BYU Studies* 26 (Spring 1986): 3-30.

Luce, Ray W. "Building the Kingdom of God: Mormon Architecture before 1847." *BYU Studies* 30 (Spring 1990): 33-45.

Meader, Robert. "The Shakers and the Mormons." *The Shaker Quarterly* 2 (Fall 1962): 83-96.

Molyneaux, David G., and Sue Sackman. *75 Years: An Informal History of Shaker Heights.* Shaker Heights: Shaker Heights Public Library, 1987.

Moore, R. Laurence. *Religious Outsiders and the Making of Americans.* New York: Oxford University Press. 1986.

O'Donnell, Thomas E. "The First Mormon Temple, at Kirtland, Ohio." *Architecture* 50 (August 1924): 265-69.

Ogden, Kelly D. "The Kirtland Hebrew School (1835-36)." In *Regional Studies of Latter-day Saint Church History, Ohio,* 63-88. Edited by Milton V. Backman, Jr. Provo: Department of Church History and Doctrine, Brigham Young University, 1990.

Olson, Earl E. "The Chronology of the Ohio Revelations," *BYU Studies* 11 (Summer 1971): 329-49.

Parkin, Max H. "Mormon Political Involvement in Ohio," *BYU Studies* 9 (Summer 1969): 484-502.

Partridge, Scott H. "The Failure of the Kirtland Safety Society." *BYU Studies* 12 (Summer 1972): 437-54.

Peterson H. Donl. "The Mormon Mummies and Papyri in Ohio." In *Regional Studies of Latter-day Saint Church History, Ohio,* 122-38. Edited by Milton V. Backman, Jr., Provo: Department of Church History and Doctrine, Brigham Young University, 1990.

Petersen, Melvin J. "Preparing Early Revelations for Publication." *Ensign* 15 (February 1985): 14-20.

Porter, Larry C. "'Ye Shall Go to the Ohio': Exodus of the New York Saints to Ohio, 1831." In *Regional Studies in Latter-day Saint Church History, Ohio,* 1-26. Edited by Milton V. Backman, Jr. Provo: Department of Church History and Doctrine, Brigham Young University, 1990.

Quinn, Michael. *Early Mormonism and the Magic World View.* Salt Lake City: Signature Books, 1987.

Riggs, Michael S. "The Economic Impact of Fort Leavenworth on Northwestern Missouri 1827-1838: Yet Another Reason for the Mormon War?" *Restoration Studies* 4 (1988): 124-33.

Russo, David J. *Families and Communities: A New View of American History.* Nashville: The American Association for State and Local History, 1974.

Rust, Alvin E. *Mormon and Utah Coin and Currency.* Salt Lake City: Rust Rare Coins, Inc. 1984.

Searle, Howard C. "Authorship of the History of Joseph Smith: A Review Essay," *BYU Studies* 21 (Winter 1981): 101-22.

Sellers, Charles L. "Early Mormon Community Planning." *Journal of the American Institute of Planners* 28 (1962): 24-30.

Sonne, Conway B. *Ships, Saints, and Mariners: A Maritime Encyclopedia of Mormon Migration, 1830-1890.* Salt Lake City: University of Utah Press, 1987.

Thornton, Willis. "Gentile and Saint at Kirtland," *Ohio State Archaeological and Historical Quarterly* 63 (January 1954): 8-33.

Underwood, Grant. "Early Mormon Perceptions of Contemporary America, 1830-1846." *BYU Studies* 26 (Summer 1986): 49-61.

Unruh, John D. Jr. *The Plains Across: The Overland Emigrants and the Trans-Mississippi West, 1840-60.* Urbana: University of Illinois Press, 1979.

Van Kolken, Diana. *Introducing the Shakers: An Explanation and Directory.* Bowling Green: Gabriel's Horn Publishing Co., 1985.

Van Orden, Bruce A. "Zion's Camp: A Refiner's Fire." In *The Prophet Joseph: Essays on the Life and Mission of Joseph Smith,* 192-207. Edited by Larry C. Porter and Susan Easton Black. Salt Lake City: Deseret Book, 1988.

Westerngren, Bruce. "A Time of Preparation: The Kirtland School of the Prophets." *Thetean* 14 (1984): 98-113.

Wheeler, Robert A. "Shakers and Mormons in the Early Western Reserve: A Contrast in Life Styles." In *Ohio's Western Reserve: A Regional Reader.* Harry F. Lupold and Gladys Haddad. Kent: Kent State University Press, 1988.

Whittaker, David. "Early Mormon Pamphleteering 1836-1857." *Journal of Mormon History* 4 (1977): 35-49.

Wilcox, Frank. *The Ohio Canals.* Kent: The Kent State University Press, 1969.

Winter, Robert. "Architecture on the Frontier: The Mormon Experiment," *Pacific Historical Review* 43 (1974): 50-60.

Women's Studies

Arrington, Leonard J. "The Legacy of Early Latter-day Saint Women." *John Whitmer Historical Association Journal* 10 (1990): 3-17.

_____. "Persons for All Seasons: Women in Mormon History." *BYU Studies* 20 (Fall 1979): 39-58.

Beecher, Maureen Ursenbach. "The 'Leading Sisters': A Female Hierarchy in Nineteenth Century Mormon Society." *Journal of Mormon History* 9 (1982): 25-39.

_____, and Lavina Fielding Anderson, eds. *Sisters in Spirit: Mormon Women in Historical and Cultural Perspective.* Urbana: University of Illinois Press, 1987.

Brunson, L. Madelon. *Bonds of Sisterhood: A History of the RLDS Women's Organization, 1831-1983.* Independence: Herald House, 1985.

Goodyear, Imogene. "'The Legacy of Early Latter-day Saint Women': A Feminist Critique." *John Whitmer Historical Association Journal* 10 (1990): 21-23.

Madsen, Carol Cornwall, and David J. Whittaker. "History's Sequel: A Source Essay on Women in Mormon History." *Journal of Mormon History* 6 (1979): 123-45.

Morain, Tom. "'The Legacy of Early Latter-day Saint Women': A Review." *John Whitmer Historical Association Journal* 10 (1990): 18-20.

Newell, Linda King, Valeen Tippetts Avery, and Valeen T. Avery. "Sweet Counsel and Seas of Tribulation: The Religious Life of the Women in Kirtland." *BYU Studies* 20 (Winter 1980): 151-62.

Scott, Anne Firor. "Mormon Women, Other Women: Paradoxes and Challenges." *Journal of Mormon History* 13 (1986-87): 3-20.

Scott, Lyn, and Maureen Ursenbach Beecher. "Mormon Women: A Bibliography in Process, 1977-1985." *Journal of Mormon History* 12 (1985): 113-27.

Tullidge, Edward W. *The Women of Mormondom*. New York: Tullidge and Crandell, 1877.

INDEX

T. Jeffery Cottle practices law in Orem, Utah. Before receiving his law degree from Lewis and Clark Law School in Portland, Oregon, he studied anthropology and public administration at Brigham Young University in Provo, Utah. Jeff's current research interests deal with early LDS Church history, historic photography, and various legal topics. Jeff has spoken in various settings in his legal profession and has presented papers at professional history association meetings and symposiums. He lives in Provo with his wife, Michaela Voss Cottle.

Richard Neitzel Holzapfel teaches for the LDS Church Educational System in Irvine, California. He has published articles in the *Ensign* Magazine, in *Brigham Young University Studies*, and in Sperry's Symposium Presentations published by Deseret Book Company. He has also contributed to the multi-volume *Encyclopedia of Mormonism*, published by the Macmillan Company. He lives in Irvine, California, with his wife, Jeni Broberg Holzapfel, and their five children.

Jeff and Richard have collaborated on several articles, on the award-winning book entitled *Old Mormon Nauvoo and Southeastern Iowa: Historic Photographs and Guide* (Santa Ana: Fieldbrook Productions, Inc., 1991), and on *Old Mormon Palmyra and New England: Historic Photographs and Guide* (Santa Ana: Fieldbrook Productions, Inc., 1991).